Try This at Home!

Try at This Home!

A Do It Yourself Guide to Winning Lesbian and Gay Civil Rights Policy

An ACLU Guidebook

Matthew A. Coles

The New Press
New York

This book is dedicated, with gratitude and love, to Robert Nakatani, of course.

© 1996 by Matthew A. Coles
All rights reserved. No part of this book may be reproduced in any form without written permission from the publisher.

Library of Congress Cataloging-in-Publication Data
Coles, Matthew A.
Try this at home!: a do-it-yourself guide to winning lesbian and gay civil rights policy: an ACLU guidebook / Matthew A. Coles.
p.   cm.
ISBN 1-56584-309-6 (pbk.)
1. Gay rights—United States—
   Handbooks, manuals, etc.
2. Gay men—United States—Political activity—
   Handbooks, manuals, etc.
3. Lesbians—United States—Political activity—
   Handbooks, manuals, etc.
4. Civil rights—United States—Handbooks,
   manuals, etc.
5. United States—Social policy—Handbooks,
   manuals, etc.
I. Title.
HQ76.8.U5C65   1996
323.3'264—dc20   95-36038

Published in the United States
by The New Press, New York
Distributed by W. W. Norton & Company, Inc.,
New York

Established in 1990 as a major alternative to the large, commercial publishing houses, The New Press is a full-scale nonprofit American book publisher outside of the university presses. The Press is operated editorially in the public interest, rather than for private gain; it is committed to publishing in innovative ways works of educational, cultural, and community value that, despite their intellectual merits, might not normally be commercially viable. The New Press's editorial offices are located at the City University of New York.

BOOK DESIGN BY Paul Carlos
PRODUCTION MANAGEMENT BY Kim Waymer
PRINTED IN THE UNITED STATES OF AMERICA
9 8 7 6 5 4 3 2 1

CIP

Contents

III. *Civil Rights Policies*

IV. *Domestic Partnership Policies*

Appendix A

Appendix B: Domestic Partnership

Appendix C: ACLU Fact Sheet

Acknowledgments

Six people were instrumental in creating and shaping this book. If not for Bill Rubenstein, my predecessor as director of the ACLU's Lesbian and Gay Rights Project, there would be no book. He convinced me that this should be a book and not a pamphlet, encouraged me to cover domestic partnership, and, not least, introduced me to my publisher.

More than anyone else, David Kirp, professor of public policy at the University of California at Berkeley influenced the shape of the book. It was his idea to base it on interviews with activists from all over the country. The original plan of the book was completely rearranged following his suggestions.

Dorothy Ehrlich, executive director of the American Civil Liberties Union of Northern California enthusiastically supported the book, allowed me to spend a considerable amount of my time as a staff attorney working on it, and helped obtain the foundation funding that underwrote a part of it.

Tom Stoddard, former director of Lambda Legal Defense and Education, knows more about how to write civil rights legislation than anyone I know, and he freely shared it with me. He helped think through and set up my New York activist interviews, the first I did.

Diane Wachtell of the New Press shifted my original focus from local civil rights laws and convinced me to make the book work for as many different kinds of campaigns as possible. She also convinced me to include the sidebar anecdotes that appear throughout the book.

Finally, Robert Nakatani my (partner? significant other? boyfriend? oh, the hell with it) lover gave me so many good ideas about methodology, structure, and content, I can't begin to list them.

Three other people deserve a special mention: Dick Pabick, my father, the late Albert Coles, and Harry Britt. They taught me what I know about practical politics. All three were talented, kind teachers, and I am deeply grateful to them.

All of the travel needed for the activist interviews, and many of the other expenses associated with the book were underwritten by a generous grant from the Joyce-Mertz Gilmore Foundation. Bob Crane of the foundation was also one of the first people to suggest that what I had learned about domestic partnership and civil rights legislation ought to be written down.

My coauthors are the activists from around the country who graciously spent time telling me about the campaigns in which they had been involved, and the great and awful things that had happened. To all of you my heartfelt thanks for what you did for all of us, and for your patience with me. To any of you I misunderstood, my apologies. I also include the names of a few people I worked closely with on policy campaigns, even though I did not interview them separately. There have been quite a few, some quite a while ago. I know I forgot a few folks. Forgive me. My thanks to the following activists: Larry Agran, Bob Anderson, Rob Bader, Betsy Barton, Jim Boone, Harry Britt, Bob Brokl, Tom Brougham, Cheri Bryant, Pat Callahan, David Chambers, Marge Conners, Audrey Covnor, the Reverend Charlotte Cowtan, John Henry Damski, Jon Davidson, John D'Emilio, Lauri Dittman, Meredith Emmet, Chai Feldblum, Terry Friedman, Rick Garcia, Ethan Getho, Jacqueline Gist, Deborah Glick, David Goldman, Joe Grabarz, Ron Gray, Buddy Greg, Bob Harmon, Jean Harris, Greg Herek, Joe Herzenberg, Lee Hudson, Joe Hughes, Andy Humm, Art Johston, David Jolly, Lisa Kaye, Barbara Klimaszewsky, Bill Krause, Jim Levin,

Rene David Luna, Rand Martin, Laurie McBride, Harvey Milk, Mike Nelson, Mary Watson Noe, Dick Pabich, Chris Perry, Sister Ardeth Platte, Fred Plummer, Sue Purrington, Alan Roskoff, Leon Rouse, Rick Ruvolo, Frederick A. O. Schwartz Jr., Mabe Segrest, Allan Shore, Tom Stoddard, Marnie Thompson, Dana VanGorder, Al Wardwell, Paula Werner, Dan Woodbridge, and to reporter Mike Thompson.

I.   *Before You Start*

---

1.   A ROAD MAP TO GET THROUGH THIS BOOK

1.1   The Setup of the Book

This book is set up so that it can be used by people doing different kinds of jobs in many different kinds of campaigns. It is designed to be useful for people trying to get legislatures to pass state civil rights laws; for people trying to get cities and towns to pass local laws; and for people trying to get universities and businesses to adopt nondiscrimination policies. It should also be useful for anyone trying get any of those institutions to adopt a domestic partnership policy. And although the entire book is focused on passing civil rights policies for lesbians and gay men, the first two parts—on getting started and campaigns generally—should have valuable information for people working for change that has nothing in particular to do with lesbians, gay men, or bisexuals.

Although the book was written for people who are trying to obtain civil rights policies, much of what it says, particularly about campaign planning, organizing, media, and dealing with opponents, should also be useful in battles against anti-gay laws and anti-gay initiatives aimed at preventing civil rights laws from ever being passed.

Moreover, the book was set up to give people performing different jobs in campaigns easy access to what they need. Reading the whole guide will give you an overview of a whole campaign. But the material is split up so that people, for example, organizing inside the lesbian/gay community or gathering endorsements from nongay organizations, lobbying or working with the media, etc., can quickly put their hands on the information they need.

This beginning chapter is designed to show you how to get the most out of the book. It explains how the material is divided up for different users, how to get the parts you need most, and how to use the numbering system of sections to get what you need quickly. It also provides a guide to the "shorthand" language used in the book.

1.2   A Chart of What's Most Important for Different Readers

1. If you are going to be doing this in a campaign:	2. If you are going to be working on passing this kind of policy, here is what you need to read:		
	Civil Rights Campaigns in General CHAPTERS	Lesbian/Gay Civil Rights CHAPTERS	Domestic Partners CHAPTERS
Overall Organizing for a Lesbian/ Gay Civil Rights or a Domestic Partnership Campaign	1–24	25–31	32–38
Overall Organizing to Oppose an Anti-Gay Law or Initiative	1, 3, 4, 6–22	25, 27–29	32, 34–36
Overall Organizing for Some Other Kind of Campaign	1–15, 17–24		
Handling Grass-Roots Organizing Generally	5–11, 13–22, 24	27–29	34–36
Lobbying a Board	8, 12, 15–23	25–31	32–38

Organizing in the Lesbian/Gay Community	5−8, 11, 15−16, 18−19, 21−22, 24	27−29	34−36
Organizing Support Outside the Gay Community	5, 7−11, 15−16, 18−19, 21−22, 24	27−29	34−36
Handling Media and Public Relations	8−10, 12−19, 21−22, 24	27−29	34−36
Giving Legal Advice	3−5, 17, 20−23	25−26, 30−31	32−33, 37−38
Getting Witnesses and Other Support for Your Proposal	8, 15−16, 21−22	27−29	34−36
Dealing with the Opposition	8, 12, 15−16, 17−22	27−29	34−36
Organizing Volunteers	8−9, 13−19, 21−22	27−29	34−36

1.3 The Way the Book Is Divided and the Numbering System

The basic idea was to break the book down into small pieces of information to make it easy to get exactly what you need. These then were organized in three sets of larger groupings to make it easy to find the piece you need by starting with general ideas and becoming more specific.

Here is how it works: The book is divided up into four major sections: *Part One:* Before You Start; *Part Two:* Campaigning for a Policy;

Part Three: Civil Rights Policies; and *Part Four:* Domestic Partnership Policies. *Part One* is this chapter and a short one on being clear about what you hope to accomplish. *Part Two* covers all the basic steps you might have to go through in a campaign no matter what kind of policy you want to pass. *Part Three* covers some of the special things you need to know about campaigns designed to get civil rights laws for lesbians and gay men (laws that say you cannot discriminate on the basis of sexual orientation). *Part Four* does the same thing for campaigns designed to get domestic partnership laws.

The chapters are divided into even shorter numbered sections. So, for example, chapter 15, "Responding to Opposition," is divided into sections on "The Basic Options," "General Guidelines for Replies," "Building a Reply—Getting the Facts," "Building a Reply—Deciding on Presentation," etc. To make it easier to find exactly what you need, and to make it easier to deal with cross-references, no two sections have the same number. Each section has a number with a decimal point in it (like this one, section number 1.3). The number before the decimal point is always the number of the chapter, and the number after the point is the number of the section. So this is chapter one, third section, and this is the only section 1.3 in the book.

1.4 Tips for Different Users

Here are some tips on how different users can get the most out of the book.

Campaign Organizers. If you are going to start a campaign, or be an overall campaign organizer (rather than just do a particular job), you should probably read through parts one, two, and either three or four (depending on which kind of law you are trying to pass) before you start. Since so many different aspects of a campaign are connected to each other, you'll need to go through all of the general material and all of the material on your specific kind of campaign to get a good idea of what a campaign looks like and what you'll need to do to put one together. You may want to do that even if you are going to work on particular parts of the campaign to get an overview. As you get organized and launch your campaign, you'll be able to just refer to sections covering particular issues to help you with problems as they come up.

People Doing Particular Jobs. If you are going to be working on just one aspect of a campaign, you probably don't need to read through the whole guide. The chart in section 1.2 shows what you need to read to do a specific job.

1.5 I Know, I Know, There's Too Much Here

No matter how much time you have and how many people you have working with you, you won't be able to do all the things that this guide suggests. You'll have to decide which things you have the resources for, and which things you think will work best for you. You also probably won't agree with all my suggestions, either. You will find better ways to do some things. And you have the same right to make your own mistakes that the rest of us have made.

1.6 Some Special Words

To make the book work for people doing different kinds of policies, but also to keep it from being too long, the guide uses some general words to cover many similar but slightly different things. Here is a list of some of the most important words you'll need to know:

Board means any person or group of people who has the power to adopt a policy. It could be a town council, a legislature, university trustees, a business board of directors, etc. It could be an individual, such as a university or a corporate president.

Campaign means any organized effort to get a board to adopt a policy. (It could include an election campaign for a referendum or an initiative, although most of the time that is not what it means.)

Constituency means whomever the board answers to. It could be voters, stockholders, the legislature, etc.

Policy means a rule that either says that lesbians and gay men cannot be discriminated against (a "civil rights" policy) or that recognizes some form of domestic partnership (a "domestic partnership" policy). The rule could be a law adopted by a government or a policy adopted by an institution. Laws adopted by cities and counties are usually called *ordinances;* laws adopted by states are sometime called *statutes*.

Civil Rights Policy means any policy that states that something can't be done to a person because of her or his sexual orientation. It includes rules about job discrimination, housing discrimination, discrimination by businesses, government, or educational institutions. These are sometimes called "nondiscrimination" or "antidiscrimination" policies.

Domestic Partnership Policy means any policy that recognizes couples in committed relationships who are not married. It includes simple registration systems in which people document their relationships, employment benefit plans, and any policy, such as a hospital or jail visiting policy, that tries to recognize nonmarital relationships.

2. Be Clear About Why You Want to Do It

This guide comes out of my own experience with twenty or so lesbian/gay civil rights and domestic partnership policies, and out of the experiences of about fifty activists around the country (listed in the *Acknowledgments*). Perhaps the most important thing all of us can tell you is that being clear at the start about why you are working for a lesbian/gay rights policy will make your campaign more focused and greatly improve the chances that it will achieve the most important of its many potential goals. It will also make working on it a better experience for you.

There are three reasons why you should work for lesbian/gay civil rights and domestic partnership.

First, policies against discrimination are a good thing to have. They give some recourse to people who lose their jobs, homes, etc., because of their sexual orientation. More importantly, they prevent discrimination. Civil rights policies (just like all other laws and rules) work because most people obey them. If you have a policy, some people who otherwise would have lost their jobs or homes won't. Moreover, the protection of civil rights policies makes life easier for lesbians and gay men. Civil rights policies ease the fear that you have to hide who you are to protect yourself.

Domestic partnership policies are also a good thing to have. People shouldn't be cut off from those they love most at hospitals, etc. Perhaps more importantly, they acknowledge the existence of important, committed, loving relationships that have been hidden.

The second reason is that by doing a campaign, you learn the process by which change is made in America. To truly make it possible for lesbians, gay men, and bisexuals to live their lives without fear and to be secure in their relationships, civil rights and domestic partnership policies will have to become the norm. One policy change alone won't do it; we'll need change on a grand scale. The only good way to learn how to change the rules is to do it. With each campaign, if you pay attention, you'll get better. If you run grass-roots campaigns, lesbians and gay men throughout America will learn how to organize and make change, which will make change on a grand scale possible.

Finally, and most important of all, the process itself is ultimately the vehicle for real change. Changing the rules, oddly enough, doesn't really change society. Think about how many laws have been passed in the last thirty years aimed at ending race discrimination. You can argue about how much progress those laws have achieved. But it would be just wrong to say that they've really ended discrimination. You change society by changing people's minds. To truly make it possible for lesbians, gay men, and bisexuals to live in peace, society has to become convinced that discrimination is wrong.

Proposals for civil rights begin a debate on discrimination directly. Proposals for domestic partnership usually generate debate on one important kind of discrimination. More importantly, they can smash some of the worst stereotypes society uses to justify discrimination. Everything from criminal laws to bans on same-sex marriage have been justified at least in part on the basis that we are unstable, shallow, flawed women and men incapable of deep emotional commitment. Keeping our relationships out of sight has been vital to maintaining that lie. Making our relationships visible—something every domestic partnership debate does—is a good way to expose it.

2.

Ultimately, change on a grand scale, changing people's minds, is always the result of ordinary women and men working on and with their neighbors. Every movement needs inspired leaders. But real change won't come from thrilling speeches any more than it will from court decisions or civil rights laws if the people who live under those decisions and laws don't change as well. Personal contact is the key to change of this sort. And personal contact with the people you need to move is exactly what a grass-roots policy campaign gets you.

Finally, you need an important warning before you start. Bring all your brains, all your energy, and all your passion to the campaign. But don't get hurt. Remember that a policy campaign will start the process of getting people organized and getting people to think about discrimination whether you fail or succeed in getting a policy passed. Even if a policy gets passed, the process of change will be far from over. Remember: the campaign is not about whether you or any of the rest of us are good or bad. Don't ever get sucked into a debate about that. The issue is whether discrimination is good or bad.

II. *Campaigning for a Policy*

---

3. YOU MAY NEED PROFESSIONAL HELP

3.1 Whom You Might Need

In most circumstances, it will be important to have a lawyer working with the campaign. As explained in the next section, lawyers can help you write, negotiate, and answer arguments against a policy proposal. If you are proposing a domestic partnership policy for a health-care plan, an economist who is familiar with health-care economics is essential. Depending on how you go about proving your case, how much you need to teach your board, or how elaborate you decide to make any public hearing, you may also need:

* a psychologist to explain that being gay is not an illness and/or the damage that discrimination does to people (*see 21.8, 28.6, 29.8*);

* a scientist to explain that we don't know the origins of sexual orientation (some MDs can do this, some psychologists can do it, some biologists can do it)(*see 21.8, 29.3*);

> * a public health expert to refute the argument, if it gets made, that AIDS or other public health concerns are a legitimate reason to discriminate (*see 29.11*);
>
> * a social scientist to help with surveys and/or to explain the damage that discrimination does to society (*see 21.8, 28.5*).

3.2 You Shouldn't Have to Pay

You shouldn't have to pay for either lawyers or experts. A volunteer policy campaign should be able to get voluntary help. More importantly, people who propose to help you for a fee are less likely to know what they are doing anyway. Particularly with law, the issues that are important to these policy campaigns are just not areas in which there is much commercial work to be done. The people who know their stuff (and are not working for the institutions you are trying to influence) either work for public interest organizations, universities, or do this kind of work for its own rewards.

3.3 Why You Need a Lawyer

Most of the writing described in chapters 23 (the general chapter on writing), 30 and 31 (the chapters on civil rights policies), and 37 and 38 (the chapters on domestic partnerships) will be easier if you have a lawyer helping you. If you are just adding sexual orientation to an existing law or policy, a lawyer is less crucial for the writing. If you are adding sexual orientation to a university or business policy, which are usually much simpler and straightforward than laws, you may not need writing help at all.

But even if you don't need a lawyer to help write the policy, you may need one for other reasons. Many of the arguments people will make against the policy will be essentially legal arguments. For example, opponents typically argue that cities don't have power to pass nondiscrimination laws (see section 6.3) or argue that discrimination is already covered by state or federal law (see sections 6.5 and 26.4). It will be much easier to sort out these claims and respond if you've got a lawyer helping you. Equally important, your replies are likely to be more credible if you've got a lawyer backing you up, or, better still, a lawyer making your legal arguments for you. This is particularly important if the legal argument you are responding to is coming from a lawyer, especially a city attorney.

In addition, opponents, members of the board, and even friends are likely to propose amendments to your policy. The effects of some will be obvious; but the effects of others will not be. Having a lawyer to help you figure out what amendments mean is especially important if you need to respond quickly.

3.4 Why You May Need an Economist

An economics expert can be helpful with a civil rights policy, providing testimony about the costs of discrimination, etc. (See section 28.6.) If you decide to propose a domestic partnership policy that involves some form of valuable benefit, an economist or financial analyst is almost essential. One of the central issues with any valuable domestic partnership benefit plan is cost. There are at least two potential kinds of cost considerations, and several ways to adjust plans to modify costs. (See chapter 36. and section 35.4.)

There is also a significant amount of information about cost in the experiences of employers who have adopted benefit plans and in several expert studies. You'll need an expert to understand and evaluate the data. Some of the studies are subtly based on very pessimistic assumptions, which don't prove true when plans are adopted. You'll need a sharp expert to find the assumptions and explain what's wrong with them.

A health maintenance organization based its first demand for a domestic partners' surcharge from the City of San Francisco on a complex cost estimate that twice included costs of childbirth, etc.

A study done for San Francisco's health plan had a so-called "optimistic prediction," which its authors later had to admit was based on a mix of favorable and unfavorable assumptions, and a "pessimistic" prediction, which

3.5

they later admitted was based on the idea that a combination of many unfavorable possibilities would all happen, something they admitted really could not happen.

Neither of these "estimates" would have been exposed without the work of a careful economist.

3.5 Things to Look for in an Expert

It is important to get the advice of an expert who does not work for an organization you are asking to adopt a policy. In-house experts, especially those who work for local government, often have a narrow view of what the institution can do. While this sometimes really reflects limits on power, sometimes it is a convenient way to get rid of people, or worse, a line to cover opposition to the policy itself.

Moreover, the pressure on in-house experts to come up with the numbers or opinions their employers would like to see is just too great. For the same reason, be wary of people who make a good portion of their living as paid consultants for similar institutions. They'll also be under pressure to get answers their clients will like.

The best kind of expert is someone who is sympathetic to your goals but who retains enough detachment to give you realistic answers, not just the answers you may want to hear. Your lawyer should know something about the law on municipal power or the powers of whatever institution you want to have adopt a policy. He or she should know something about state and federal civil rights laws. He or she should also be willing to do some research, stay with you throughout the process, and appear in public to answer questions.

You may have to put this ideal adviser together using several different persons. A legal advisory committee can be made up of people with different training; it also allows the work to be spread.

3.6 Tips on Finding an Expert

First, call the lawyers, doctors, economists, etc., you know who will be sympathetic. Even if they are not right for the job, they are your best shot at finding someone who is. Ask people working with you on the campaign, and then friends, if they know of an expert who might be willing to help or who might know someone. Call them and ask them for referrals if they themselves can't help.

If you cannot find someone local outside the institution you are working on, (and, perhaps, even if you do), try going to the nearest university. See if there is a lesbian/gay student group or a chapter of the National Lawyers Guild or a similar national organization that supports lesbian/gay rights. Students are often able to get help from sympathetic professors.

You can also get help from national and regional legal organizations that support lesbian/gay rights (Lambda Legal Defense, the ACLU). Some, like the ACLU, have regional affiliates and chapters that may be able to help with day-to-day advice.

4. SCOPING OUT THE PROCESS AND THE PLAYERS

4.1 Introduction: No Two Alike

Before you do anything else, you've got to do some basic research. There are many different models for running businesses and universities and for governing cities and counties, each with different structures and policy processes. Even among similar institutions (like universities) the variety is enormous. For example, some cities are structured like the federal government and most states: they have administrative branches headed by powerful elected executives (usually mayors) who must approve policy, and elected legislative bodies (although usually one body instead of two) who must pass it. But some have executives with no formal role in adopting policy. In others, legislative power is split among two or more bodies, some of which aren't even elected.

Since there aren't one or two general models for how institutions are organized or how they work, this guide can't tell you for sure what to expect. Instead, it goes over some of the things you'll need to find out, and some of the things you can do to get the information you need.

This chapter covers research on the process of getting a policy adopted, both what you need to know and how you might find out. Chapter 25 covers finding out what kind of civil rights policies exist already; chapter 26 covers finding out what kind of civil rights policy is possible; and chapter 32 does the same thing for domestic partnership.

4.2   What You Need to Know About Your Target Institution

The first thing you need to find out is who makes policy. Although someone usually has final say, the answer is usually not one person, like a mayor or a college president, or one body, like a city council or a board of trustees. The answer usually describes a process in which many officials and several bodies play a part. Chapter 20 reviews most of the steps in a typical city government process.

You also need to find out what each of the officials and bodies involved in the process is supposed to do—what their jobs are generally and what they are supposed to do in policy adoption in particular. This is important because it will help you understand the different ways different people are likely to think about your proposals and because it may help you spot someone going beyond his or her authority.

> **In San Francisco, the first proposal for a law banning sexual orientation discrimination in employment, housing, and public accommodations came back from the city attorney's office as an ordinance about "Housing Discrimination Against Homosexuals." In addition to leaving out jobs, businesses, heterosexuals, and bisexuals, the new version took out most of the enforcement mechanisms. The city attorney was unwilling to consider modifying the proposal until the board of supervisors pointed out that his job under the charter was restricted to approving laws "as to form," not substance. After the board threatened to pass the law without his review, he relented and restored the rest of the bill.**

You need to know the sequence of the process and how a policy proposal moves through it. Sometimes there are options on sequence (you may be able to start in any one of several commissions, your proposal could be assigned to any one of several committees) and you need to know this so you can evaluate the options. Chapter 20 lays out in more detail some of the possibilities with city governments.

You need to know what it takes to move a proposal from one stage to another. Sometimes the rules say a proposal should be referred to an official, but it keeps going to the next stage unless he or she stops it. Sometimes the proposal will move forward only if the official approves it.

Most processes have both formal rules and informal rules. Sometimes the unwritten rules are observed more rigorously than the formal rules. (See chapter 20.)

> **The rules for the New York City Council say that any proposal considered at a public hearing must be voted on by the committee that held the hearing. But year in and year out, the chair of the committee in which the proposed lesbian/gay civil rights bill had its hearings simply refused to schedule a vote. By long-standing tradition, no council member ever challenged a committee chair's decision to bury a proposal this way.**

You need to find out how officials get their jobs. Are they appointed? If so, by whom? Do they serve for terms or until they are removed by the person who appointed them? Which officials are supposed to represent people? Officials can represent districts, geographical areas, or groups of people defined by shared characteristics (e.g., alumni, union members). All of this is important to figuring out how to lobby officials and which endorsements matter most.

Some institutions, especially cities and counties, have unofficial "political" structures. In some locales, there are elaborate political party organizations, with committees in every ward (usually a geographical subset of a district). In others, particularly those where there aren't two viable political parties, people organize through political clubs, unions, and the like.

Finally, when you work for government policy, you need to find out the extent to which voters can become directly involved in making policy. *Initiatives* are laws that are proposed and passed by the voters. *Referendums* are elections on whether to approve or repeal laws passed by legislative bodies. *Recalls* remove public officials. Are any of these devices allowed? To minimize the chance that one of these tools will be used to defeat or repeal your proposal, you need to know at the start if they are available and how they work. (See chapter 24.)

4.3   What You Need to Know About the Players

Find out who the political players are. Not all persons who hold the same or similar offices (like members of a city council) are really equal players in the process. Some, because they are widely respected, are particularly effective legislators, or, because they have access to money and volunteers, may be far more important than others.

For many of the same reasons, individuals who are not formally part of the process at all may be crucial players. Members of policy-making bodies may defer to people in other positions or sometimes to people with no office at all.

Even where there is no strong tradition of informal political organizations, officials may defer to people with whom they have worked a lot in the past or people who have helped them in the past. Organizations not formally a part of the process can also be crucial players. In a classic "union town," important policy doesn't get made over the objections of organized labor.

In many parts of the country, religious groups wield important influence. Many people think of civil rights for lesbians, gay men, and bisexuals and domestic partnership as posing moral questions. You need to know which religious groups and which religious leaders are important. (See chapter 16.)

Learn about the institutions of the lesbian/gay community. In some places, there is an elaborate lesbian/gay subculture, with retail businesses, professionals, bars, etc., all identified as gay, and with a gay press, usually one or more local or regional weeklies or monthlies. Some towns have gay community centers. In many towns there are lesbian/gay religious groups, especially in the more progressive churches, and lesbian/gay civic, political, and social clubs. Even in the least-developed gay communities, there are often interlocking social circles of gay men and lesbians.

4.5

4.4 You Need to Know a Bit of History

Spend some time finding out the civil rights history of your institution. At the very least, you are likely to find things that happened in the past and comparisons with your proposal. For example, if an important institution like a church took a leadership role in a past civil rights campaign, you may be able to appeal to its pride in what it did in that battle to get support for your proposal.

4.5 Getting the Information — People

The best source of information is often someone who has been paying attention to the politics of your target institution for a long time. These observers tend to fall into three groups, each with its own strengths. If you can, try to find someone in each group.

* Observers associated with likely allies, such as a member of a local ACLU or NOW chapter, are valuable because they will be paying attention to issues connected to yours. They'll be particularly helpful with figuring out who is likely to be an ally on your issue and who is likely to be an opponent.

* Inside observers, such as members of the board or their staffers, are valuable because they know the process intimately. They should be helpful with both formal and informal rules and structures.

* Detached observers, such as reporters or some career bureaucrats, are valuable because they don't have the interests of the first two groups. They are most likely to tell you about influences the first two groups may be reluctant to acknowledge. Often, reporters for the alternative press—

weeklies or monthlies that identify themselves as offering views and perspectives other media do not—may be most willing to talk with you.

If you approach people you don't know (and don't have a contact for) in any one of the three groups, be forthright about why you want to talk with them. Being coy can make you an enemy later. People who retired from working in any of the three categories can make great sources. They often have more time to talk, and they often enjoy the process of reflecting on what they used to do.

4.6 A Warning About Friendly Advice

While there may be no better source of information than friendly insiders, their advice needs to be evaluated with caution. Sometimes the board members most friendly to cutting-edge proposals are professional gadflies, those who enjoy taking on difficult policy questions even if there is little or no hope of success. Sometimes they are not as interested in the policy process, and, not being particularly effective legislators, they are not able to give the most insightful advice about it.

Occasionally, the most friendly policymakers will become resentful when a campaign begins working with moderates. While this may be understandable, make sure that it isn't skewing their suggestions about whom to approach.

"No vote," Chicago's enthusiastic organizers insist, "is a dirty vote." They say proudly there was not a single member of the council with whom they wouldn't talk, or a single member whose support they spurned.

Unfortunately, avoiding tough issues is one of the ways to success in politics. Friendly politicians are sometimes apt to be discouraging because lesbian/gay civil rights is usually a tough issue. Remember, to some outsiders, no time is likely to be the right time for either domestic partnership or lesbian/gay civil rights.

4.7 Getting the Information—Reading

A few cities publish helpful guides explaining how they work. You can usually get a copy of the institution's charter and basic rules. For cities, charters usually set out how the policy process works in some detail, although they frequently make difficult reading. City boards sometimes publish their operating rules as well.

Business charters are usually called "Articles of Incorporation" and they rarely provide helpful information. The corporate "bylaws" will at least give you the board's formal operating rules. Universities are typically more like businesses than cities in terms of which documents are helpful.

A good way to begin your research is simply to devour the local press or company newsletter. If you follow a couple of local issues carefully, you are likely to pick up the outlines of the structure, some idea about the informal structure and who is important in it, and the names of possible sources in all three classes of observers.

4.8 Getting the Information—Watching

Go watch the board in action. It will be easier to do this if you already have a rudimentary idea about structure and process. In any case, direct observation will quickly answer many questions that reading about an institution raises. You'll learn a lot about who the players are and the subtle dynamics of the process as well.

If you can, find one or two policy proposals and follow them through the process. One good way to get practical knowledge of the mechanics is to identify a proposal at the end of the process and trace it back. Most boards publish calendars or agendas, and you can scan them to find a promising proposal at the end of the line. Most boards have files with "dockets" for each proposal, tracing its progress. For most government institutions, these are open to the public. The board's clerk or secretary will often be happy to tell you how your board works.

Once you've traced a policy proposal back from the end, try to follow a couple of proposals from the start. If proposals begin in a committee, go to committee meetings for a while until you see a proposal that you want to follow. If they begin with members of the board, they will usually be introduced at board meetings.

Finally, follow every election campaign as closely as you can. You'll find out where board members stand on issues, which organizations endorse which individuals, and which individual and group endorsements seem to mean the most.

4.9 Getting the Information—Allies and Opponents

As you work to find out who plays a part in making policy, try to begin categorizing people and groups as likely allies, likely foes, or those in the middle. You can do this by asking helpful observers where people stand and by paying close attention while you read and listen. You may want to pay particular attention to how the key individuals you have identified vote or speak on certain issues. (See chapter 17.)

5. BASIC DECISIONS ABOUT THE CAMPAIGN

5.1 Introduction: What this Chapter Covers

This chapter and chapter 7 cover important basic decisions you should make about your campaign right at the start.

This chapter covers:

* which type of policy you should propose—domestic partnership or civil rights;
* should the campaign be noisy or quiet;
* should lesbians and gay men do the campaign or should it be done by a broad coalition (when you decide this, you'll be deciding whether the campaign will be about lesbian and gay rights, or other civil rights as well);

* should you have a large grass-roots campaign or will the campaign be done by a small closed group (in either case, you'll need to think about how to build a core group to run it);

* should your organization be created just for the campaign or should it be designed to continue after the campaign is over.

Chapter 7 covers focusing the campaign and getting started.

5.2 Civil Rights or Domestic Partnership?

The most basic campaign decision is whether you are going to propose domestic partnership or civil rights. Most people think that civil rights are ordinarily the first step. The idea is that basic protection against losing a job or a home is almost essential before you can meaningfully work to make relationships more visible.

Civil rights are also usually an easier first sell. Most Americans think that people who are qualified should be hired and people who do their work shouldn't be fired. It isn't a great leap to say that if people are being denied jobs or are fired for other reasons, they need legal protection.

The idea of domestic partnership—recognition of nonmarital relationships—is somewhat foreign to many people, as is the idea that lesbians and gay men have partners at all. If your institution's civil rights policy doesn't cover sexual orientation, and if there is no overriding state law that forbids discrimination, civil rights will usually be your first choice. But not always.

> **After the governor vetoed a statewide lesbian/gay rights policy in 1991, a group in Marin County, California, decided to campaign for a county policy.**
>
> **At first, they planned to push for a county-wide version of the civil rights law the governor vetoed. But basic research showed that a county law would apply only to county government itself and parts of the county where there weren't town and city governments.**

> They also found that local businesses were much more opposed to a civil rights law, that the county supervisors seemed open to either, and that the lesbian/gay community seemed more excited by the prospect of a domestic partnership law.
>
> They decided to propose a domestic partnership policy, which was passed a year after the veto and just a few months after the governor approved a statewide civil rights law.

If you already have full civil rights protection, domestic partnership might seem like the logical choice. But again, not always.

> In the late 1980s a school board in a conservative Northern California town was asked to adopt a policy forbidding sexual orientation discrimination against teachers and students. Both topics were actually covered by state law. The proponents of the policy believed that almost no one (lesbian/gay or heterosexual) knew that discrimination was illegal. They also believed that most of the town hadn't thought about the issue, and that among those who had, opinion was divided. They concluded that despite the state law, they still needed to make civil rights the issue.

Basic research should tell you if you already have a civil rights law and if it is as comprehensive as it could be. (See chapters 25 and 26.) Preliminary organizing in the lesbian/gay community should tell you what lesbians and gay men would most like to have. (See chapter 6.)

5.3 Noisy or Quiet?

How quiet can a campaign for a lesbian/gay civil rights law be? Consider Flint, Michigan. There were no public hearings. Organizers asked lesbian and gay organizations not to write letters to council members or the media. Council members were lobbied in private. When the bill came up for a vote, only its number was read aloud (truly, this was the bill that dared not speak its name). There

**was no debate. There also was no opposition. The bill
passed on a voice vote.**

The case for a quiet campaign is simply put: You are more likely to lose if there is a public fight over the policy. If your campaign is quiet, it is possible that potential opponents won't even know about it until it is over. Some people who might vote for you if the policy is unopposed will abandon you if the opposition turns out.

Moreover, some potential opponents on your board may not take a stand against you if you don't make the debate public; if none of their colleagues is speaking out, they may be afraid of appearing bigoted and narrow-minded if they take a public stand against the policy. Also, some people are very uncomfortable talking about lesbians and gay men and will turn against you if you force them into any public debate on the subject.

> **In Raleigh, North Carolina, council members who agreed
> early to back a policy did so explicitly on condition that
> the whole thing be kept quiet. Partly they feared con-
> stituent anger, especially if strong religious opposition
> formed. But, as one organizer said, it was also "a southern
> thing. People down here just don't talk about sexual orien-
> tation, or sex for that matter."**

The case against the quiet approach is also easy to lay out. Once your opponents do find out about it, your policy can be repealed by the board that passed it, amended to death, or even put on the ballot. (See chapter 24.) You are likely to have a tougher time convincing people to support your policy if it looks as if you tried to sneak it though.

Stealth campaigns also don't get much real progress even if they do win. Quiet campaigns are almost always done by a very small group of activists (it is virtually impossible to keep a grass-roots campaign quiet), so they don't do much to get the community organized. Since they don't put civil rights or relationship recognition for lesbians and gay men on the public agenda, they don't start the public debate, and they don't begin the process of changing the way most people think about lesbians and gay men.

A policy adopted as a result of a stealth campaign may not even be much good as a policy. If nobody knows about it, people don't know to obey it. People who are discriminated against, for example, may not know they have a right to complain.

A bit ruefully, the backers of Flint's civil rights policy admit there wasn't much celebrating when the city adopted a civil rights policy. Most lesbians and gay men didn't know about it, and even those who did know about it "didn't feel much connection to it." Although the backers believe there is very significant discrimination in Flint, they now think the policy was just the very start of dealing with it, and a more modest start than they had hoped it would be.

5.4 A Lesbian/Gay Community Campaign or a Broad Coalition?

Every campaign should try to get support from throughout the community. (See chapter 9.) This section addresses whether the campaign will be directed by lesbians and gay men or by a broader coalition.

If you plan to propose a domestic partnership policy, the campaign will almost surely be run by lesbians and gay men. Many heterosexual couples choose not to marry, and society's failure to recognize their relationships has consequences as tragic and unfair for them as it has for lesbians and gay men. Nonetheless, the availability of marriage, and the fact that most straight couples decide to get married at some point, has made it virtually impossible to get large numbers of heterosexual unmarried couples involved in domestic partnership campaigns.

But campaigns in which broad coalitions take a direct, "hands on" role are possible with civil rights. Indeed, if you want a broad civil rights policy that either covers other groups for the first time or improves coverage for everyone, you will have to do a broad coalition campaign. But you cannot decide to campaign for a law to protect some other group. If you try, you are likely to incur their opposition, not their support (you are also likely to lose). By the same token, if you want a campaign to which other groups in the community will fully commit time, money, and effort, the campaign will have to encompass their policy goals as well.

Begin by deciding whether you would want a broad coalition effort if one were possible. There are several advantages to a broad coalition campaign. Other community organizations are likely to bring you more contacts with the board. A coalition campaign is likely to bring more allies than you could pick up by yourself. It should bring more workers, making it possible to run a larger, more thorough campaign.

A broad coalition can also mute one popular opposition argument, i.e., that lesbians and gay men shouldn't be treated like other groups protected by civil rights laws. A broader coalition that includes African Americans can also help prevent opponents from employing a favorite tactic: driving a wedge between lesbians and gay men and African Americans, and trying to get black churches actively involved in the opposition.

Coalition campaigns have two potential drawbacks, both preventable under most circumstances. The first, assuming you don't want a quiet campaign, is that lesbians and gay men could get lost in the campaign. This is unlikely if there is active opposition (opponents usually want to highlight the presence of lesbians and gay men because they think it is the least popular civil rights policy issue).

You can prevent lesbians and gay men from disappearing if you and your coalition partners agree that among the campaign's regular speakers will be an open lesbian or gay man, that there will be an open lesbian or gay man in the smallest core group directing the campaign, that sexual orientation discrimination will be prominently featured at hearings, in media and other campaign events, in literature, etc.

The other serious risk is that lesbians and gay men will get dumped. Most coalition campaigns at some point face offers from potential opponents to support the policy if lesbians and gay men are left out. Opponents frequently offer to support the policy if the proponents will amend it to diminish protection for lesbians and gay men alone. All members of the coalition must agree at the start that no one will accept a policy that excludes any part of the coalition or that includes terms ultimately unacceptable to any part of the coalition.

If you think you might want to have a coalition campaign, you need to learn whether it is realistically possible. Your basic research will tell you what kind of broad policy might be possible. If the institution you are focusing on has no policy now, or if it could be improved for all groups, a broad-based coalition is possible. If neither, look to see if there are other groups that could be covered by the policy who are left out. If so, you could create a coalition effort with them. (See chapter 25).

If policy benefiting other groups is possible, get the names of the leading local organizations for those groups. Use the same basic research techniques to get the information. (See chapter 4.) Make sure you don't inadvertently take sides in any community disputes; if there is more than one significant organization in a community (and there usually is), contact them all.

Tell the organizations you contact what you know about existing policy and how it could be improved. Tell them about your plan to campaign for a civil rights policy on sexual orientation and ask if they are interested in trying to obtain or improve a policy for their group.

> **Concord, California, had no civil rights law when lesbian/gay activists began contacting other organizations about passing one. Eventually, a coalition of African-American, feminist, Japanese-American, Latino, and lesbian/gay groups got together to campaign for a civil rights law. The council passed a law prohibiting all "arbitrary discrimination." When fundamentalists placed an initiative on the ballot to repeal the law, but only as it applied to lesbians and gay men, the coalition held. All the groups worked to keep the law intact. Although the vote was close, the initiative passed. Almost all the members of the coalition then joined in a lawsuit, which invalidated the initiative, and restored the law.**

Sometimes other groups are willing to participate in a coalition campaign for a broad law, but, frequently because they already have the protection they need under other laws or policies, they don't really

5.4

want to lead the effort. You can design a coalition campaign in which lesbian/gay groups essentially run the campaign and do most of the work, but you need to be careful.

Though your partners in this kind of campaign may be somewhat passive, they are more than endorsers, since the policy you are proposing deals with their issues. If you are going to keep their support, you can't exploit them. They must be part of every important decision, and they must be kept informed about every important event. You must be sure speakers from your partners are part of every press conference, every important campaign statement, every event. Everything you do must be sensitive to their issues as well as your own.

Chicago had a comprehensive law, but it didn't cover discrimination based on disability, marital status, source of income, or parental status. Lesbian/gay activists contacted disabled and women's groups. Both agreed to join in a campaign to try to add all those categories, along with sexual orientation. However, both made it clear that since they already had protection under state and federal law, they expected lesbians and gay men to lead the campaign and do the lion's share of the work.

Almost from the start, the disabled and women's groups were told the council would pass the law immediately if sexual orientation were left out. All those proposals were rejected. Although it took several years of hard work, a strong law covering all the coalition partners eventually passed.

One of the reasons the coalition held so well is that the lesbian/gay organizers demonstrated a real commitment to disability issues. As one disabled activist put it, "every event, every speaker's platform was accessible. When they weren't sure how to handle an issue, they asked us first. We were part of every decision. Eventually, the gay community itself started to reach out and welcome us in, with businesses adapting in ways the law didn't even require. This is a coalition that will last a long time."

5.5 The Straight Strategy

So far, this chapter has assumed that lesbians and gay men ought to be at the center of any campaign. That seems almost self-evident. A campaign can't convincingly make the argument that lesbians and gay men are entitled to equal treatment if we are invisible. As one Chicago organizer put it, "It's your law, and your lives, and your stories the campaign will be about."

A few organizers disagree. They feel that campaigns are most likely to succeed if the most visible proponents are heterosexuals. These organizers particularly favor having the public parts of the campaign promoted by individuals who, because they are either clerics or ethnic minorities, can easily refute some of the common opposition arguments.

> One organizer has practically made a career of putting together campaigns based on a "religious strategy." He lines up local religious support by approaching most likely supporters first, then using their support to get endorsements from others. He uses nondiscrimination statements from national organizations wherever possible to get local ministers to agree. He then goes to the city council with a campaign built entirely of ministers, rabbis, and other clerics. He uses religious leaders for all public statements and all lobbying. The strategy has succeeded in several places.

Even if one disagrees with the "straight strategy," there may be situations in which there is a good chance to pass a policy but in which it isn't practical for lesbians and gay men to play much of a role in a public campaign.

> A rare opportunity to pass a civil rights law came about in Saginaw, Michigan, when the local newspaper printed a sympathetic story about a destitute man forcibly thrown out of his apartment when his landlord found out he was gay. The incident happened just as the city was about to adopt a new fair housing law. Saginaw had no organized gay community, and lesbians and gay men in the town were

still frightened by several "near riots" at a gay bar when people showed up with clubs and rocks and beat patrons.

The campaign to add sexual orientation to the fair housing code was lead by a longtime civil rights activist on the city council and the African-American staff person for the human rights commission, both heterosexuals. With support from several of the area's prominent local religious leaders, the proposal passed. Unfortunately, the lesbian/gay community is still almost completely unorganized, although some say the law has made them feel a bit more secure.

5.6   The Campaign Organization: Symphony or One-person Band?

A TALE OF TWO CITIES

Late in negotiations over San Francisco's lesbian/gay civil rights law, the critical board member whose vote was needed to pass the law reached agreement on language with the person doing most of the lobbying. "When can you check with your people?" the board member asked. "If it's all right with me," said the lobbyist, "it's all right with my people." The board member marveled at the disciplined organization of the gay community. The lobbyist didn't tell him he really had no "people," that the whole campaign was being done by a few insiders.

Chicago's campaign was run by an organization called "town meeting." Anyone who showed up at any meeting was a member, entitled to vote. Some meetings had hundreds.

While the San Francisco example is a bit extreme, many campaigns have been run by just a handful of people. But grass-roots campaigns that involve as many people as possible are usually better. First of all, size itself is an advantage. With a large campaign you can do more. For example, you can have one lobbyist for each board member, or you can send representatives to every organization from which you want an endorsement. Large campaigns can also lobby constituents, set up tables, and canvass neighborhoods. They enable more people to come into direct contact with lesbians and gay men. (See chapter 18.)

Size isn't the critical difference between a grass-roots campaign and a small group campaign. Grass-roots campaigns are open; their meetings are public, as publicized as possible, and people are encouraged to join. You won't be able to have a large campaign if you don't run a grass-roots campaign. But having an open campaign doesn't guarantee that it will be big. The greatest advantage of an open campaign, in addition to the potential that it could become large, is that it will help organize the lesbian and gay community and teach as many people as possible how to make change. That, of course, is one of the primary goals of a policy campaign. (See chapter 2.)

5.7   A Core Group to Run the Organization

Whether you opt for a single mass organization, such as Chicago's town meeting, or a coalition of new and existing organizations, as New York City did, you'll have to deal with the fundamental tension between the urge for democracy and the need for some authority structure to make the campaign work.

> **The actual wording of civil rights policies is almost always decided in the last moments before the final vote, as crucial votes are won and objectors placated with last-minute changes. In San Francisco, it was the minimum number of employees for the law to apply; for the state of California, it was the description of what kind of reform a court could order. In both cases, decisions about what the campaign would accept had to be made by one or two individuals at the last moment.**

It is probably impossible to avoid creating a small group and giving it the authority to make certain important decisions. Negotiations and unforeseen events can't be managed otherwise. Politicians frequently insist on working with single individuals or at most small groups. While secrecy shouldn't be a big issue, you need to be careful with information if, for example, you want to time its release for maximum effect, or if you have a supporter who is nervous about being publicly identified.

Most campaigns solve the problem by having a large group (either everyone involved, which is typical with a mass organization like Chicago's, or a large group of representatives of other organizations, which is typical with umbrella groups) make basic policy decisions. Small groups or individuals appointed by the large group take responsibility for carrying out the decisions. These small "core" groups must have the authority to make important decisions when situations like negotiations or the need to respond publicly to something require quick action. Most campaigns keep their core people accountable by giving them rough guidelines for the most important areas and by requiring that they periodically report back to the larger group.

Those in the core group should be people who don't want to run for office or receive appointments from politicians. People who do are sometimes easily diverted. Perhaps more important, never asking for anything personal is the best way to get and keep credibility with both the larger campaign organization and with the board members, staffs, and politicians.

Try to get a mix of veterans and rookies in your core group. Experience and history are very helpful—you don't want to repeat somebody else's mistakes. People who've been around often know the best way to get to decision makers. But experience needs to be tempered by a fresh perspective; just because something didn't work two years ago doesn't necessarily mean it won't work now. Try for political diversity in your core group, which will make it easier to work with the board members and others.

5.8 The Future of the Organization: A One-shot or an Enduring Player?

Should your campaign organization be an ongoing organization or a special organization created just for the campaign, to be disbanded when the campaign is over (or some hybrid)?

If you use an organization that existed before the campaign, the members may already know some of the people you'll need to influence and will already have their own organization and systems in place. Organizations set up specifically, but designed to continue, also offer more to your prospective allies—support on their issues in the future. With planning, such organizations can offer the lesbian and gay community vehicles for future action.

On the other hand, existing organizations carry baggage with them: enemies from the past both inside and outside the campaign, previous stands on issues with which people whose support you now need disagreed, etc.. Ongoing organizations also usually have other issues on which they are working. A one-shot has no mixed agendas, so it is focused and harder to divert with compromises in other areas. Not having existing structures can be an advantage. With a one-shot, you can tailor your organization to the single task at hand. If you fail, you don't damage existing community organizations.

6. ORGANIZING IN THE LESBIAN/GAY COMMUNITY

6.1 Introduction: What this Chapter Covers

If you want the lesbian/gay community to learn about organizing for change, you'll need to have a grass-roots campaign. Most campaigns start fairly small, and in some places, people may be so afraid to be open that you'll never get more than a handful of people involved.

The first step in putting together a grass-roots campaign is to run the idea by the community to see if there is support. This chapter will look at how to do that with an organized lesbian and gay community and without one. Then it will move on to building support for the campaign within the lesbian/gay community. It will finish with some tips on running a mass grass-roots campaign organization.

6.2 Running the Idea by an Organized Lesbian and Gay Community

If the community has visible leaders, start by meeting with them and explaining what you would like to do. At this stage, take a broad view of who a leader is; if some people in the lesbian/gay community treat a person as a leader, contact her or him. If the community has organizations, talk to their leaders. If you can, try to get permission to go to a meeting and present your idea to the members of the organization.

Finally, if you can, try to hold at least one open, public community meeting to discuss the idea. (See section 18.2, on how to get people to meetings.) Circulate sign-up sheet at meetings for people who might want to work on a campaign later if you decide to go ahead.

If the leaders and the community are generally positive, you should go ahead. If they are all against the idea, you probably shouldn't. More typically, you'll find something of a split. There is no easy formula for what to do then. Sometimes when people say the time isn't right, it isn't. A policy campaign could spark a backlash which, if the community isn't organized enough to respond, could be a serious setback.

> **Some of San Francisco's best-known lesbian and gay leaders refused to support the campaign to get a nondiscrimination law passed in 1977. They said the voters weren't ready for it, and that it was unfair to pressure friendly politicians. Enthusiastic activists went ahead, anyway. Although the campaign was tough in many ways, the law passed and there was no public backlash.**
>
> **A group in San Jose defied similar conventional wisdom in 1979 and got a law passed there. Within days, opponents had gathered enough signatures for a referendum. The law was rejected overwhelmingly in an election campaign for which the lesbian/gay community was unprepared.**

Pay attention to the warnings of people who understand the political process and have worked it effectively, especially warnings that are reasoned out and don't depend too much on an emotional reaction to your proposal. Be respectful of other views; if most people disagree with you, there's probably a good reason. On the other hand, if you've done your basic research and the objections really do seem based on fear of change, don't be afraid to disagree.

6.3 Running the Idea by a Community That Is Not Organized

How do you contact the lesbian/gay community if it does not have visible organizations or leaders? First, try finding the community through other organizations that are generally supportive of lesbians and gay men. The more liberal churches, particularly the Unitarians and the Quakers, frequently have significant numbers of lesbian and gay members. You can often put notices on church bulletin boards or in newsletters asking to meet members of the community. The church may let you speak to a membership meeting. Sometimes, a minister will know local lesbians and gay men and will contact them for you. Feminist bookstores, women's organizations, local chapters of the ACLU or the National Lawyers Guild, and similar organizations are also a good source for first contacts. Try the same techniques you would with a church.

When you've made a few contacts, you might try asking people to invite their friends to a meeting at which you will explain what you propose to do. See if you can use a few meetings like that to generate others. You want to make sure that you don't wind up talking to one circle of friends.

> **There was no organized lesbian/gay community in Berkeley, California, in 1978, when one person thought that Berkeley should have a nondiscrimination law comparable to the one San Francisco had just passed. He called a few friends, persuaded them to call friends, and scheduled a meeting at his house. He invited one of the San Francisco organizers to come explain how it was done, and the campaign was underway.**

Hold a public meeting, although it may be difficult to get anyone from an unorganized community to come. An unorganized community may be supportive but unwilling to work directly for the policy. Many people may fear that they'll lose their jobs or homes if they campaign openly. You may need to think about using one of the alternative campaign models if most members of the community are unwilling to work openly. (See section 5.5.) If you do use an alternative model, try to involve as many lesbians and gay men as you can, at whatever level. Be especially careful to think about how you can use the campaign as a step in community organizing.

6.4 Building Support in the Lesbian and Gay Community

If you've run the idea past the community and decided to go ahead, you'll need to keep building support in the community. Enlist the support of as many community leaders as you can. Use the logrolling and lobbying techniques described in chapter 17 that you'll use later to line up the support of policymakers. Go after those most likely to support first, and, if you can, approach them with people they know and respect.

> **Although there was a group of visible lesbian and gay leaders who didn't support the campaign for San Francisco's law, they didn't publicly oppose it either. By the time these leaders were approached, organizers had already lined up enough support that this group, although it didn't agree with the plan, was afraid to be identified as opposed to it.**

Obviously, with both leaders and organizations, keep in mind your eventual goal of obtaining their support when you do your "run by" effort. Ordinarily, you shouldn't ask for endorsements when you are consulting people about whether to do a campaign; you shouldn't have decided whether you are going ahead at that stage. But you should approach those who are least likely to oppose first, so that you don't build a groundswell against a policy before you've decided. Finally, efforts to line up support from lesbian and gay leaders and organizations should continue throughout the campaign. Welcome support whenever it comes.

6.5 Staying in Touch with the Community

Start the campaign with a public meeting. Try especially hard to get the word out about this meeting (see chapter 18 for tips); try to use the newsletters and meetings of organizations that already support you to help. They may be a great source of campaign volunteers.

At the meeting, briefly sketch out the goal and the elements of an ideal campaign. Mention any support or endorsements already lined up. If some popular leaders are willing to come to the meeting and allow their names to be used in your publicity, so much the better. Circulate a sign-up sheet and ask people to say in which parts of an ideal campaign they would most like to participate. Make sure people include their phone numbers.

The campaign should have regular public meetings. If you organize as a grass-roots campaign, these will be your organization's regular meetings. Even if your campaign is done by a small organization or an umbrella group, you should hold regular public meetings at which you report back to the community about what you are doing. It may be easier to get people to this kind of "report back" meeting if you do it in conjunction with existing organizations.

You need to reach people who can't or won't come to public meetings. In addition to building support, this will help you turn out supporters when you need them. Try to convince a gay paper or an alternative paper to let you have a regular column to report on the campaign. (See section 13.9 on working with the gay press.) If that fails, write up a newsletter and regularly circulate it in the community (see section 12.6). A single sheet is fine (two-sided won't work if, for example, you want to put it up on bulletin boards).

> **In one New York City campaign, organizers published a weekly information sheet for the lesbian/gay community. It briefly reported on the progress of the bill. It also informed people which members needed to be contacted**

and how to contact them, and it told people of upcoming events. Since it was done as a single sheet printed on both sides, it was easy to distribute.

Stay in regular communication with the organizations that have endorsed the campaign or that are being generally supportive. Offer short progress reports for their newsletters, or ask permission for a member of the organization to report briefly at their meetings.

Finally, use events and gatherings. Get permission to set up booths at lesbian/gay pride parades, block parties, and street fairs in gay neighborhoods as well as at events that may attract likely supporters, such as prochoice rallies and street parties in liberal or progressive neighborhoods. Your booths should always include sign-up sheets for the campaign in addition to information about voter registration and how to contact policymakers. (See chapter 17.)

6.6 Using Events to Galvanize Support in the Community

As further explained in section 10.2, a galvanizing event is an incident that can be used to focus attention on some of the problems your policy would address. These incidents may involve opposition to or support for lesbians and gay men individually, or for the community as a whole. Sometimes, you can create events that galvanize community support. The keys to using galvanizing events are to focus people's reaction on the policy campaign and to keep track of people who react strongly to the event.

Just as galvanizing events can be a way of getting the public to see the need for a policy, they can be a way of rallying support in the lesbian/gay community. (See section 10.2.)

In Greensboro, North Carolina, a group formed to promote the lesbian/gay march on Washington in the mid-1980s stayed together after the march to run a series of local hearings on AIDS. After the hearings, they quietly began working on a nondiscrimination policy.

Not long after, the city council decided to ban parking

6.6

on Commerce Street at night. The street had become an informal gathering place for lesbians and gay men. At the next council meeting, the march group showed up to protest the ban. So did about forty other lesbians and gay men. The march organizers obtained names and phone numbers, and the campaign organization was born.

The protest at the council meeting served as a galvanizing event that got the nondiscrimination campaign underway. Protestors complained that the city was insensitive to the lesbian/gay community. The council asked the Human Rights Commission to look into the charge; this led to hearings and, eventually, to the policy.

Some events, like bad court decisions or an attack on the community by a politician, will result in a spontaneous demonstration. If that happens, get someone from the campaign to speak at the demonstration and make the connection to the campaign. Pass around sign-up sheets. If you've had time to schedule a post-event public meeting or if a public campaign meeting was already scheduled, announce the time and place as often as you can. Pass out flyers announcing the meeting and briefly describing the campaign. If you haven't had time to schedule a meeting, announce that one will be called, and tell people where to find out about the time and place.

If the event doesn't result in a spontaneous demonstration, schedule an open public meeting to discuss the event. Have the campaign sponsor the meeting and have at least one speaker draw the connection to the campaign, describe it, and ask for volunteers. But don't focus the meeting entirely on the campaign; let people discuss the event in whatever way they wish. Again, be sure to circulate sign-up sheets.

7. PUTTING IT TOGETHER — THE CAMPAIGN PLAN

7.1 Introduction: What this Chapter Covers

Before you can get your campaign underway, you need to make a plan for passing the policy and design a campaign organization to carry out the plan. This chapter assumes you'll run a grass-roots campaign, but much of what it says applies to closed campaigns as well. If you are going to run a coalition campaign, you'll need to do most of the things described here with your coalition partners.

7.2 Who Is the Audience for Your Campaign?

No question generates as many apparently contradictory answers as the question about who your audience is when you run a policy campaign.

> Every time Chicago organizers heard a tactical suggestion they thought was aimed at the wrong audience, they'd refer to it as a "blimp." The term came from one activist's idea that the campaign should rent blimps to fly over Wrigley Field during Cubs games. The blimps would display short slogans in favor of the civil rights law and lesbian/gay rights in general. "The blimps missed the point," the organizers say. "Every tactic should be judged by the answer to this question: Will this win us votes at the board? The board is the audience."

On the other hand:

> "Your campaign should focus on the public, not the city council," says one of the activists who worked longest on New York City's campaign. "Getting the law is no good if people don't understand it. Besides, the real point of the campaign is to end discrimination by changing the way people think. Every campaign debate should be looked on as an opportunity to explain the lesbian and gay community to the public."

These answers may not be as contradictory as they look at first. You'll never get a policy passed if you don't concentrate on the board that has the power to pass it. On the other hand, policies passed without support among those to whom the board is ultimately accountable may not be around for long.

7.2

> In Irvine, California, a law was repealed by an initiative soon after it was passed; repealing the new law in Greensboro, North Carolina, was one of the first acts of a new council elected shortly after it was passed. In both cities, organizers believe they might have avoided the repeals if they had built up more public support for the law before it was passed.

The problem with the "blimp" plan was not so much that the public shouldn't be part of your audience as that the plan tried to reach the public in the wrong way. It didn't focus on the most susceptible people, and it didn't focus on the best way to persuade them. These two problems (along with focusing on "selling" lesbians and gay men instead of selling the policy; see chapter 8) are the most common problems with campaign plans.

To get your campaign focused, write up a "passage plan" that includes every step in the process for passing a policy. (See chapter 20, which lays out some of the possible steps, and chapter 4 on research.) The last step should be support among whatever "public" the board ultimately answers to. For a city, this would typically be voters. With a university, for example, it may be the university community, the alumni, the state legislature, depending on who makes the decision and to whom they answer.

The usefulness of the plan is likely to depend on detail; the more you put in, describing each player at each step, the more helpful the plan will be. The last step should include a description of all the constituent groups (the "publics") to whom the board answers.

> Students at one university in the West spent months putting together a campaign to convince the administration on campus to recognize domestic partners in housing. They succeeded, only to learn that the policy couldn't be

changed without the approval of a central administration for the whole multi-campus university system.

Next, fill in the names of the people involved at each step. Include people who are not direct participants in the process but are most likely to influence those who are. Then add the names of all the organizations whose support might influence the participants.

You now have a map of the process.

7.3   Make a Plan for an Ideal Campaign

For each step in your plan, list the campaign tactics that, if you could get all the resources you needed, you think you might be able to use at that step (while you shouldn't be conservative at this stage, do be realistic). (See chapters 9–13 and 17–22.) Some tactics will involve using people at one step to get the support of people at another.

Along with tactics, list the messages that you think are most likely to work with the individuals at each step. Where you have more than one person at a step, your list may differ from person to person. Then list the tactics you might be able to use to support the messages. (See chapters 8, 15, 16, and 22.)

Deciding which tactics and messages are most likely to work shouldn't be just a "gut call." During your research, you should have spoken with people experienced in local politics who can give you solid information about what does and does not work. You also should have talked to people who've done lesbian and gay civil rights campaigns. Estimate the amount of money you would need to use for each of the tactics or your list. Don't make up the numbers out of thin air; talk to people who've done similar things.

Now you have a plan for your ideal campaign.

7.4   Make a Real Plan

Real campaign plans need to be flexible. Your resources are likely to change as the campaign goes on and you pick up support. Your experiences will change your ideas about what works and what doesn't. The process described here should be going on all the time, and you should stop and go over the whole plan from time to time.

* List your resources. Who is willing to work, what skills do they have, what kind of time do they have? How much money do you have, how much could you raise, and what would it take to do it?

* Go back to your ideal plan and match your resources up to it. Draw up a practical plan that includes your map through the process but lists only those campaign tactics you realistically think you can use.

* Do a time version of the plan. Focus on 1) logrolling techniques, 2) the sequence that some steps in the process must follow, and 3) the sequence you've chosen for others. Then decide the order in which you'll execute the steps in the plan. (See chapters 4, 9, 10, 20, and 21.)

Now you have a real plan. Don't forget to keep adjusting it as you go along and things develop.

7.5 How to Design Your Campaign Organization

The work in the campaign plan has to be divided up and assigned to the people who are going to do it. Once jobs are assigned, people need to coordinate with each other so that the phases of the campaign are in sync and people don't duplicate each others' work. Whatever design you adopt for your organization, it should build both division of tasks and coordination into its structure.

If you have a very small campaign, all you may need to do is divide up the work so that each worker is in charge of some aspect of the campaign, and have the whole group meet regularly.

If the campaign is large, or if you think you may eventually get larger numbers of volunteers, you may want to create a steering committee of those in charge of each part of the campaign, and have that committee meet frequently. A core group might propose a division of work to present to the entire campaign for approval at a public meeting. You may need to change the design as the campaign progresses.

You may decide that some things could be better done if the division were changed. As the campaign progresses, you may not need to do some things at all anymore.

Whatever design you decide on, it is probably a good idea to have someone in charge of running any large public meetings. Some person or group (it could be the whole steering committee) also needs to make up agendas for the public meetings. At some point, you may need to do this for the steering committee as well. And make sure that by the end of the campaign, some person or small group has the authority to negotiate the final terms of the policy.

7.6　Train Your Volunteers

Everyone who works on the campaign should understand the proposed policy, the case for it (chapter 8), and the answers to the opposition (chapters 15 and 16). The best way to do this may be with regular speakers' training. Have groups of volunteers meet (fifteen to twenty, not many more). Have members of the core group explain the policy, the case, and the answers. Encourage the volunteers to ask questions. You want to be sure they understand, and this is a good way to find out where your explanations and arguments need work.

Have your most experienced media person explain how to talk to the media. Have your most experienced public speakers explain how to tell groups about the policy and ask for their support. Not everyone will have to speak in public or talk to media. But everyone needs to answer questions they get asked by friends or by people on the street when you set up tables or walk precincts. The media/speaking sections of the training, because they emphasize clear, terse explanations, will be a help to everyone.

7.7　Keeping Lists of Members and Volunteers

If you have a list of members and volunteers (and you should), make it as secure as you can. Only one or two persons should have responsibility for keeping it. (If they have access to a safe or a strong box, so much the better.) You should make it policy that any-one can have her or his name removed from the membership list right away just by asking. It should be policy that the list is never shown to anyone outside the organization for any reason.

If the law regulates your organization, it may not be possible to keep the list confidential, and people should be told that before they sign up. It is also always possible that a hostile government agency or someone else exploiting the courts could get your membership list, and people should always be warned that no one can guarantee confidentiality.

7.8 Communications within the Organization

You should set up a regular system for communicating to the lesbian and gay community and the public at large what the campaign is doing. (See sections 6.5, 12.6.) This will be invaluable for lobbying and for rallying people. You should also set up an internal phone tree for emergency meetings or unexpected events (e.g., surprise public hearings). To create a phone tree, each member of the organization takes the phone numbers of a small number of other members and agrees to call them with emergency messages as soon as she or he is called. The best trees have one or more managers who have the whole tree and can cover calls if someone can't be reached.

7.9 Some Other Tips on Running a Campaign

There is no best way to run a campaign's meetings or its day-to-day business. Your campaign will develop its own processes. Here are a few general tips that may make it easier at the start. First, check with your lawyer to find out if the law in your area regulates organizations set up to work for the kind of policy you want to pass. In most places, unless you are working for a state law, this probably won't be necessary, but it is important to check at the start.

Someone with basic bookkeeping skills should be in charge of the campaign's finances. Although most campaigns won't involve a lot of money, you might want to look into the possibility of getting a bond for your treasurer. Call a local insurance agent. If the law requires campaigns like yours to make reports on finances, your treasurer needs to know that at the start so that your books can be set up to make the reporting easy, and so that pledge cards and donation cards ask for the right information.

You need to have some basic ground rules for your public campaign meetings. You may want to consider:

* limiting the length of comments in debate
* setting times for each item on the agenda, allowing the group as whole to vote to extend them
* recognizing people who've not spoken before those who already have
* agreeing to use some published set of rules (like Robert's Rules of Order) for situations where you have no rules
* creating rules about how people can add items to the agenda
* having each part of the campaign briefly report on what it has been doing at each meeting.

You should try to get a regular meeting time and place. It is much easier for people to keep track of the meetings that way.

7.10   Campaign Tone and Style

Don't skip this section; it may be the most important of them all.

The two great enemies of a successful campaign are emotion and exaggeration. Most Americans like to believe that we consider policy through rational processes, and, to most people, rational process means mostly unemotional process. If you run a campaign in which your messages are delivered with an emotional pitch (no matter what the messages are), even sympathetic people are likely to think your case for the policy is so weak you can't state it dispassionately. Some people will buy into old stereotypes about lesbians and gay men and use your own tactics as a reason not to adopt the policy.

It is very difficult to remain calm when some of the arguments made against you, even if delivered with a veneer of reason, amount to nothing more than attacks on our humanity, driven at best by ignorance and at worst by hate. But your chances of making people see that are much greater if you stay calm. You can't ignore attacks, but you ought to react as if you are strong enough to rise above them.

This is not to say that occasional emotional appeals do not have their value. They do; but they need to be thought through and carefully timed. (See section 22.8.)

Opposing a nondiscrimination policy is not the same thing as committing a mass murder. But analogies that farfetched and worse— repeals of civil rights laws have been compared to the Holocaust— have been made. Exaggerated comparisons destroy a campaign's credibility because they make it look as if the campaigners have no perspective. Exaggerated claims pose a similar problem. If you say there are hundreds of discrimination stories and you present only two, people will think the problem turns out to be far less serious than you stated. They may think you were lying to them.

The campaign's overall tone should also be the tone of its individual workers. In hearings, at public meetings, with the media, in conversations with board members or leaders, be rational and don't exaggerate. Never swear, never lose it. Never leave a meeting under circumstances that make it impossible to meet with the same people again.

7.11 Planning for the Future

The campaign will end when your policy is passed. It may end before that if an attempt fails and people want a break before trying again. If your campaign ends without a policy, make sure that whatever information and materials the campaign has put together are saved and accessible to anyone who may want to try again or try with a different institution.

Very few campaign organizations survive in any form once the campaign ends. Some people see this as a failing. It may just be unavoidable. Campaigns are very demanding, and most people want to get away from intense activism for a while once the campaign ends. Even people who want to keep working will usually want to work on different things. A single organization may well be unable to accommodate them all, and, if the organization was built for the campaign, it may not work well for any of them.

It probably isn't a tragedy if the organization just ends. The people who worked in it have become involved in politics and acquired valuable skills. Most of them will stay active. Many of them will have built alliances with other organizations, and those won't disappear either.

However, with a little planning, you can make it more likely that the energy and knowledge your campaign has marshaled will not be lost. Think about the kinds of organizations politically active people in your area tend to use. They may be political clubs, civic associations, caucuses of unions or churches, etc. While the campaign is going on, ask the people involved to think about how they might want to stay involved in politics, either by joining existing political organizations or by setting up new ones, or new caucuses in existing ones. When the campaign does end, have a post-campaign meeting, and ask members of the campaign to present their ideas for future activism. Then let nature take its course. And make sure the post-campaign meeting is a victory party. Whether the policy was passed or not, you won if you got people involved, acquired skills for them in the process, and put the issue on the table.

8. BUILDING A CASE FOR THE POLICY

8.1 Introduction: Why You Need to Have a Case

Every policy campaign needs to have a "case" for the policy; that is, a statement that makes the most important arguments for adopting the policy and answers the most important questions about it. You need to develop your case at the very start of the campaign, so that all your literature, all your public statements, and everyone working on the campaign uses the same basic messages.

This chapter explains the basic elements of a case statement and how to decide on primary arguments. (Chapter 27 reviews primary and secondary arguments for civil rights policies at the time this was written, and chapter 34 does the same thing for domestic partnership policies.)

8.2 General Guidelines for Case Statements

Your main goal should be to make the statement brief and understandable. Do your best to avoid jargon and technical language.

> In 1988, a Southern California member of Congress sponsored a statewide initiative on HIV that, if passed, would have amended about fifteen state laws. The case statement for the opposition campaign, including all the elements of a good case statement, fit neatly on one two-sided sheet. Although the campaign did regular volunteer trainings, the case statement was clear enough that they were largely unnecessary.

A case statement is a working document; you should keep changing it as you go through the campaign and refine your messages. As new issues become important during the campaign, you may want to put in new elements and drop others that no longer seem important.

> In one of San Francisco's three domestic partnership campaigns, opposition at first argued the law would be too costly. As it became clear that voters understood that it was a "registration" law that had no cost, opponents shifted their attack to claims that the law weakened the status of marriage. The campaign's case statement had to change the focus of its section on answering opponents accordingly.

A case statement doesn't have to be written down. The advantage of writing it out is that it is easier to incorporate into literature and materials you use to train volunteers. The downside to written statements is that people sometimes become bogged down in grammar and style. While you need a good case statement, don't spend the entire campaign writing it. Although the case statement is usually the basis for literature and training materials, it usually isn't distributed itself. However, its contents shouldn't be any great secret, and you should never put anything in it that you would be unhappy to see in a newspaper.

8.3   The Four Major Elements of a Case Statement

A case statement should have four major elements. Each element should be set out in one fairly simple statement. You can elaborate if you need to with a couple of sentences giving details or explaining a point.

The first element should be an explanation of what the policy does. This should be a concise statement of the major parts of the policy.

> **For example, if you were proposing a comprehensive civil rights law for a city, your basic explanation might say: this law states that people can't have their homes or jobs taken away or be refused service simply because they are lesbian, gay, bisexual, or heterosexual.**
>
> **If you were proposing an all-encompassing domestic partnership law for a city, your basic explanation might state: this law says intimate, committed couples can register their relationships, and can visit each other in hospitals. If one partner works for the city, she or he can get her or his partner on the health plan.**

Make sure your lawyer is satisfied that whatever you say is accurate. You can add an explanation of the details that are most likely to be interesting to the board and its constituency if you think you need to.

The second element is a short summary of your main argument, followed by a few sentences of elaboration if needed.

> **For example, for an employment policy your basic argument might say: since everyone in this society has to work to survive, people who do their jobs well shouldn't lose them just because the employer doesn't approve of who they are.**

49

> **For a "recognition" domestic partnership policy, it might say: in hospitals, no human being should be separated from the person he or she loves and has made a life with because society says they can't marry.**

The third element is short statements of any important secondary arguments for the policy.

The fourth element is answers (you know how long) to the major questions about or objections to the policy. (See chapters 15, 29, and 36 for some typical objections and responses.)

8.4   Formulating and Choosing the Basic Argument

Most policy campaigns serve many purposes. Most civil rights campaigns, for example, are part of larger movements that aim to get society to accept a group it has marginalized. Often, policy campaigns are aimed in part at getting a community organized. Sometimes an important part of the aim is to get the public to start thinking about an issue. While all of these are perfectly legitimate reasons to do a policy campaign, they are usually not the most persuasive arguments for adopting a policy.

To boards and their constituents, the best reasons for adopting a policy are usually connected to what the board's job is and the practical effects of the proposed policy—what it would actually do if it were adopted. The best arguments for a policy are arguments that explain why it would be good to have a policy like the one you propose. This may seem obvious, but more than once in the past, policy campaigns have instead wound up focusing on something completely different.

> **In the late seventies, one Northern California town considered adopting a policy that would have banned discrimination in employment. Most of the debate on the policy, from both sides, was not about employment but whether it was acceptable to be gay. In several other communities, much of the debate about civil rights policies has focused on whether those who opposed the policy were bigoted or fanatical.**

Most of these campaigns were unsuccessful. Although there were many reasons for that, one surely was that they failed to focus on what the policy did.

When you've got your explanation of what the policy does, think about why it would be good to have it. Most of your reasons are likely to be built around the idea that something undesirable or unfair is happening (or could happen), which the policy is designed to stop or prevent. For example, the classic civil rights argument is that people are losing jobs because of sexual orientation and not ability, and that the law is designed to keep that from happening. (Chapter 27 covers some typical basic arguments for civil rights policies. Chapter 34 does the same thing for domestic partnership.)

Two factors should help you decide which argument to use as your main argument. The first is resources. Most arguments are made up of some factual and some moral propositions. For example, the classic civil rights argument described above is based on the factual claim that people lose their jobs because of sexual orientation, and the implicit moral claim that people shouldn't lose jobs if they have ability and do their jobs well. You should make this the centerpiece of your campaign only if you will be able to produce: 1) evidence that people lose jobs, and 2) support from recognized moral authorities that people shouldn't lose jobs except for lack of ability (if a proposition is near universally accepted, like this one is, you may not need too much support for it).

The second factor is which arguments your board and its constituents are most likely to find compelling. To make decent predictions about this, you should do a little attitude research.

8.5   Doing Attitude Research

First, check whatever opinion polls you can find. National polls on attitudes towards lesbians and gay men are usually done every year. You can find them either through a newspaper with an annual index (like *The New York Times*) at most local libraries, or through a computer news data base such as Nexus. When you think about how to use polls, make sure you think about ways in which the group sampled is similar to or different from your board and its constituency.

Talk to people who have recently carried out policy campaigns with similar boards. If you've heard about campaigns in the media, check the stories for leads on the people who did them. Most activists are very willing to spend time sharing their experiences. Ask them what did and did not work. If you don't know of any similar campaigns, call one of the national lesbian/gay organizations for a referral.

Finally, and perhaps most importantly, talk to people in your area; ask them what they think about a proposed policy and gauge how they react to different reasons for adopting one.

> **In one of San Francisco's domestic partnership campaigns, the proponents got a little help from some marketing professionals and a local politician. The politician included a domestic partnership question in an issues poll he was doing for other purposes. The professionals did a little market research. Both found, to the surprise of the campaign, that of all the possible arguments for the policy, people responded most strongly to the argument that lesbians and gay men should be able to register their relationships to have them officially recognized.**

Make sure that you talk to people who reflect the diversity of your board and its constituency, not just people inclined to favor a policy. (On the other hand, you probably shouldn't bother with likely die-hard opponents.) Try talking to representatives of business, moderate political groups, moderate churches. Talk to some of the same professional observers you approached in your basic research on the board. (See chapter 4.) Talk to some sympathetic politicians, especially those you will expect to support you. You run the risk of alerting people to your coming campaign, but as long as you are quietly asking about ideas and you don't plan a stealth campaign, you are unlikely to start a counter-campaign or do much harm.

9. ENDORSEMENTS

9.1 Endorsements Are Essential

No matter whose statistics you believe, lesbians and gay men are a small minority of the population. There is no way you can win a campaign without widespread support from other people. One of the most important techniques for getting both public support and the support of politicians is getting endorsements. You need endorsements both from organized groups and from individuals who are respected, either generally or by the board members you are trying to reach.

9.2 Basic Research

The strategic planning covered in this chapter requires a little basic research. You need to know what political, civic, issue-based, ethnic-based, religious, and social groups exist in your area. You need to know which ones typically make policy endorsements, who their allies are, whom and what they have endorsed in the past. You need to find out how they communicate with their own members, whether they are connected to any national organizations, what their stands on civil rights for lesbians and gay men and on related issues are. Use all the basic research tools described in chapter 4. Following local media, especially newspapers, is likely to be particularly valuable here.

Before you approach any local organization that is affiliated with a national organization, contact the national one and find out if it has a nondiscrimination or domestic partnership policy of its own and whether it has a position against discrimination or is in favor of domestic partnership. Many churches, unions, professional organizations (such as the American Bar Association and the American Psychological Association), and civic organizations have both national nondiscrimination policies of their own and official positions in favor of them. Local endorsements are usually easier to obtain if you have the organization's national policy in hand.

Find out what stand the group has on the issues most important to it. You need to do this to avoid being inadvertently offensive.

For example, it isn't smart to send someone who works for a health insurer to get the endorsement of a union that has just been told premiums have increased so much that its members will now have to pay part of the cost.

More important, this information will be critical in seeking endorsements from groups which aren't natural allies (see section 9.3).

9.3 Developing an Endorsement Strategy

In most parts of the country, the groups most likely to support you simply if asked will not be enough. You'll have to do more than round up the support of the "usual suspects." You will have to convince moderates and other groups that might be more reluctant to support you as well.

Map out an endorsement strategy at the very start of your campaign. The basic technique for going beyond natural allies takes time. In addition, there are lots of groups that might support you that will stay neutral if the other side gets to them first, and there are potential opponents you might neutralize if you get to them first. Finally, the more endorsements you line up early, the more it may appear that passage of your policy is a foregone conclusion. This can discourage the opposition and make your job significantly easier.

The best plans are usually based on "logrolling," which is using one endorsement to get another. You start by approaching one of your most likely supporters, get its support, and then move to a slightly more doubtful group that is connected to the first group (or greatly respects it). When you ask the second group for its endorsement, you tell them about the endorsement from the first group. Keep moving progressively from your most likely supporters to your most doubtful ones. As you pile up endorsements, it will be harder for people to resist.

Start by making a list of natural allies, folks who are most likely to support you either because of their political views in general or because they specifically support civil rights for lesbians and gay men. Next, make lists of groups you think might be "logrolled" into support. Think about surface connections; for example, the endorsement of one religious group may help you get that of another group that shares many of the same beliefs. Also, return to your basic research; the support of one political club may help you get the support of another club that frequently works with the first.

Finally, think about the board you'll need to persuade and do some targeting. Concentrate first on the endorsements that you think will be most helpful in convincing your board. For example, it looked like the main opposition to adding sexual orientation to the fair housing policy in Saginaw, Michigan, would come from religious groups. That posed a serious problem, since several members of the council were deeply religious and several others had very religious constituencies. Organizers began their campaign by securing the support of several prominent religious leaders before the policy was publicly introduced and having those leaders present when the policy was announced.

9.4 Finding Your Natural Allies

It should be easy for you to identify who are your natural allies. Typically, they'll have already expressed support for lesbian/gay civil rights or they'll have an ideology that will make it likely they'll support you. So, for example, the local ACLU, NOW chapter, and the local Unitarian church are all likely supporters. Local human rights commissions and commissions on the status of women are often willing supporters.

Labor unions are often overlooked. Many unions have nondiscrimination policies at the national level, and locals are often required to abide by them. Unions frequently have considerable knowledge about local politics and considerable experience with lobbying. Their advice is often valuable, their help sometimes invaluable.

For example, professional lobbyists appeared at the New York City Council for the first time in history when the Teamsters Union brought two down from the state capital to lobby for the lesbian/gay rights bill. Teamster lobbyists spoke with a special persuasive force because the union had a political action committee that contributed a lot of money to local political candidates.

9.5   Beyond Natural Allies

Once you move beyond organizations that are already committed to lesbian and gay rights, getting endorsements is harder. Showing that you have the support of other groups or individuals who are respected helps; but most people will need to be convinced that they should support the policy.

This usually means two things: First, you need to be ready to show that the policy is a good idea. (See chapters 8, 27 and 28, 34 and 35.)

Second, you need to show that you deserve support. Sometimes showing why the policy is needed will do that. But with many groups, you'll have to show that your policy fits the group's agenda. This is why you need to know the organization's position on the issues important to it. Think about how your policy fits the organization's own agenda, as an extension of its policies (for example, as helpful to a church's policy that no one should be without a job or a home) or as a reflection of the same underlying philosophy (for example, a union's commitment to the idea that people shouldn't lose jobs for reasons that don't have to do with ability).

While you should be ready to make the case that the organization should see your policy as connected to its agenda, you should do so respectfully. Never assume that because you see a connection that you are entitled to an endorsement, and never lecture a group about the meaning of its principles.

Perhaps as important as arguing a connection, you should show (as opposed to state) sensitivity to the organization's concerns. For instance, Chicago lesbian/gay organizers helped cement a tentative coalition with disabled groups by holding their early organizing meetings in accessible places before anyone from the disabled groups had to point out the need.

If you want to get the support of African-American groups, show that you are committed to equality by reaching out and bringing African Americans into your organization at the start.

Sensitivity also means acknowledging the pioneering work others have done and, while respecting the struggles of others, not presuming to understand them. No one who is not gay really knows what it is like to be gay in America. The same is true for other groups who've suffered discrimination. (See section 27.4.)

9.6   Asking for Endorsements

You will have a better chance of getting an organization's endorsement if you ask for it with the support of one of the organization's leaders or another individual respected by the organization. Try to have a leader accompany you when you ask for the endorsement or, failing that, to give you a letter of support. If possible, get a lesbian or gay member of each organization you approach to ask for the endorsement. People usually find it more difficult to say no to a colleague.

> **Quite unexpectedly, the county Democratic Committee endorsed the proposal to have the city of Greensboro, North Carolina, add sexual orientation to the list of ways in which it would not discriminate. The Democratic party's national policy against discrimination didn't hurt. But organizers felt the county committee voted to endorse the policy because one of its members came out in an impassioned speech asking for the endorsement.**

You should also recognize that asking for an endorsement is an opportunity to persuade people that discrimination against lesbians and gay men is wrong. Always ask for a little time to speak and lay out the basic themes of your campaign. Even if an endorsement is a sure thing, explaining your position may win over some members who disagree or who don't care. Also, remember that any chance to appear in public is a chance to dispel some stereotypes. Even if only one person can speak to a group, it doesn't hurt to send a small delegation that reflects the diversity of the lesbian and gay community.

If it looks as though you will not get an endorsement, ask for the opportunity to return and explain at greater length why you are right. If it appears as though an endorsement proposal is going to fail, it is better if you can persuade the group to postpone the vote until a later presentation. Once the proposal has failed, it will usually be tougher to get the organization to reverse itself.

9.7   What Endorsement Statements Should Say

Like requests for support from candidates, endorsement statements pose a specificity dilemma. If the statement is very general —like a stand against discrimination, or in favor of the principle of civil rights—it may blunt the effect of the endorsement. Politicians who want to ignore it can simply say that those who made it didn't deal with the problems in your specific proposal. Sometimes politicians or groups who have made endorsements in general language will then use the specific proposal as an excuse to back off, claiming to support the concept but not the specific proposal.

On the other hand, if your policy is complicated, it will be much harder to get endorsement of a detailed draft. People are understandably nervous about backing detailed proposals and will usually want to study them at length to make sure they contain no hidden surprises. Worse, if you have to change the proposal in any significant way as you negotiate, you give an organization feeling some pressure a different excuse to back off: they can say the proposal is significantly different from the one it endorsed.

The best tactic is probably to suggest a statement that backs the principle of nondiscrimination and gives a general description of the proposal. For example, if the proposal were for a city ordinance to ban discrimination by the city, its contractors, and all employers in the city, you might suggest an endorsement like this:

> *[Name of organization] condemns discrimination against lesbians, gay men, bisexuals, and heterosexuals. It supports the proposal to have [name of city or institution] adopt a [policy, ordinance, law, etc.] banning sexual orientation discrimination by [name of city or institution], its contractors, and employers in [name of city].*

[Name of organization] urges all members of the [name of body which is considering the nondiscrimination proposal, e.g., the city council] to support the proposal.

If the organization has a national policy against discrimination, you may want to refer to it in the proposed endorsement statement. It is probably a good idea to give the organization a copy of the draft proposal as it exists. However, you should tell the organization that while the general principles will stay the same, the details could change as the campaign evolves.

When you ask for the endorsement, ask for a written copy of the resolution or the minutes containing it. This may be useful in written materials. It may also help if the organization later comes under pressure to withdraw its support.

9.8   Asking for More than a Statement

Before you approach any group, consider things other than just the support that it might be able to give you. The ACLU may be able to get you legal help. Human rights commissions and similar bodies may be able to give you advice about city politics. Groups such as NOW and the Unitarian church frequently belong to civil rights coalitions and can help obtain endorsements from other members of the coalition and the coalitions themselves. Membership organizations may be willing to let you ask their members to call, write, or meet with board members. You can ask people to help through newsletters or at public meetings of the group.

Ask the organization to agree to send a representative to any public hearings on the proposal and, if possible, to lobbying sessions with critical members. The organization is most likely to agree at the moment it endorses your proposal. Like a written endorsement, a commitment to send a representative will be helpful if the organization later comes under pressure to disavow or play down the endorsement.

Occasionally, groups may be willing to give you "nonnegotiable demand" support; that is, a commitment not to support anyone who does not support your policy. It is essential that you send a representative of the organization to visit the members of the board and tell them or get this support stated in writing.

For example, when the Teamsters Union in New York got behind the proposed nondiscrimination law with "nonnegotiable demand" support, the head of the union told a group of council members: "If you don't support this, you won't get another dime of union money."

9.9 Keeping Endorsements

Your first campaign is not likely to be your last. The odds are that it will take more than one try to pass your policy. You could face repeal efforts in the future, and you are likely to face related issues in the future. You need to keep the allies you make.

If the only thing you ask for is a statement of support, it probably isn't necessary to recontact a group until you thank it for its support at the end of the campaign (which you should do no matter how it comes out). If you ask for more—if you ask for representatives at board meetings, help with lobbying, and especially if you ask for advice on the campaign or help getting other endorsements—you should keep the group posted as the campaign progresses. The greater the commitment you seek, the more the group is likely to be resentful if it feels that you contact it only when you can exploit its support. At a minimum, you should report back to your major supporters on important developments (approval by subcommittees, major endorsements, etc.) and on important upcoming events (rallies, hearings, etc.).

If you keep people informed, you are also likely to get more people to attend hearings and perhaps to obtain useful information or advice that you wouldn't have known to seek.

10. GETTING ON THE PUBLIC AGENDA

10.1 Introduction: What this Chapter Covers

This chapter is about using events or making things happen to get the board and the public to think seriously (or more seriously) about the need for a policy. This is often a good way to start the public phase of a policy campaign. Most of the strategies covered here can also be used to support your arguments during a campaign.

To use events effectively, you'll most likely have to use one or more of the tactics covered in other parts of the book. This chapter will refer specifically to some of them. The last part of this chapter covers a few public campaigning techniques that are not covered elsewhere.

10.2 Using Galvanizing Events to Get Public Attention

A galvanizing event is an event that illustrates some of the problems your policy is designed to remedy. It could be prejudice against lesbians and gay men, neglect of the gay community in policy-making generally, or the specific kinds of discrimination a civil rights policy will cover. It could involve the specific kind of recognition a domestic partnership policy will provide.

> In Raleigh, North Carolina, the campaign for a nondiscrimi-
> nation policy began when a church that had allowed
> the predominately lesbian/gay Metropolitan Community
> Church to meet in its building got bomb threats. The
> threats led one of the church's heterosexual members to
> organize a meeting, which in turn led to a church-organized
> public hearing on anti-gay prejudice and discrimination.

The first step in using a galvanizing event is to develop an explanation of how the event ties into your policy proposal; for example, how it illustrates the need. If you can do this with one of your basic themes, so much the better.

Next, make the connection for the audience you want to work on— the lesbian/gay community, the board, or the public—using the techniques for lobbying that audience. (See chapters 17, Lobbying; 6, Organizing in the Lesbian/Gay Community; 18, Mass Action; 13, Working with the Media; 21, Public Hearings; 9, Endorsements.)

If you want to use an event to begin the process of adopting the policy, you can approach members of the board and ask them to introduce the policy because of the event. If you want to start a bit more gradually, use the galvanizing event to organize one of the pre-introduction events described in section 10.3.

10.2

> **In Durham, North Carolina, a civil rights campaign began when a gay man was killed at a sunbathing spot as a result of what began as an anti-gay assault. Largely in response to the crime, a group of lesbians and gay men began making plans for the city's first gay pride march while seeking endorsements from progressive political organizations. When they asked the mayor for a proclamation supporting the parade, he held a public hearing on it. The proclamation he issued lead to an attempt to recall him. Durham's nondiscrimination policy was adopted with the mayor's support after the recall was defeated.**

While many campaigns have either been sparked or significantly advanced by anti-gay violence, sometimes more mundane examples of discrimination work well also. People are often better able to identify with lesbians and gay men who suffer discrimination in situations with which most people are familiar. It is also often easier for people to see the connection between the incident and a policy if the incident is something the policy would directly address.

> **In Saginaw, Michigan, the stage may have been set for a housing nondiscrimination policy by a violent attack on the patrons of a gay bar. People went to the bar with clubs and crowbars and physically assaulted people leaving the bar.**
>
> **But the policy was actually introduced in response to an eviction. A member of the city council proposed the amendment after a landlord evicted a gay man because, as the landlord admitted to the local papers, he disapproved of gay people.**

You can also use events that show lesbians and gay men being left out of community processes when they ought to be included.

> The policy process in Flint, Michigan, got started because the local **AIDS** prevention campaign was focused on heterosexual transmission. Protests that the use of African-American women in campaign posters reinforced stereotypes led to an education program at which the city began to acknowledge that gay men had been ignored completely.
>
> In Greensboro, North Carolina, the process was sparked by a new parking regulation that would have eliminated an informal lesbian/gay evening gathering spot. Apologetic city leaders admitted they hadn't consulted the gay community because they didn't really know there was one.

10.3

Making Things that Get Public Attention Happen

Boards or their committees usually hold public hearings when they have specific policy proposals before them. But other organizations, such as human rights commissions and church groups, often hold more general hearings on community problems. (See chapter 21.) Policy campaigns can be started with public hearings on discrimination in general, with public hearings on the lesbian and gay community, and with hearings on related issues.

> In Irvine, California, the mayor appointed a special commission to investigate all forms of discrimination in the city. The commission spent five months doing research and holding hearings with twelve community groups. At the end, it recommended that the city adopt a comprehensive civil rights law. (Orange County, North Carolina, went through a similar process.)
>
> In Greensboro, North Carolina, the city's human rights commission was persuaded to hold a series of hearings over a two-month period, covering anti-gay violence, police abuse, medical and psychological facts about being gay, discrimination, religious views about being gay, and

> **the legal aspects of a nondiscrimination policy. In the end, the commission made a detailed set of policy recommendations to the city council.**

You can start a policy campaign with a "little policy" campaign, an effort to get a policy passed by a small subunit of your institution. For example, if you ultimately want to get a university to adopt a nondiscrimination policy, you might start by asking a few carefully selected campus organizations to adopt one. If, ultimately, you want to get a policy from a city, you could ask its parks department or school board first.

One of the advantages of a "little policy" campaign is that if you succeed, you will usually get people from the organization that adopts it committed to nondiscrimination policies. They may then be strong allies when you move on to the next level.

> **In Connecticut, passage of local laws in Stamford and New Haven were important to setting up passage of the state law. They started a public debate, enlisted the support of moderate politicians in the two towns for a state law, and helped persuade some state legislators that supporting a state law wouldn't arouse the ire of voters. They also helped organize local communities for the statewide campaign.**
>
> **Berkeley, California, one of the first cities to include domestic partners in its health plan, was worried about cost. Domestic partners were included first in the school board's dental plan, then the school health plan, then the city's dental plan, etc.**

You may also be able to create events that illustrate some aspect of the problem at which the policy is aimed. Think about marches, gay pride rallies, proclamations in support of the Stonewall anniversary, petitions to a government, etc.

> **After the parking hearing in Greensboro, North Carolina, activists drew up a formal "complaint," listing the ways in which they believed the lesbian and gay community was mistreated. The complaint formed the basis for the human rights commission hearings, which resulted in the recommendation for the policy.**

10.3

> **In Durham, North Carolina, while the pride march was in the planning stage, a group of librarians had the public library mount a display on the lives of lesbians and gay men. The display caused a vigorous debate about lesbians and gay men in the local newspaper, in its letters column, and in community organizations.**

10.4 Speakers Bureaus, Information Tables, and Knocking On Doors

There are at least three techniques, borrowed from political campaigns, that you can use to build public support for your proposal.

First, set up a speakers bureau and market it aggressively. All you need to do is train a group of volunteers to speak about lesbians and gay men and why the policy is important. Put together a list of all the civic organizations you can think of, from garden clubs and churches to political clubs, committees, schools, and business clubs. Call them, find out who is in charge of programs, and offer to send a speaker. You can send speakers to organizations you might ask for endorsements later. You can also send them to groups that either cannot or would not endorse your proposal.

Second, set up public information tables on street corners, in shopping centers, and the like. First, check any local rules on where such tables are allowed and whether you need a permit. From a table you can distribute information about events and the policy itself, and you can ask people to sign endorsements, petitions, and postcards to the board. (See chapter 18.)

One of the great things about public information tables is that they put supporters of the policy in direct contact with the public. While a single short encounter with a gay person may not change the mind of a confirmed homophobe, it can begin the process of encouraging many people to reexamine their ideas about lesbians and gay men. It can also help destroy some common stereotypes (e.g., that all gay people are white men).

> **Organizers in Durham, North Carolina, set up tables in shopping malls while campaigning against an attempt to**

recall the mayor, who had signed a general proclamation against discrimination. They tried to have at least one gay person and one heterosexual at each table. The hope was that the gay person could talk directly about being gay and answer questions, and that the straight person would help demonstrate that recall opponents had political support outside the gay community.

Organizers are convinced that one of the most important benefits of the plan was the direct encounter with homophobia that some of their heterosexual supporters got. (Organizers in Irvine, California, had a similar experience.)

Finally, if you have a large number of volunteers, you should consider informational "precinct walking" in carefully selected places. Precinct walking simply means going door-to-door in a certain area, ringing bells and knocking on doors, and asking people you encounter to support the policy.

Precinct walking can bring you support because you'll find supporters you wouldn't find any other way, and because people will often agree to do things that they might not otherwise do when asked face-to-face. It can also win you new supporters, particularly among people who don't have strong feelings on the issue. A personal request for support is often critical with people who are undecided. The drawbacks to precinct walking are that it requires a lot of effort, and some of your volunteers are bound to have unpleasant experiences with people they encounter.

If you do precinct walk, make sure you have literature to give people who ask for more information. Also, be sure to have some device for getting a commitment on paper, like a support postcard or a petition. Do a little careful research before deciding where to walk. Try to pick areas likely to have a high proportion of fence sitters, weak supporters, and weak opponents. Try to pick areas where the statements of support you are seeking will do you the most good; for example, statements of support from voters might have the greatest impact on a board member who is not in a safe seat, one who is undecided about the policy.

11. USING ELECTORAL POLITICS

11.1 Introduction: Three Reasons to Get Involved in Politics

This chapter covers things you can do through electoral politics to advance your campaign. It applies mostly to campaigns where you are trying to get a board that has been elected by voters to adopt a policy. You can use electoral politics most effectively in:

* creating a lesbian/gay constituency
* building working relationships with board members and others who have a role in adopting policy
* getting public attention for your issue.

Building a constituency is important because one way to get politicians to pay attention to you is to show them that there are voters who care about your issue. Building working relationships is important because politicians, like most people, tend to respond more favorably to people they know. Getting public attention is important because politicians are likely to deal with issues they believe voters generally care about.

Most of the tactics covered here will help with at least two of these aims. All of the tactics covered here except one involve elections for office directly. The chapter also talks about getting lesbians and gay men appointed to boards and commissions. Appointments are often a result of being involved in the electoral process, and they are the principal way (short of electing lesbians and gay men to office) to get lesbians and gay men into policy-making positions.

11.2 Keep the Campaign Organization Out

It is probably not a good idea to have your campaign organization itself involved in electoral politics. First, because you'll need broad support to pass the policy, it is best to be nonpartisan. Since candidate endorsements make enemies as well as friends, they are likely to narrow your support rather than expand it. Second, candidate endorsements almost unavoidably involve considerations other than your policy, and organizations that make them are likely either to compromise the policy goal or compromise what they see as the lesbian/gay community's overall best interest.

There are two exceptions to this general rule: voter registration and candidates' nights/issue questionnaires. Voter registration doesn't involve taking sides in an election, so it can't really hurt; it is also about the most apple-pie electoral thing you can do (nobody is publicly against it). Candidates' nights and questionnaires about candidates' positions on the policy make politicians take sides on your issue. Since these techniques don't require you to choose between rival contenders (both can side with you if they want) and since they are focused precisely on your policy, they avoid most of the risks that accompany other kinds of involvement in electoral politics.

While your campaign organization ought to stay out of electoral politics, the individuals who do get involved may find that having an organization is essential. To use involvement in politics effectively, lesbians and gay men must be a visible presence. It is often easiest to be visible if you are identified with an organization such as a lesbian/gay political club. In addition, as explained below, sometimes you need to deploy people strategically to have much impact, and you can do this best with a political organization.

The obvious solution is to have the individuals either get involved in the election through an existing lesbian/gay political club or set up a new one. The political organization should not be merely the campaign organization with a different name. Some of the policy campaign leaders should focus primarily on the policy and stay out of the election. At least a few of the campaign's leaders and most important workers should stay out of election campaigns so that they can work with whomever wins.

Finally, in some electoral races, people who work in the policy campaign will disagree about who is the best candidate. You shouldn't discourage people from working for opposing candidates. If members of your campaign work on both sides in an election, it will buttress the nonpartisan status of your campaign. It may also make it easier to work with the eventual winner.

11.3 Registering Lesbian and Gay Voters

In many states it is easy to register voters, and almost anyone can do it. The first step is to find out what the local rules are. Most cities have a local official called a registrar of voters, who will explain what is necessary. If your town doesn't have a registrar, call your city council representative and find out who is in charge.

Remember, the idea is not to register any voter but to register lesbian and gay voters and to make sure politicians know you are doing it. Make your drive as visible as possible and as lesbian/gay identified as possible. To recruit lesbian and gay voters (and for visibility), focus your drive on lesbian/gay events and places. Even if you don't have an annual lesbian/gay pride parade or rally, you and your friends have Christmas parties, birthday parties, etc. If there is no lesbian/gay neighborhood, register outside lesbian/gay or gay-friendly bars and businesses. Try setting up a table labeled "lesbian/gay voter registration drive" in a part of town where supporters are likely to found.

If your state allows it, you can add a voter registration drive to things you are already doing. For example, think about coordinating it with a postcard campaign, with collecting discrimination stories, or with inviting people to public hearings. (See chapters 18, 21, 28, and 35.) Keep a count of how many people you register so that you can inform the politicians. If state law allows, ask people you register if they want to sign up for your campaign organization either as potential volunteers or to receive notice of important events like public hearings.

11.4 Candidate Questionnaires

More policy campaigns have used candidate questionnaires than any other single tactic. Typically, the questionnaires ask candidates if they will support the policy proposal. Sometimes they ask related questions about lesbians and gay men.

As discussed earlier, the trick to questionnaires is the right degree of specificity, not so broad a question about discrimination that candidates can later oppose the policy's details, not a complete draft of the policy that requires a full close reading.

A good compromise might be: Will you support a human rights ordinance that will make it illegal for the city or its contractors to discriminate in hiring, firing, or on the job on the basis of sexual orientation?

Or ask: Will you support an amendment to the city's human rights ordinance to make discrimination based on sexual orientation an illegal type of discrimination?

11.5

> **San Francisco organizers kicked off their campaign for an ordinance in 1977 by sending all the candidates for the upcoming board of supervisors election a draft civil rights ordinance and asking if each would support it. They received more than they bargained for when an incumbent in a tight race decided to bolster his stance with liberal voters by introducing the draft. The organizers hadn't lined up a sponsor for the bill, and the incumbent who introduced the draft was far less interested in working to pass it than he was in getting votes with a gesture. Fortunately, a good sponsor by the name of Harvey Milk got elected that year.**

11.5   Candidates' Nights

A "candidates' night" is an event where candidates explain their positions to an audience and usually answer some questions. They are often sponsored by political or civic organizations, and typically all the candidates for a given office are invited. In a smaller town, all the candidates for all the offices might attend, though sometimes at different times. Usually the public is welcome, although sometimes the meetings are open only to members of the sponsoring organization. In some ways, candidates' nights are better than questionnaires because they may permit you "follow-up" questions in which you are able to confirm the depth of a candidate's commitment or get specifics on any reservations.

If other organizations are holding candidates' nights, attend if you can and ask about support for your policy. If the event is open only to members, join. Ask other local organizations to co-sponsor a candidates' night with your organization. You may want to sponsor your own candidates' night. To attract candidates, you will probably need to have participated in some aspect of electoral politics (a registration drive or the first part of a campaign for a policy) to show that voters care about your issue, or to show that your support is otherwise valuable (for example, that you could provide campaign workers).

Even if you sponsor or co-sponsor your own night, attend other candidates' nights to make candidates who dodge the issue by dodging your event take a stand.

11.6

Raleigh's campaign for a civil rights ordinance really began with a community public meeting on discrimination against lesbians and gay men. After that successful event, the sponsors held a candidates' night for the upcoming city council election. While not all those running came, a few serious candidates did, and came away impressed by the organizational skills and energy that went into the public meeting on discrimination. A woman running for the first time pledged unambiguously to support an ordinance. She got the support of a group of dedicated volunteers. She won and sponsored the ordinance, which passed.

For questionnaires and candidates' nights to work, lesbian and gay voters need to know what the candidates have said. Use all the usual techniques for communicating with the lesbian/gay community: the lesbian/gay press, posters and flyers in gay business and gay-friendly businesses, etc. (See section 13.9.) You might also try providing the candidates' answers to the mainstream press.

11.6 Involvement in Mainstream Political Groups

Small organizations are the basis of most local politics—as the source of the money, and, often more important, the volunteers on which local politics runs. The form these organizations take varies enormously from city to city. Some cities have town and ward committees for each party, others have political party affiliated clubs, others work with "nonpartisan" (meaning not party-identified) civic associations.

> **In many parts of the country, lesbians and gay men are involved in politics through progressive organizations instead of lesbian/gay groups. As one activist from Durham, North Carolina, put it, "In the South, it isn't very easy to be either queer or progressive, but it is a lot easier to be progressive than it is to be queer."**

11.7

Working in mainstream organizations makes you known to some of the people you'll have to influence. The more volunteer work you do in mainstream clubs, the more others feel obligated to pay attention to you when you raise issues. As with any involvement in mainstream activities, your very presence will change some people's attitudes toward lesbians and gay men. If you work well with people, you'll build personal alliances that can be very helpful in your policy campaign.

Volunteer work may be an essential first step toward getting appointed to a commission. Once you've been involved with a mainstream organization for a while, you may want to get together with other lesbians and gay men and set up a lesbian/gay caucus or subcommittee, to ensure that everyone knows you are there.

11.7 Working for Candidates

Some activists think you should stay out of partisan politics while working on a policy proposal. Political campaigns, they say, are too time consuming, and the risk that you will alienate board members whose votes you'll need later is too great. This is probably good advice for most campaign leaders and visible lobbying workers.

On the other hand, few things build working relationships with politicians better than helping them to get elected.

Moreover, if one of your supporters is targeted because of his or her support for the policy, you will need to help. While the campaign organization itself should be neutral, its leaders should actively rally supporters to the board member under attack. Nothing will damage a campaign more than the board members' belief that they may be voted out of office if they support it.

Crude as it sounds, try to help winners. The point is to get people who know you (and to a certain extent, who owe you) into policy-making positions. If you have to choose between two candidates who are both supportive of your policy, you should usually pick the one most likely to win, not necessarily the one most ideologically compatible. Look for candidates to whom your effort might make a real difference, for example, candidates involved in close races. It may make sense to work in a small race rather than a large one. Five people each working in two city council races may have more impact than ten working in a mayor's race.

Think about marshaling and deploying your forces. If you've got ten people who can volunteer, it is probably better to have them work in a couple of campaigns than to spread them out, so that you've only got one volunteer in each. With volunteer forces, you can also move from campaign to campaign; for example, have seven people precinct walk for one candidate one weekend, and make phone calls for another the next. But don't get cute and have the same people work for opposing candidates.

Working for first-time candidates can often pay extra dividends. Politicians tend to have a special affection for those who supported them early. It is also sometimes easier to convince first-timers to support a lesbian/gay policy. Since they are often scraping together the support they need, they may be more willing to risk losing some supporters if they can pick up significant support from lesbians and gay men. Incumbent's paralysis—from fear of losing any support—usually hasn't set in yet.

To understand deployment, you need to know what activities each campaign has planned and when. If you come offering volunteers, most campaign managers will give you this information. General visibility, as always, is important. But here the idea is to make sure that the candidate and his or her organization knows that lesbians and gay

11.7

men are volunteering. You can usually do that by telling the candidate's staff where your volunteers come from when you show up. Don't wear gay pride T-shirts while precinct walking if that is not what the candidate wants.

Aside from volunteering for whatever the candidate's campaign has planned, you can introduce the candidate to the local gay community.

> **By the late seventies in both New York and San Francisco the "gay bar tour" had become an institution in local election campaigns. Lesbian and gay organizers would take politicians, clearly identified with buttons and name tags, to bars and restaurants, and have them introduce themselves to as many people as possible. Sometimes, owners would agree to stop the music briefly to allow a thirty-second or so stump speech.**

You can also arrange a "meet the candidate" session in bookstores, other businesses, or even in people's homes.

11.8 Getting Lesbians and Gay Men on Local Boards and Commissions

There are two advantages to getting lesbians and gay men appointed to local boards and commissions. First, they become political players; the politicians know them, and politicians will respond more readily to people they know. Second, and far more important, if you get appointed to the right commission, you could be helpful in moving policy along, by holding hearings, making recommendations, or developing evidence. In many cities, the first suggestion for a policy has come from a commission, such as a human relations commission. Often the commission's position was promoted by a lesbian or gay activist. (See section 10.3.) Although human rights commissions are an obvious choice, commissions on the status of women and civil service or personnel commissions are also good places to begin a campaign or to help it along. The great danger with appointments, just as with elective office, is that getting a person in office will become the end not the means. (See section 11.9.)

Getting appointed to local boards and commissions is easier in many places than you might think. Sometimes there is virtually no competition, and all you need to do is tell whomever makes appointments that you are interested. Even where things are not quite that easy, if you demonstrate a real interest in what the commission does—by attending meetings, offering to help out with minor tasks—you will often seem a logical choice for an appointment if you ask when there is a vacancy.

> The campaign for a policy in Flint, Michigan, was led by a lesbian who was a member of the City Human Rights Commission. She met the chair of the commission while she was serving on a YMCA task force on violence against women. He was impressed by her work. After she expressed interest in the commission, he recommended her for the next vacancy.

Asking is critical. Very few political appointments go to folks who wait humbly for recognition. The other way to get appointed is by doing political work for a party or an official, and then asking. Especially in larger cities, this is the way most people get appointed.

If is not possible to get someone on a commission, think about the possibility of getting the board you are working on to appoint a special commission to study discrimination against lesbians and gay men, or to study the need for local civil rights laws or needed revisions. While special commissions are generally less influential than standing commissions, they let you focus on your problem.

11.9 Running Lesbian and Gay Candidates

Running a candidate for office typically takes at least as much time, money, and sophistication as a policy campaign takes. While it usually makes no sense as a tactic in a policy campaign, it might, however, when the resources are available. This is a high-risk strategy that can pay off if it works. The risk is that if you fare badly in the election, you could lose most of your credibility. If you can't make even a good showing running one of your own, politicians are likely to conclude that you are not a significant enough force with the voters.

There is also the risk that if you do well, people will become confused about what is important. Far too many candidates who run at first to help with an issue come to think they are the cause. You reap most of the benefits of running a lesbian or gay candidate by running someone once and making a good showing. But few people who run can resist the temptation to have a go at it again, which will siphon time and money away from the policy campaign.

If your candidate loses but makes a respectable showing, you'll send a wake-up call to his or her opponents, and usually to most of the rest of the politicians. The message is that you have the three things politicians respect most—energy, the ability to raise money, and voters who care. They will pay attention to you, not just because your opposition is a potential threat but, perhaps more important, because your support is a potential asset.

> **Convinced they were not being taken seriously enough by politicians on the board of aldermen, Chicago activists decided to run an openly gay candidate for the board. They picked a district that had a large number of lesbian and gay residents. It was represented by someone who officially supported the policy but was unwilling to do much to get it passed. They raised more than most candidates, and they used state-of-the-art techniques. Although the gay candidate lost, it was a close race. The victor became one of the policy's most vigorous supporters.**

Of course, if you should actually win, you've got a player who, in the right office, can directly help the policy along. You've also got a colleague among the politicians, and most politicians are responsive to people they work with and whose help they may need. Harvey Milk once said that the most important thing about his election was that it stopped the other members of the board from referring to fags and dykes when they were meeting in private.

Don't try to run a candidate unless you can get the money, volunteers, and professional help you'll need to make a good showing. The point about professional help can't be overstated. Money and work alone are not enough to win elections. You need a pro who knows how to win elections in your area (techniques vary enormously from place to place). You also need pros to tell what a respectable showing is, so that you can gauge the risks.

Since this strategy succeeds or fails almost entirely on the basis of how well you do this, don't pick the office that might be most directly helpful to your campaign; instead, pick the office that presents the best chance to do well. If your policy-making body is elected by district, pick the district where you'll get the most votes (unless you stand to make an enemy out of an important supporter by doing that) instead of the one represented by your most implacable opponent. If it looks as if you could come close, or even win a run for, say, the water board, but are not likely to do well in a election for the city council, go for the aqua.

12.1

> **True political professionals do more than dispense clichés from armchairs. They analyze voting patterns and electoral techniques to find out who votes and what they respond to. In Connecticut, a gay man won election to the state House of Representatives by defeating a party leader in what was thought to be a traditional Democratic working-class stronghold. The challenger picked the district because a careful analysis of census reports and results of earlier elections convinced him that the district consisted mostly of minorities, and that local leadership had failed to recognize this and respond to the changes. He later went on to lead the successful effort to enact Connecticut's lesbian/gay civil rights law.**

12. DEVELOPING LITERATURE

12.1 Introduction: What this Chapter Covers

This guide has many suggestions for using written literature in your campaign. This chapter is designed to show you the different kinds of literature you may want to use and how to prepare them. At the end it gives a few suggestions about how to use literature effectively.

Try to get professional writers and designers to help you with all of your literature. The greatest message in the world is of no help if your audience doesn't read it. Attractive design and clear, direct writing are essentials, not luxuries.

12.2 The Purposes of Campaign Literature

Most campaign literature is designed to serve one or more of these purposes:

* to get your messages out,
* to tell people about your support,
* to inform and mobilize your supporters.

12.3 Basic Pieces Most Campaigns Need

Virtually every campaign needs a few key pieces.

First, you need a piece that makes the case for the policy: a sheet or brochure that explains your main argument and your most important secondary arguments about why the board should adopt the policy.

You need this piece for people who don't know about the issue and who haven't taken a stand as well as for supporters and endorsers, who need to know what your basic argument for the policy is, especially so that they can explain it (and their support) to others.

It should be easy to draw this piece out of your case statement. (See chapter 8.)

Second, you need a piece that answers most of the arguments being made against the policy. This kind of piece can often be done as a "question/answer" or "myth/truth" piece, in which you quickly summarize the objection in a "question" or "myth" and then respond to it. One of the advantages the question-and-answer format has over myth/truth is that it allows you to state the opposition's position in your own words.

You need this piece for the same reasons you need a basic case piece. You may be able to combine these two pieces, depending on how long your arguments are. On the other hand, it may be a better idea to keep them short and separate.

Third, you'll want to have a list of all the organizations and important individuals who support your proposal. Keep this on file in a computer if you can, since you'll have to update it often. For the same reason, don't make too many copies of any single version.

Fourth, if the board you are working on represents constituents (for example, the way a city council represents voters), you probably need a constituent contact piece. This tells people who their representative is, how to make contact, and what to say. If the board governs a geographical area, the easiest way to tell people who their representatives are may be with a map. Consider updating the constituent contact piece regularly with information about who needs to be contacted most and where the members of the board stand on the proposal. (See section 20.14.)

12.4   Special Issue Literature

If an issue becomes particularly important in the campaign, you may want to devote a special piece to it. The advantage of this kind of piece is that you can explain your argument in greater detail and use your expert sources. Special issue pieces can be particularly helpful for your allies, who may not know how to respond to some arguments from the opposition. Late in their campaign, Connecticut organizers put out a daily information sheet for legislators. Typically the sheet would provide in-depth answers on specific fact issues, and detailed arguments.

Special issue pieces don't have to be structured as conventional arguments. For example, if you want to do something on why you need a nondiscrimination law, you could do short summaries of strong witness testimony under the headline "We Need a Lesbian/Gay Civil Rights Policy."

You may also want to do special pieces that respond to particular opposition tactics. If you do, remember not to attack, and to keep the emphasis on your arguments.

> Opponents of a civil rights policy in Durham, North Carolina, circulated recall petitions to remove a mayor who had supported a lesbian/gay pride day march. Policy supporters set up tables near the petitioners in shopping areas. For their tables, the supporters prepared a special flyer with the headline THINK BEFORE YOU SIGN. It emphasized arguments that a recall election would not be a good thing for Durham.

12.5 Endorsement Lists and Other Support Literature

If you think the board you are lobbying is worried about one particular group of constituents, or if some members of your board respond more strongly to some groups, prepare a special list of supporters. For example, if board members whose votes you need are small business advocates, write up a list of small businesses and business associations that support the policy. You can also put together special lists of local or national organizations that have endorsed either your policy or civil rights in general. Connecticut organizers, convinced that legislators were worried about religious opposition, put together a list of all local and national religious organizations that had endorsed civil rights for lesbians and gay men. They distributed the list of over 150 organizations to every legislator a few days before the final vote.

If you are working on a political board, you could write a piece on polls that show most voters support civil rights for lesbians and gay men. You could also do a piece on the fact that legislators who vote for lesbian gay/civil rights don't suffer politically for doing so. (See section 17.11.)

12.6 Sheets and Newsletters for Communicating with Supporters

If you have a sizable grass-roots campaign, you'll need to communicate regularly with your volunteers. (See section 6.4.) If you decide to do a regular "sheet," try to standardize as much as you can.

It will save time, and it will help your supporters find what they are looking for. For example, part of your sheet could be a regular box with the names of the board members who most need to be contacted. Another could be a box with upcoming events listed. Try to get the basic format set up on a computer.

You might want to do a special sheet explaining how the board works; this could be combined with a "how to contact your representative" piece. If there are hearings that will include public testimony, you may want to do a sheet explaining the ground rules. (See section 22.10.)

12.7 **Writing Campaign Literature**

There are a few very important guidelines:

* Make your point in the first sentence; provide context, background, explanations later. You simply cannot count on most people to read all of anything, even a half-page flyer. Your only chance to get to many readers will be with that first sentence. Even if you think a word of explanation is essential to make your point, make the point first and give the explanation right after it.

* Write short sentences, use basic English, and avoid jargon. Sentences that run on and on, or contain obscure words, usually have to be read twice. You can't count on people to read campaign literature twice.

* Don't lie, exaggerate, or attack your opposition.

* Don't say anything in writing you aren't willing to have the whole world see. (See also sections 13.1 and 13.5.)

(See the guidelines in chapters 8, 15, and 16 on how to put together the text for message pieces.)

12.8 **Hot Tips on Design**

Try to put everything on a single sheet. It's much cheaper and the likelihood that anyone will read a long handout decreases with each page. But don't use tiny type, tiny margins, or omit spaces between paragraphs. Remember that printing on both sides of a sheet is fine as long as you don't want to tack up the piece anywhere. If you want to post it, you'll have to stick to one side.

When you start putting a piece together, think about all the different ways you might be able to use it. See if you can write one piece to fill multiple needs. For example, you may be able to create a newsletter that is also a meeting notice and that can be posted.

12.9 Hot Tips on Use

Every time you set up a table or a booth, your basic case and basic answers material should be on it. If you register voters, find out if it is legal to have campaign literature on the table; if it is, do it. Every time you go to speak to another group either to ask for support or to give information, bring literature and ask for permission to pass it out. Have literature at public hearings. Anytime you visit an undecided board member, leave behind your basic case and basic answer pieces. Put your phone number on it so that the member can contact you with questions.

13. WORKING WITH THE MEDIA

13.1 Introduction: What's Covered Here, Where Else to Look

Everybody knows the media is important. It may be the most effective way of getting the attention of the board you are lobbying and the public. And whether you want attention or not, the way you come across if the media does cover your story may be the most important factor in whether you get the policy passed.

Dealing with the media effectively means planning what you do and acquiring communication skills. This chapter covers some of the basics on both of those things. For more guidance, there are usually several good books on dealing with the media available at any time. Get a guide and read it before you start.

13.2 Basic Goals and Ground Rules

The basic goal for all your dealings with the media should be to get your messages about the policy out to your audiences (the board and its constituencies). It is not to explain or justify lesbians and gay men to the world generally; it is not to answer whatever questions you are asked; and it is not to get your picture on TV so that you can wave to Mom.

Never lie to a reporter. If you are found out (and you will be most of the time) you'll lose your credibility with reporters (and with the public if the lie becomes a part of the story). Better just to say you don't want to talk about something.

Gross exaggerations are as bad as lies.

Don't try to use media to advance a side issue or carry out a vendetta against some person or organization. Reporters are likely to see what you are doing, and, again, your credibility will be shot. Don't say anything to a reporter that you don't want to read about in the paper or hear about on TV. Commenting "off the record" or "Not for attribution" frequently blows up in your face, if for no other reason than that people are often able to guess correctly where the comments come from. If you don't want a message attached to the campaign, don't deliver it.

13.3 Getting Organized

You need either a person or a small committee in charge of coordinating your media operation. At the start of your campaign, put together a list of all the electronic and print outlets that reach any significant part of your audience. Your list should include when each outlet appears (or broadcasts) and what the deadlines for each are. You can usually get deadlines by calling and asking. You need them for announcements and for scheduling events and press conferences. Your list should include the names of reporters who cover the board on which you are working, and the editors who supervise them. Some outlets list reporters' names and beats; sometimes you can figure it out by reading the papers or listening for a few days. As you go along, you'll be able to refine this list. Include on the list any columnists or public affairs shows followed by the audiences you are trying to reach. Get their individual deadlines if you can. Organize your list so that it will be easy to call or fax the outlets and let them know when an important event is about to happen; this will make it easier to mail written releases, etc.

Select designated speakers and have them do all or most of the interviews and media appearances for the campaign. Your coordinators don't have to be the same people as your designated speakers. The coordinators need to be good organizers. The speakers need to be comfortable speaking in public and able to follow some basic guidelines on how to speak to the media (the guides may seem straightforward, but most people find them difficult to put into practice). Your designated speakers represent the campaign, so they should project the image you want people to have of it.

13.3

In New York City every opinion essay put out by the campaign was signed by a woman and a man, at least one with an "ethnic" surname. Every press conference included a small panel of speakers that was balanced for gender and included a racial minority. Every important press statement was made, at least in part, by a woman or a minority.

This was not the result of ideas about what was "politically correct." The campaign wanted to combat the widespread idea that all gay people were economically comfortable white men. The campaign thought that notion had made it difficult to get some needed votes on the city council.

You also may want to have speakers who, by their very presence, will help answer some argument being made against the policy or will help with an organizing problem.

> Organizers in Greensboro, North Carolina, used a promi-
> nent heterosexual political leader as one speaker because
> they wanted to convince the council that the policy had
> political support outside the gay community.
>
> Saginaw, Michigan, organizers believed most of their
> opposition would be religious. As their primary speaker
> they chose a prominent, middle-of-the-road local minister.

Train your speakers. Put together the tips in this chapter with ideas you get from the media books, articles, etc. If you know an experienced spokesperson, ask him or her to design and run a training session. Otherwise, have your media coordinators and your speakers do it themselves.

Make sure that some or all of your coordinators, your speakers, and your policy people are prepared to act as an emergency response team if something comes up that needs an immediate response. The members of the team should be able to get in touch with each other quickly at any time.

13.4

13.4   Building Relationships with the Media

The first tip is almost too obvious: make friends with reporters whenever you can. Be friendly, and do what you can to make their jobs easier, especially by telling them about events ahead of time (see below, section 13.5), and by making the materials you give them as useful as possible (see below, section 13.6).

If a paper or an electronic outlet ignores the lesbian/gay community, or if much of the coverage seems based on outdated ideas about lesbians and gay men, you may want to try to meet with the editors. First, decide if the problem is with the outlet's news stories, its statements of opinion, or both. Usually, different groups are in charge of news and opinions (i.e., editorials). Editorial pages often reflect the views of an outlet's owner. Editorial page editors are more likely to have a strong ideological position on civil rights for lesbians and gay men. If you have a problem with news coverage or with both news and editorials, you are more likely to make progress if you can meet with the news editors apart from the editorial editors.

> **Greensboro, North Carolina, activists asked for a meeting with the news editors of the local paper after it carried a story referring to a lesbian/ gay rights march in Raleigh as an "AIDS" demonstration. They explained the difference and used the meeting to give the editors basic information about lesbians and gay men, and about living as a gay person in the area. Activists were able to use the contacts they made in this meeting to get coverage for the campaign to pass a civil rights ordinance.**

News coverage is more important than the editorial page because many more people read the news pages. But don't give up on editorial editors. Local political leaders often follow editorial pages closely, and having the support of editorial editors (and the implicit support of the paper's top management) can often improve news coverage.

> **For years, New York newspapers were hostile to the proposed lesbian/gay civil rights law, with the *Daily News* referring to "fags and swishes" in an editorial and *The Times* ignoring the campaign. When *The Times* editorial board finally agreed to meet with the supporters, it cross-examined them aggressively. But the supporters had come prepared to prove the law was needed, and the meeting led to a supportive editorial and improved coverage.**

Editors may resist requests to meet. A supporter, a helpful politician, or a community group that has a relationship with the outlet may be able to set up a meeting for you. Approach a meeting with editors the same way you would approach any meeting with an important local political player. Be calm and use reason. If you have complaints about coverage, be specific and be ready to show plainly why the stories were inaccurate, etc., or why similar events got covered when lesbian/gay events did not. If you are going to try to convince the outlet to support your proposal, be ready to make the same arguments you would to a board or a community organization, and be ready to prove your points.

It may be worth the trouble to establish relationships with local columnists, especially those who write about civic affairs, or gossip columnists. They are often more influential than editorial writers. If you know someone who knows the columnist, use your contact. If you get an appointment, be prepared to make your case the same way you'd make it to a board member.

> **A few Catholic members of New York's city council came out in support of the civil rights bill. The bill's backers are convinced that essays by local Irish Catholic columnists applauding those members for their courage kept the members from backsliding, and encouraged others to join them.**

13.5 Getting News Coverage

The best way to get your message across through the media is in news coverage. Many more people follow it than read guest editorials or listen to public affairs or public access programs. News stories have more credibility than plainly partisan letters or public service announcements.

If you know that a potentially newsworthy event, like a public hearing or a vote, is coming up, make sure the media knows about it in advance. Fax or mail written announcements and call reporters and editors you know, especially sympathetic ones. If you think you may be able to get a supportive editorial, make sure the editorial editors get separate announcements and calls. If a newsworthy event is being sponsored by an official board or by a neutral community group, try to convince the sponsor to put out the press announcement. Media outlets that are not particularly interested in your campaign will be more likely to come.

If you have any role in scheduling an event, whether a demonstration or a hearing, or in setting its agenda, keep the various media deadlines in mind and make sure that the message you want to put out is effectively conveyed with the media present.

If a potentially galvanizing event occurs, like a vivid example of discrimination (see chapter 10), call the reporters and editors you know, tell them about it, and offer comments. If you have time, put a press briefing together. Make sure you explain the tie between any event and the policy. If you call reporters about an event that is not local, make sure you explain the local angle in your call or release. The local angle can be the policy, but be as specific as you can about how the event relates to it.

Put together a press packet to give to reporters each time one begins covering the campaign and also to give out at major events. The packet could contain a copy of the proposed policy, your basic pieces explaining the case for the policy, your answers to the opposition, and lists of your endorsers (see section 12.3), and the announcement and/or the release for the event in question. Highlight the background materials that relate to the specific event a reporter is covering.

13.6   Press Releases and Announcements

Press releases are model stories; they should include everything you might want to have a media outlet cover. Press announcements are designed to get reporters to come to an event. They should say when and where the event is and should provide a brief description of what the event will be about. They should not include the whole story, because busy reporters will be less likely to come if they do. For most events, you should do both. Send the announcement out in advance. Hand the release to reporters who come, and fax or deliver the release shortly after the event takes place to the outlets that didn't make it so they can cover the event.

Try to write your releases like stories, not like the "puff" pieces a public relations officer might write. Your sentences should be short. Write in active voice. Avoid adjectives. Don't exaggerate. Put in usable quotes: short, pithy statements that sum up your position, not long expositions. Remember that news stories aren't written like essays. They begin not with background but with the core—the most important, exciting part of the story. They should then go from the most important details to the least. They don't have conclusions.

Since your release should read like a story, if you have time, attach a written statement from the campaign that will read like a statement made at a press conference. Some reporters don't like working off releases. This can be written like a statement of position. Any quotes from the campaign you put in the release should be from the statement.

13.7 Letters, Guest Editorials, Public Access, and Talk Shows

Letters to the editor are probably the best-read part of most editorial pages. If readers are writing in about your campaign, be sure that you respond. At times you may want to respond officially on behalf of the campaign, if, for example, a letter makes a charge against it. But letters from individuals usually stand a better chance of being printed, so have campaign volunteers write as well.

In Durham, North Carolina, the controversy that led to a nondiscrimination policy was sparked in part when the library did a display around lesbian/gay pride day. For weeks after the display was announced, the letters to the editor column of the local paper carried a vigorous debate on the propriety of the display, and of civil rights for lesbians and gay men generally. Within a few days, almost everyone in town was following the letters debate

Letters can also be a way to get your message out if you are having trouble getting coverage. Most papers will print only short letters, and will edit long ones to get them down to size. Try to keep control of the content and avoid being edited. Watch the column to see the average length that the paper prints, and write to that length. Write letters the way you write releases: put the core up front, be terse and direct.

Many newspapers print guest opinion columns on their editorial page or the page opposite it (the "op-ed" page). Whether you see guest pieces in your local paper or not, call the editorial editor and ask if guest pieces are ever used, and if so, how long they should be, if there are other requirements. Guest editorials can be more formally written than releases and letters, but complex, stodgy writing is the reason most people avoid editorial pages. If you really want to have an impact, keep your sentences short, write in the active voice, and use simple, direct English. Start with something exciting. With guest editorials, it often helps to be pushy. Instead of mailing it in, hand-deliver it. Ask if the paper will print it. If the editor is discouraging, ask what you could do differently to give it a better chance; then do so and redeliver.

Many radio and TV stations allow people to do short "free speech" messages or public service announcements. Call each in your area and find out its policy and the length and technical requirements. If a radio or TV station comes out against your policy, ask for time to reply. Although they use scripts, radio and TV are essentially spoken media. Your message will sound more natural if you prepare and deliver it like a short talk rather than reading a short essay. Begin with your main point and finish with one snappy sentence that sums up your position.

In some areas, cable TV runs a public access channel that sets aside time for local public service announcements. (When you call to find out what the cable company`s policies are, ask if you can use your own producer if the campaign has access to someone with experience.) Radio talk shows can be a good way to get your message out, but be careful: most hosts are experienced manipulators of the medium. If a host is hostile, the odds are she or he can either get you to lose your cool or twist your message, both serious mistakes. Unless you are very experienced, turn down hostile shows.

13.8   Avoiding Coverage

Chicago organizers adopted an "anti-media" strategy. They believed they could pass a civil rights ordinance without general public pressure on the council, and that they could generate enough pressure on the council from the lesbian/gay community through the gay press alone. They also believed that if the ordinance did become a public issue, there would be considerable pressure on the council not to pass it.

They decided to keep the ordinance out of the press. Except for one press conference to announce widespread support among organized religions, they called no press conferences or briefings. They almost never called main-

> stream media, and they talked to reporters as little as
> possible. They did no ads, wrote no letters, and turned
> down all requests for talk shows.

The risks of a stealth campaign are discussed elsewhere (see section 5.3). But even if you decide to reject the Chicago strategy, there may be times when you will want to minimize a story. Before you decide to minimize a story, think about whether that is really a smart thing to do. If there is a part of your policy that could be very controversial, you may want to avoid highlighting it, but you should always be ready to defend it. If your opposition has made what seems a telling point in the press, running from the media will make it look all the more telling (see section 13.3).

13.9

If you do want to minimize a story, pay attention to deadlines. Just as you can schedule things to gain media attention, events scheduled after deadlines have passed or that occur when the media have left stand less of a chance of being reported. In most places, Friday and Saturday newscasts and Saturday newspapers have the smallest audience. Sunday and Monday are the reverse and doubly dangerous because they cover slow news days, and small matters can become exaggerated. Check the patterns in your local press.

Just as direct, vivid quotes tend to get used, long colorless statements tend not to. The least quotable answers are those that take no distinct stand and invoke no strong images. Qualifiers ("sometimes," "perhaps") make bad quotes. If you don't pause in the middle of a comment, it will be harder to edit it. If you are going to refuse to answer a question, avoid saying "no comment" if you possibly can. It sounds as if you are hiding something. Say "that's personal," or "I need to check on that."

13.9 Working with the Gay Press

Use the lesbian/gay press as a part of your campaign if you can. Use it to announce the campaign itself and campaign meetings, and use it to help with lobbying, information gathering, and public events. (See sections 6.4, 6.5, 7.8, 12.6, 18.3, 22.10, and 28.2.)

> **Chicago organizers treated the local lesbian/gay press as if it were a newsletter for the campaign. It publicized all organization meetings. It published a series of drafts of the policy on behalf of the campaign organization and invited community comment. It put out alerts with the names of council members who needed to be pressured. It told the community which members should be left alone. It notified the community about rallies, public hearings, and council meetings.**

The lesbian/gay press are newspapers and newsletters (usually monthlies or weeklies) marketed to lesbians and gay men. In some parts of the country they operate statewide or regionally, and in some places different cities have their own. If there is no gay press in your area, see if there is a "bar" magazine or newsletter (an informal gossipy publication usually passed out in bars, etc.) or a newsletter for a committee group or a lesbian/gay caucus of a church or civic group. If there is, try to convince its publisher to begin carrying stories and information about the campaign. Many lesbian/gay newspapers started as "bar rags." If there are no potential bar magazines, think about starting a small campaign newsletter to be distributed in bars and other lesbian/gay and gay-friendly businesses.

To work with the lesbian/gay press effectively, you must give it the respect you give the mainstream press. It should get all the same announcements, releases, packets, etc., that the mainstream press receives. Cultivate lesbian/gay press contacts just as you would cultivate contacts in the mainstream press.

To get the active support of the lesbian/gay press, you'll need to get the editors and owners behind the campaign early. Contacts can be critical. If the editors don't know you, they are much more likely to hear you out if you come with someone they do know and respect. Don't assume that editors in the lesbian/gay press will automatically support your effort. They tend to be conservative (just like the editors of most mainstream media). Be prepared to lobby them as you would the editors of a mainstream paper, staying matter-of-fact, and proving every point.

13.10 A Word About Advertising

Advertising isn't a practical tool for most campaigns. You most likely won't be able to afford it. And even if money isn't a problem, advertising is not usually an effective tool for passing civil rights policy because it is aimed solely at your secondary audience—the public—instead of at the board. Since everyone knows it is partisan and paid for, it has less credibility than any other forms of media. Moreover, selling ideas isn't like selling soap. Except in some initiative election campaigns, Americans generally don't rely on advertising much in thinking about policy.

Nonetheless, there are a few times when it makes sense to consider advertising. If all else fails, you can use it to publicize your meetings and, if you do a regular ad, to do some kinds of campaign education (names of members who need to be contacted, etc.). In some parts of the country, advertising is often used to publicize endorsements. In some places, it is widely used in local initiative and referendum campaigns.

Pay close attention to other local efforts to see if any use advertising, what kind they use, and whether they use it successfully. Talk to local political pros about whether they think advertising is important. If you do use it, try to target your efforts on the groups you need to reach and who may respond. Campaign information directed at those who want it and can't get it elsewhere is more likely to work.

Use a pro with experience to help design your ads, tailor the messages, and pick the vehicles. Advertising is too quirky and too expensive for amateurs.

14. MEDIA APPEARANCES

14.1 Introduction: What this Chapter Covers

This chapter covers preparing to talk to reporters and tips on how to be effective with both print and electronic media. To make the chapter easier to read, the term "readers" will include "viewers" and "listeners."

14.2 Getting Ready: An Audience and a Message

Before any media interview, think about who the audience is. With whom do you want to communicate? Most of the time the audience will be the readers, not the interviewer. Think about who this interviewer's readers are. It can vary enormously from paper to paper and station to station. Decide what message you want to send to these readers. Remember, when you think about targeting a message, although it is smart to focus on the specific audience, you can't limit the dissemination of what you say. So, while you should tailor your remarks, don't say anything you would not be comfortable having another audience hear.

Develop a quotable way to put your message across. You need to be able to sum it up in a short sentence or two. The summary should take no more than seven to fifteen seconds to deliver. It should use the kind of words average people use in conversation. For example, you might summarize a job fairness argument by saying:

> *It comes down to this: In a world where you've got to work to eat and have a roof over your head, it isn't fair to let someone who does a good job be tossed out of it because the foreman doesn't approve of her.*

Also, the phrases you use and any analogies you draw should be colorful.

When you get called for an interview, ask the reporter what she or he wants to talk about before you agree to do it. This is completely defensible; you wouldn't talk with a reporter if you didn't know anything about the subject. Most reporters will willingly fill you in. Offer suggestions about the story—what it might emphasize, or ways in which it might be better if the focus were changed a bit. Reporters often don't know where they are going with a story idea at first, and you may be able to shape the story significantly.

Once you know what the interview is to be about, consider whether you can bridge from that topic to the message you want to deliver. Most of the time, you can do that easily. For instance, if the message you want to get at is about job fairness, and the interview is to be about whether the policy will interfere with religious freedom, you can bridge to your message like this:

> *We are for religious freedom; the government should never interfere with matters of conscience. But that doesn't mean people's beliefs should be able to control whether someone with different beliefs can work. [Then segue into your job fairness point.]*

If you can't bridge to your message, ask yourself it there is a message which you think is important to convey to this audience and which you can tie to the interview. If not, you probably should not do the interview.

Once you know your message and your bridge and have a quotable summary ready, prepare the arguments you'll make in support of the summary. Most of them should be in colorful shorthand as well— no more than twenty seconds or so to deliver. You can give reporters more detailed explanations, but both print and electronic media are unlikely to use anything more than the summary of your position and maybe the shorthand argument.

The bridge, the summary, and the arguments are your rap. Practice your raps (you'll have more than one, since you have more than one message). Don't memorize your raps. If you do, they'll sound wooden. But run though them enough so you're familiar with each and comfortable when you answer questions. As you run through them, you'll refine both your ideas and your way of conveying them. Try to figure out what the tough questions may be and their answers, and develop a rap to deliver the answer in the interview. Again, practice the rap but don't memorize it. If you find it helpful, get someone to practice the interview with you. Tell them to be skeptical and tough.

14.2

14.3 Getting Ready: Pre-interview Research

Always read the morning newspaper on the day of an interview and the evening newspaper from the day before. The reporter will probably have read them, and if there is anything in either related to your campaign, it will doubtlessly come up. In fact, it may well have prompted the interview. If there is a locally popular news or public affairs program on the radio or TV (whether local or national like NPR's "Morning Edition" or ABC's *Nightline*), tune in.

Find out everything you can about the reporter coming to see you. Your media committee should keep a log of stories (print and electronic) so that you know what each reporter has said about the campaign and any related issues.

14.3

14.4 Being Interviewed

First, be yourself; warmth and enthusiasm work with most reporters. Never get into an argument with a reporter, especially not on tape.

With TV and radio interviewers, ask to talk for a few minutes before the taping begins. This is particularly easy with TV, since the person operating the camera will usually be setting up. If you describe your position and main points in a pretaping conversation, you will often find that the questions will be pitched right at you when the interview starts.

Whenever you can, use the points you've decided to make when you answer the reporter's questions. Don't leave them to a summary at the end; they are far less likely to get into the story.

If you disagree with something the interviewer states in a question, say so when you start to answer. Especially with radio and TV, never answer another point first and then register your disagreement. The disagreement must come right after the question, or the question and an answer may get broadcast while your disagreement is cut.

If you are asked a hypothetical question, give a hypothetical answer and make sure you say that the answer is hypothetical. If you think the hypothetical is farfetched, say that before you answer, and respond to the question itself only if you think it raises a concern your audience may care about.

For example, if a reporter asks, "What would happen if a court ruled that your law required hiring quotas," you might say:

> *That's a farfetched hypothetical. There are laws like this all over the country, some of which have been on the books for over twenty years, and no court has ever done anything like that.*

If a question gives you a set of choices, you don't have to accept them; you can offer your own alternative.

For example, if a reporter asks, "So, when it comes down to a choice between additional burdens on small business or rights for homosexuals, you say we should choose the homosexuals," you might reply by saying:

> *We don't face that kind of a choice. Not discriminating doesn't cost anything, and experience under the laws in other states and cities shows these laws don't impose new costs on small businesses.*

Don't accept guilt by association, either, and don't speak for others. For example, if a reporter asks, "Isn't your ultimate goal, like ACT-UP's, to radically restructure society?," don't try to explain what ACT-UP's goals really are. Instead, just say what your goal is.

If a reporter asks you a slew of questions at once, take advantage. Say you'll be orderly in answering, then pick the question that makes it easiest for you to get to your message, and answer it.

Don't get drawn into a discussion about things unrelated to your proposed policy or the topic of the interview, such as gay marriage or religious dogma. If a reporter gets far afield, bring him or her back to the topic of the interview. When trying to bring a reporter back to the topic, use your bridges if you can. If you can't, just say, "You asked me here to talk about the proposed civil rights law. Here's what we think about [the topic]"; then, go into your message.

14.4

14.5 Some Special Tips About Radio and TV

If you are going to be on a show, watch or listen to it first. Get a feel for the interviewer and how the show works. Make sure you find out when the show will be on and how long it is. This will tell you something about your audience and something about how many points you can cover (in a half-hour show, two or three is usually all you can get to).

With electronic media, it is critical that you put your message into a ten- to twenty-second answer. Always make your summary point first in an answer, clearly and cleanly. That means make it without qualifiers, ifs, ands, or buts. After you've made it, expand on it by providing background. Since you have no control over how the tape will be edited, this gives you the best chance to get your point in.

Don't restate the other side's position; this merely gives them air time. If you have to say something about their argument, put your spin on it.

If you get interrupted by another guest on a show or by a reporter or host, don't speak louder or faster. You are likely to appear out of control if you do. Keep your voice and face steady and keep talking. Most important, stick to what you were saying. That will highlight the fact that you were interrupted. If you respond right away, you'll legitimize the interruption. If you want to respond, do it when you finish your point.

When you are on TV, *smile* (unless you are talking about something tragic). TV tends to make people look more dour than they are. If you don't smile, you are apt to look unfriendly. Don't ever get angry or antagonistic. It will usually look like you think an important point against you has been made. At best, you'll look excitable, which is not the image you want for a policy debate.

If you are making a public information announcement, look at the camera. If you are being interviewed, always look at the reporter. In an interview, you'll look evasive if you look at the camera instead of the reporter. On a show with multiple guests, look at the host or the interviewer. Never look at the monitor (you'll look shifty on screen).

Always assume that you are on camera. TV likes to use "reaction" shots of people listening to someone else speaking. Never react in a way you wouldn't want the world to see. Never fidget or become agitated; it looks like you think the other speaker has scored an important point. Also, always assume that any microphone is on. (Remember former president Ronald Reagan's "joke" about the bombing of Russia beginning in five minutes?)

If a TV show offers you makeup, take it. The offer usually means the lighting they are using will make you look pale and sick if you don't.

Richard Nixon refused makeup for the first televised presidential debate against John Kennedy. People who listened to the debate on the radio and only heard what was said thought Nixon had the best of it. People who saw the debate on TV thought Kennedy did. Nixon's pasty appearance and five o'clock shadow helped cement the "Tricky Dick" image that haunted him during the campaign.

15.2

---

15. RESPONDING TO OPPOSITION

15.1 Introduction: What this Chapter Covers

This chapter describes how to respond to arguments from the opposition. It covers how to decide what your response ought to be and how to get the information you need to make it and shape it. (Chapter 29 deals with some of the opposition arguments aimed at civil rights policies. Chapter 36 deals with arguments against domestic partnership policies.)

15.2 Focus on the Point of the Campaign

There are three basic options for responding to anything your opponents do or say: You can appear to ignore it; you can reply; or you can modify your proposal. Within each option, there is a wide range of possible responses. There is only one rule for deciding which option to use and how to shape your specific response: Keep focused on the point of the campaign.

Your aim is to get a policy adopted. The best response to something the other side does may be to dispel a myth about lesbians and gay men, to reveal the dishonesty of the argument. But you should never respond because you want to even the score with the other side or because you've always wanted to get a particular message out. Since your aim is to get the policy adopted, your response should always be calculated to persuade the uncommitted members of your board and its constituency. If that isn't your primary justification for a particular response, you shouldn't make it, no matter how tempting it might be.

15.3   The Basic Options

Organizers in Irvine are convinced that their attempt to keep a civil rights policy failed because they decided to keep emphasizing their message and not reply to charges from the opposition. "We overestimated the sophistication of the voters," they said, "and we failed to answer questions they had."

Organizers in both New York and Chicago think they picked up supporters by not replying to opponents who made outlandish charges about gay people. "The crazier they looked, the saner we seemed."

Never truly ignore anything your opponent says. You might decide not to reply if you are convinced that an opposition argument has had no impact or inadvertently has helped you with the uncommitted middle. But if you do that, you run the risk of overestimating what people know about lesbians and gay men. Most of the time, you should at a minimum respond with the truth about whatever facts are claimed in the opposition argument.

Unless you are convinced that an opposition argument has cost you uncommitted votes that can be regained only by changing the proposed policy, you should usually try to reply before you agree to modify. Although modifications may take away an opposition argument, they almost never reduce the fervor of the opposition itself. You should modify your proposal only if uncommitted board members are truly convinced that the opposition has a point, or if they are so worried about the effect of the argument on constituents that you need to neutralize it.

If a board member is set on modifying the proposal to diminish opposition, encourage him or her to "smoke out" the opposition by offering possible amendments in exchange for support from the opponents. More often than not, this tactic reveals that an amendment will never satisfy the opposition.

> **During the course of an early effort to get a policy passed in a midwestern town, one council member reacted to objections of religious conservatives about gay ministers by preparing an exemption for clerical employees. When he asked for the opponents' reaction, they raised a new objection to another part of the law. The member prepared an amendment for that, and the opposition raised still another objection. Eventually, concluding that the opposition would never be satisfied, the member withdrew all of the amendments.**

15.4

15.4 General Guidelines for Replies

Here are a few important guidelines for putting together a reply to any opposition argument.

First (in general), *you shouldn't attack your opposition*. This may be the "broken record" theme of this guide. (See section 7.10.) One of the most important unstated rules of public discourse in the United States is that everybody is supposed to act as if the process is calm, deliberate, and focused on the merits of the proposal. Attacks on the opposition, like arguments made with a primarily emotional pitch, break that rule and almost always hurt those who use them.

Worse, attacks on your opposition frequently make them appear sympathetic. The attacks can actually gain supporters for the other side. Attacks may work in campaigns for office. They don't work for proponents of civil rights policies.

**Organizers in Irvine, California, are convinced they hurt
themselves by constantly saying that opposition to their
policy was "mean-spirited." "People saw that message as
a personal attack on our opponents, most of whom were
religious, and they didn't like it."**

The hardest part of trying to live with this guideline is that it works
out to be one-sided. Much of what even moderate opponents say turns
out to be attacks on the character of lesbians and gay men. But most
people think that we make at least some of those arguments "fair
game" by proposing a civil rights policy in the first place. This isn't to
say you shouldn't respond to such attacks. It is to say that you should
respond calmly with the truth, and not return the attack in kind.

Second (and equally important), *don't let the need to reply divert you from
either your campaign plan or your affirmative messages.* You need to make sure
arguments against adopting a policy are answered. But overcoming
claims that a policy shouldn't be passed isn't the same thing as convincing people that it should. Three techniques may help with this:
First, try to make your replies affirmatively, without mentioning the
attack. If, for example, the opposition claims that the law will be bad
for business, have your economics expert explain that the law on the
whole will be good for business. She or he might refer to claims to the
contrary only if asked.

Second, try to tie your reply into your main messages. For instance,
if the opposition claims the policy will force employers to hire lesbians
and gay men, your reply might say:

> *This is a bill to restore ability and willingness to work as the
> important things on the job. It doesn't allow people to be fired
> because of who they are, and it doesn't require people to be hired
> because of who they are. This law is about merit.*

Finally, try to work your replies into your existing campaign plan. If
you want to play up your union endorsements, ask union representatives to deliver your answer to a charge that relates to jobs or business.

15.4

15.5 Building a Reply — Getting the Facts

First, get the facts. Almost every opposition argument contains some type of factual claim. Usually, the argument at the least distorts the facts; often, it makes factual claims that are simply not so. Since you may need to reply quickly to a charge if it catches the public's attention, you need to have sources for response lined up in advance. Pay attention to the arguments opponents of lesbian/gay civil rights are making around the country as you begin your campaign. Try to get expert sources in each area covered by the argument opponents have made elsewhere.

> **At the time this was written, two favorite arguments of opponents were that discrimination was already covered by state and federal law, and that being lesbian or gay is a choice and, therefore, not appropriate for coverage by a civil rights law.**
>
> **Good responses to these arguments could be built on the facts that state and federal law do not forbid sexual-orientation discrimination; that being lesbian, gay, or bisexual is not a matter of whimsy; and that, in any case, civil rights laws aren't restricted to things that are "accidents of birth," and in fact civil rights laws protect people on the basis of things such as religion and marital status, which are much more "chosen" than sexual orientation is.**
>
> **To build these responses, you would need experts in human sexuality and civil rights law.**

The best experts for the response itself are likely to be experts with state or national reputations. For example, a law professor, law school dean, or head of a state civil rights commission could be powerful explaining civil rights laws. Try to get people who will seem to be a bit above the fray, or people whose expertise is well established and who are not a part of your campaign.

At the same time, to help you build your response, you should get local experts to work with the campaign. They can tell you what the facts are and point you to the most likely experts to use in a response. If you can't get a local expert to help, try contacting potential state or national experts yourself. If you can't identify any, call national professional associations, like the American Psychological Association, etc. You can also call the national lesbian/gay civil rights organizations to ask for leads.

15.6 Building a Reply — Deciding on Presentation

Sadly, truth by itself is often not enough. Your success in refuting the opposition with the truth may depend on how you present it; thus, part of your campaign planning should be to find out which positive arguments your board and its constituents are likely to accept. (See section 8.5.) When you do that attitude research, keep the focus broad and find out as much as you can about attitudes to possible responses as well. Use that information to shape your response.

Also, never twist the truth or play games with the facts by saying something that is technically correct but that you know is giving most listeners the wrong idea. When you have your reply planned, run it past some of the people you've used to decide what will persuade the board and its constituents so that they can confirm that you are on the right track.

15.7 Anticipating Opposition Tactics

Assume your opponents have the evil twin of this guide, which describes a contrary tactic for just about every strategy and tactic set out here. Assume they'll do everything you'll do and more. And assume that they've read this guide. Don't ever count on surprise. Then, be ready for a few tactics opponents often rely on.

Get your religious campaign ready at the start. It will usually be easier for your opponents to mobilize religious supporters, and they will often use a member's own religious faith to pressure him or her. You can neutralize this some if you already have religious endorsements. (See chapter 16.)

For example, in Connecticut and New York, opponents organized parochial school children to write and call state legislators and to ask their parents to do the same. In some places, busloads of parochial school children have been brought to a board to lobby against a bill.

Organizers in New York believe that the archdiocese transferred priests who testified for the bill out of the city. They also believe that representatives of the archdiocese met with council members and threatened them with excommunication if they supported the bill.

Knowing the rules and having your lawyer on call at the start is critical. One of the best ways to kill a policy proposal is with procedural maneuvers by insiders. (See chapter 20.)

> **The city attorney in Flint, Michigan, quietly slipped a "poison pill" into that city's law, changing the words in a seemingly inoffensive way, which made the law unenforceable.**
>
> **The city attorney in Milwaukee almost singlehandedly defeated that city's bill with a series of adverse procedural rulings at the final vote (the proponents knew the procedural rules as well as he did and avoided disaster).**
>
> **The city attorney in San Francisco drastically restricted the reach and enforcement of that city's proposed law until proponents, armed with respected legal experts, forced him to back down.**

15.7

Finally, be ready for what is now a favorite tactic, a last-minute attack more or less based on the argument that the policy is part of an "agenda," the ultimate aim of which is unbridled sexual license. You must have your own endgame campaign tactic that vividly illustrates your basic message and what the bill achieves. Since you can't know what the opposition will do at the end, and since they are unlikely to leave time for a reply, your message must be positive—an implicit repudiation of whatever they say. For example, have a locally important moderate religious or political leader who is willing to endorse your campaign make the announcement on the eve of the vote. Have him or her restate one of your major themes in the strongest possible terms.

> **The weekend before the public was to vote on an initiative to repeal Concord's lesbian/gay rights law, 15,000 lurid videotapes describing the "homosexual agenda" were distributed to homes in the city.**
>
> **In Irvine, what organizers describe as an "obscene" flyer was distributed days before a repeal election.**

16. DEALING WITH RELIGION

16.1 Why It's So Important

Much of the opposition to civil rights for lesbians and gay men is based on the belief that being gay is somehow immoral. "Moral" opposition to domestic partnership is often even stronger. For many Americans, religion is the primary source of guidance on morality. In most parts of the United States, you won't be able to pass a policy if the only religious voices that your board hears are speaking in opposition.

16.2 The Goal for Your Religious Strategy

Your primary goal should be at best to isolate the fundamentalists as your only religious opposition, or at the least, to make sure there is a serious division in religious views. A division will reduce religious influence; if there is no single message about the morality of being gay, board members who might otherwise defer to a religious view may pay religion less heed. Weak supporters who fear religious opposition may feel more comfortable.

> In New York, both supporters and opponents were able to get leaders from most religious denominations to back their positions and work for them. Opponents got priests and rabbis to testify against the law and to lobby council members individually. Supporters matched them, denomination for denomination. In the end, most of the organizers in New York think that the religious lobbying didn't change a single vote.

Isolating the fundamentalists is even better because their opposition is usually tinged with a prejudice that borders on hate. When they are alone, this is more likely to surface, and the violence of their prejudice will often push people to your side. For instance, as passage of the New York law began to look more likely, the largely religious opposition got more venomous and more offensive. Proponents think that helped them by demonstrating to skeptical members and an initially disbelieving media just how bad attitudes towards gay people were.

Some advocates argue for "low profile" campaigns to try to avoid alerting religious opposition. The general drawbacks to the stealth approach are described in section 9.3. Sometimes though, it may be the only way to handle potential religious opposition.

> **Organizers in Flint, Michigan, are convinced that if there had been a public debate over the ordinance, they would have lost because of the opposition of conservative churches. In Flint, well over half the members of the council belonged to conservative churches. While most of them were willing to support a measure they knew the church opposed if it could be done quietly, they felt they could not support the policy if there was a confrontation with the churches.**

16.3

16.3 The Strategic Plan

At the outset, you should decide whether you want to have religious leaders involved as primary proponents of the legislation, as active participants in the campaign, as public supporters, or if you are modestly aiming at neutrality or "soft" opposition.

> **In Milwaukee, in Hawaii, and to a large extent in Wisconsin, the campaign organization was made up entirely of religious leaders brought together by one organizer. Although all three of those campaigns were successful, the failure to include the lesbian and gay community in the effort has some of the same drawbacks as a stealth campaign.**

In part, the level of involvement you aim for depends on what kind of commitment you can get and what the cost of the commitment would be.

> **In Connecticut, the Catholic church was willing to officially not oppose a civil rights bill if the text stated clearly that it didn't apply to church employment of clerics and to**

> **parochial schools. That seemed a small price to the organizers, who agreed.**

In part, the level of involvement you want should depend on your board. If religion is very important to your board, you may want as much as you can possibly get.

> **After a young man was thrown out of his apartment for being gay, the original proponent of Saginaw's [Michigan] nondiscrimination policy brought the idea first to several of the town's progressive ministers. She believes that the policy passed because those ministers became the primary public speakers for the policy, although the campaign was carried on by others. The ministers were already respected in the community, and they dispelled the notion that supporting the policy would amount to support for immorality. That, she says, made it possible to focus the debate on the issue of equal access.**

If religion is important to your board, plan to preempt the issue; raise it on your terms before someone else brings it up. This means deciding on the level of religious involvement and getting commitments for support before your proposal is publicly announced, and probably before all or most members of the board know about it.

16.4 Basic Research

You need to do a little basic research to decide on the level of involvement you want and to put your plan into action. Find out how important religion is to your board. How often is the board addressed by religious leaders; and how important do the views of religious leaders seem to be in the board's decisions. (See chapter 4.)

No matter how important religion seems to be in general, find out how important it is to the individual members of the board. Biographies may give you important clues. You can usually get a biography by calling a member's office and asking for it. See if the member is listed in one of the many Who's Who publications. If the member doesn't have a biography, just ask the office what church she or he belongs to. Newspapers and observers should also be helpful here. (See sections 4.5, 4.7.)

With both boards and their individual members, some religions and some clerics are likely to be more important than others. Look for these details: Who seems to speak to the board most, who does the board seem to pay most attention to, what are their denominations, what are the denominations and parishes, etc., of the individual board members; then you can focus your religious recruiting efforts. Get people who know about religion to make sure that you are asking the right questions. It isn't enough to know that a person is Jewish or Christian. You need to know what branch of which denomination and who is the pastor or rabbi of the member's synagogue or church.

Next, find out what kind of support you can line up. You need to do two things: First, find out where the churches you've decided are important stand on civil rights for lesbians and gay men. Many churches have adopted national policy statements. You may be able to get copies by calling one of the national lesbian/gay organizations or by calling the national offices of the individual denominations.

16.5

Second, scope out the local scene and locate a couple of clerics who will probably support the policy. Start with the more liberal denominations (the Unitarians are a good bet). To find them, check the religion section of the local newspaper for stories and listings of Sunday sermons. If there is a lesbian/gay religious group in the area, its members are likely to be the best source. Religious universities and religious social justice organizations (like Catholic social services) can also be a good source of likely supporters.

16.5   Lining Up and Consolidating Your Religious Support

When you've located a couple of supporters, ask them to help you finish your plan by identifying others who might be brought on board, particularly those in the sects and denominations you've targeted.

Next use "logrolling" and the national endorsement statements to line up commitments. Go to your most likely supporters first and use the commitments you have and the national statements to bring them on. Then use their names with the next most likely group. If you are seeking more than just endorsements (if, for example, you want people to appear at a press conference or lobby other clerics or board members), you need to think each time about what to ask for. With a relatively strong supporter, it may make sense to ask for a full commitment at the start. With others, you may want to ask for support at first. Many people find it easier to campaign for a policy after they've committed to it.

16.6   Using Your Religious Support

Put out the message that the policy has religious support early and as positively as possible. If you can, have one or two prominent religious leaders at whatever press conference or event you have to announce the proposal publicly. For example, in Chicago, organizers put together a special "religious" press briefing, at which they had supporters from all the denominations they thought important announce support for the policy. Religious opposition seemed less important to the council after the briefing.

Whether you have religious leaders at an event to start the campaign or at a special event, have a list of all your religious supporters and all of the national support statements for the press. Make the tone positive; your speakers should explain why they support the policy, and they should avoid any reference to religious opposition unless the press brings it up.

Religious supporters who are willing to lobby should be thoughtfully deployed. Match the cleric to the board member as closely as you can. An individual's own rabbi or priest is probably the best match; nuns can be especially effective with people who attended parochial schools, and, as with lobbyists, people from the district are best.

> **Nuns who appeared at press events and lobbied for the policy in Chicago resisted wearing clerical garb. Organizers eventually convinced them they were much more effective, especially in individual lobbying, when they did.**

Even if a cleric is not willing to lobby personally, he or she might let someone else connected with the church do so and speak on his or her behalf.

Although a Wisconsin bishop would not himself lobby, he did let an aide call legislators and ask, "Are you with us on this one?" Organizers thought that was very effective.

Organizers in Connecticut probably did the most comprehensive job with religion. First, they put all the national support statements into a book and sent it to each member of the legislature. Next, they identified the affiliation and congregation of every member of the legislature. They then put together a religious lobby plan, which called for an organizer, with national support statement in hand if possible, to call each legislator's parish minister and ask the minister to contact the legislator. If he or she would not, the organizer called the bishop (or whomever in the next stage of the hierarchy) and asked him or her to make the contact. If that didn't work, they would go to some other figure prominent in the denomination.

16.7   Don't Bash the Opposition or Get Sidetracked

Bashing religious opponents by referring to them as the "religious right" or "fringe fundamentalists" just doesn't work. It never turns people away from those you are attacking, and it often makes you look intolerant. No matter what you think of a person's views, everyone has a right to participate in the process and the fact that a person's views are motivated by conservative religious dogma does not change that. Attacking church involvement in the process as a violation of tax or lobbying laws is also generally ineffective. People are not impressed, and the government never does anything about it. Time you spend on this is likely to be wasted.

Finally, don't debate the policy on religious terms. You'll almost never succeed against a pro. To the extent there is a dispute about god's views on civil rights laws, let your clerical supporters take it on. Your line should be that although people motivated by religious conviction have every right to speak and participate (in a pluralistic society), policy shouldn't be based on one group's dogma.

---

17. LOBBYING

17.1 Introduction: Three Ways to Lobby

There are three ways to lobby: visiting board members; getting cards and/or phone calls to them; and focusing direct action on them. The first is essential. The second, if you have the resources, is always helpful. People are divided about whether the third works at all. In any case, it should be used selectively. (Phone/card campaigns and direct action are covered in chapter 18.)

17.2 Planning Your Lobbying Campaign

The first step in planning a lobbying campaign is to take stock of your resources. If you are planning to lobby a small city council, and you have a large campaign, you might be able to lobby every member and to visit each frequently. If you need to lobby a representative town meeting (a form of local government with many representatives) or a large board of trustees, and your organization is fairly small, you'll have to focus your efforts on a portion of the board.

Even if you will be able to carry on a fairly comprehensive lobbying campaign, set priorities right at the start. Generally speaking, put the greatest effort into those who are not committed but whose votes you think you might sway. Include in this group people who may have taken a position but who don't appear to have a firm view. The second order should be those who have told you they support you, but who are neither sponsors of your proposal nor working directly with your organization. You need to keep their votes. The committed opponents come last.

When you divide the council into these groups, keep three things in mind: First, *never assume that you know how someone is likely to vote on the basis of stereotypes.* Politics is full of people voting against type, and people are more likely to cast unexpected votes on civil rights for lesbians and gay men than they are on most issues. You need hard information.

Second, *don't ever completely give up on anyone.* Virtually every organizer who has worked on a civil rights policy has triumphant stories of implacable opponents who were turned around by a well-thought-out approach or an unpredictable event.

Third, *don't ever assume that a vote is completely safe until it has been cast.* Virtually every organizer also has stories of betrayal by a supposed ally. These stories are often accompanied by rueful admissions of not having kept tabs on the ally.

Dan White, the San Francisco supervisor who later murdered Mayor George Moscone and Supervisor Harvey Milk, was the only member of the San Francisco board of supervisors who voted against the city's lesbian/gay civil rights law in 1978. Until the moment of the final vote, White publicly supported the bill. He was chair of the committee that conducted public hearings on the bill, and he actively helped organizers present their case. At the close of the hearing, he made a long impassioned speech about the need for a lesbian/gay civil rights law. He apparently changed his vote not because of anything having to do with the law, but because Harvey Milk refused to support White in an effort to keep a halfway house out of White's district.

17.3

17.3 Identifying Allies and Opponents

Identify likely allies and likely opponents not only among members of the board, but in other political positions. You may pick up votes on the board by getting the endorsement of an official who is not on the board, but who is a close ally of a board member or who the board members think they need to cultivate. Members of part-time boards frequently rely heavily on the advice of other officials and bureaucrats. Figure out which individuals may be influential in getting support on the board.

There are many ways to help identify potential allies and likely opponents. If a similar policy has been proposed before, find out what stand the current members took and, if they voted, how they voted (again, don't take this as the final word on your bill—stands and votes change). Look for proposals that people who support lesbian/gay civil rights would likely have supported as well (and that opponents would likely have opposed). For example, in Wisconsin, organizers initially tagged all members of the legislature as likely supporters, opponents, or undecided on the basis of votes in the previous sessions on abortion, race discrimination in housing, and decriminalization of sodomy.

The best way to begin finding out about important votes, and another good way to get information about board members, is to talk to people who pay attention to the local political scene. Talk to reporters, gossip columnists, or politicians you know are supportive. Talk to people in organizations who are logical allies, such as feminist groups, the ACLU, more progressive churches, etc. Ask the people you talk to for their opinions about where the members stand and about important votes on other issues.

Browsing through old newspaper files is another good way to get some sense of your board members. Most public libraries keep the local paper, often on microfilm.

> **Like most newspapers in smaller cities, the Greensboro [North Carolina] *Record and News* doesn't compile an index of the stories it covers. The local library in Greensboro does one of its own, but there's no reference to the index in the card catalogue, so the only way to find out about it is to ask at the desk.**

If the library doesn't have the local paper, the paper itself probably keeps either microfilm or back issues, and most papers are willing to let people do research. Newspapers usually make up their own indexes or "morgue" files and arrange them by person. In addition to stories about the board, look for stories about speeches, election campaigns, and political positions the members of the board may have had in the past.

If board members publish newsletters, either the library or the board itself may keep them. And there is always the direct approach.

Call the board member's office and ask if she or he has public positions on any issues related to lesbians and gay men. Ask for any relevant literature. Try to have "informal" conversations with board members in which you ask for their general views on civil rights for lesbians and gay men or domestic partnership. You can often do this at public "meet the member" events, or by asking for a short meeting. If the member asks why you are interested, you should be honest and say that you are thinking about proposing a policy.

Be flexible. As you learn more, your sense of where people stand is likely to change, so be ready to move people around and change them from category to category while you lobby.

17.4 Finding Out What It Will Take to Get a Vote

While you are doing the research on where people stand, get information that can help you persuade people when you begin lobbying. Look for anything that might help you make a connection with the member: a political connection, an intellectual connection with the issue, or a personal connection.

Most people in public office want to get reelected, elected to a higher office, or both. That means that they usually have ties to other politicians whose help they will need, and that there are interest groups and community leaders to whom they pay attention. Look for the obvious things, like whom members endorse and who endorses them. But also look to see whose dinners they attend, to whom they present awards and commendations, etc. Look especially for connections to your political allies, your endorsers, etc. Be careful with information about associations rather than views; it can be misleading. Try to get some knowledgeable friends to help you evaluate the information, and don't overestimate its value.

> **In many Boston parishes, no one goes to an annual communion breakfast unless he or she is a friend of the parish. On the other hand, in New York, the archdiocese used to have an annual event that every politician in town went to, no matter how chilly his or her relations with the church were.**

Find out which organizations the member belongs to, especially which church, if any. Find out how seriously she or he seems to take religion. If any of the organizations to which a member belongs has a good official stand on lesbian/gay civil rights, you'll want to tell the member that when you lobby. You'll want to do the same thing if his or her church has a good stand, or a local bishop or pastor does. You may want a member of the organization or the church to visit the member with you.

Find out where members live, where they grew up, where they went to school, who their spouses are, and who their children are, and where the children go to school. Find out if anyone in your organization is close to family members or close friends of a board member. Time and again, votes have been obtained by spouses and children who lobbied at home.

In Chicago, the vote of a council member who everyone thought would oppose the law was obtained by a long-time friend and supporter who came out to the member and explained in very personal terms why the law was important.

Some New York City activists are convinced that one critical vote was secured by a very persuasive "mistress." Almost everyone who worked in New York was convinced that some council members who leaned against the bill were persuaded to change because their children worked hard to persuade them that the bill was right.

17.5   You Need to Meet in Person

You should insist on personal meetings with every council member you want to lobby. It is much easier for someone to mislead you about where she or he stands if you talk on the phone or through an aide. You can never know if your written materials get read, but you'll know your message was delivered if you make your case in person. Perhaps more important, people without terribly strong views of their own are likely to be coping with strong appeals from both sides.

Your chances of being listened to as you make your arguments are stronger if you have a personal relationship with the member. The most successful campaigns usually assign specific members of the campaign to specific members of the council. This makes building relationships possible and it makes it easier for the organization to keep track of its progress with the member.

> The final successful campaign for New York's law used an "insider/outsider" strategy for lobbying. In addition to the "insider" lobbyists who kept in touch with members, "outsider" lobbyists from other grass-roots organizations, usually more skeptical about the process, lobbied some members. Some board members felt more comfortable with the outsiders, some with the insiders.

Establish a friendly relationship with the member's staff. Staff often exercise considerable influence over a member's schedule, and may decide whether you get in to meet the member at all. Most members also look to this staff for advice on the substance of proposals that come before them. Since members are usually too busy to do all their research themselves, they'll frequently ask staff members to get the answers to questions that interest them. You want to be sure that you are at least one of the people the staff member calls for answers.

17.5

You should have at least one major meeting with every member in which you make your case for the law, reassure the member, and pitch any angles you think may be particularly effective with this member. Obviously, anytime a member has questions you should be ready to meet with him or her again to answer them, and you should meet with a member anytime she or he does or says anything publicly that might reflect or have an impact on how he or she views the policy.

You should also have as much contact as you can with people who are undecided or who you think might be swayed. The more you make them think about the policy and your arguments, the more likely movement will occur. Members will think about the issue, at least briefly, every time they see you. You should simply stop by to say hello if you can, and be ready each time with a one- or two-sentence argument about why the member should support the policy. When you can, give the member a written fact sheet or explanation that supports the argument.

Finally, don't neglect your positive votes. The other side may be lobbying them. Again, you should just stop by and say hello frequently, and make sure that each time you easily but unmistakably reaffirm the members' commitment.

17.6   When to Lobby Whom

As you decide whom to lobby, think about logrolling. The idea is to go to your most likely allies on the board first, and get their commitments. Go to less-committed folks next and tell them about the commitments you have. Go to more doubtful people after that, and so on.

Board members, like other people, are more likely to do something if they know other people will do it. Make sure you tell members who have said they'll support you that you are going to tell others. If they are reluctant to let you do that, assume the commitment is not solid and that the member needs more work. If the commitment is solid, see if you can get the board member to talk to the next colleague in line, either privately or with you (obviously, make sure the two are at least politically friendly before you ask).

17.7   Who Should Visit

Even if you are able to assign a campaign worker to every member, other people whose presence may help convince the member should visit at least once. You may want some of these people at your first major meeting with the member, and you may want them at later meetings as well. Your research on what the member cares about will tell you whom to bring. As mentioned above, you should think about political allies, union or business groups, community leaders, and religious leaders.

Organizers in both New York and Chicago put together "nun squads" to lobby Catholic council members. Clerics

> make particularly effective lobbyists because so much of
> the opposition to lesbian/gay civil rights laws tries to por-
> tray itself as motivated by religious morality. Pro-civil
> rights clerics not only provide an answer, but they give the
> member a certain amount of cover with religious con-
> stituents. The organizers also thought the "nun squads"
> were particularly effective with members who had
> attended parochial school. They had a tendency to look at
> their shoes and mutter, "Yes, Sister," while being lobbied.

It is usually critical for at least some of the people who visit to be constituents—people who live in the district and who are registered to vote. It is very good to get at least one lesbian or gay constituent to visit. Too many members think they don't have any. Perhaps as effective are constituents who are parents of lesbians and gay men. Most board members will identify more quickly with parents than they will with lesbians and gay men themselves.

One way to find constituents is to keep your volunteer lists sorted by ward or district. If you live in a fairly large city, the easiest way to do this is to get a zip code map, a district map from the city, and draw the lines from one onto the other. You can often find zip code maps in the phone book or at local stationery stores. The city should have ward or district maps. Sometimes cities have descriptions of the districts that say which addresses are where. If neither of these works, you may just have to look at the district map and sort.

The best way to find constituents is often by word of mouth. Organizing begins at home. Ask your friends and family if they know anyone who lives in the district and who is gay or who has a gay child or parent or brother or sister. Look over your list to see if any of the organizations that have endorsed you are located in or have subgroups in the district. Look at lists of district political clubs and service organizations. They may be able to help you find constituents.

Never allow anyone to meet with the member and lie about living in the district. Your credibility will be blown if the lie is discovered, and lies like that are all too easy to discover.

If you can, have your visitors reflect the district. If there are important racial or ethnic blocks in the district, try to get both lesbians and

17.7

119

gay men and parents from all the principal groups in the district. This will help keep the member from thinking that the issue is only important to one group in his or her district. You may help smash some myths while you are at it.

17.8 Preparing for Visiting

Anyone who goes to visit a member should have a basic familiarity with the proposed policy and the major themes of the campaign. If you've got a case statement and answers to important questions or replies to opposition arguments, make sure every prospective visitor has read them. (See sections 12.3–12.5.) Some campaigns put the case statement and all the major issue papers into a briefing book that all visitors get well before they visit. You should run at least one training session for visitors. Go over the basics of the policy, review the major arguments for it and your answers to the arguments of the opposition. Go over some of the tips for effective meetings that are set out below. Demonstrate some of the questions people are likely to get. You won't be able to get every visitor to a training session, but try at least to talk to all of them on the phone and go over the most important points.

Whether your contact is by meeting or phone, tell every visitor not to guess at answers to questions the member asks. Visitors should take down any question to which they are not sure about the answer and say that someone from the campaign will get back to the member.

17.9 Giving Out Written Materials During Visits

There are three theories about giving written materials to members while visiting. Some campaigns put together briefing books with endorsement letters and short papers on all major issues and give them to members at a major meeting. Some campaigns issue short briefing papers and letter packets throughout the campaign and try to stop by members' offices for short visits when each is issued. Some campaigns provide written materials during visits only if the member asks for something, and some even send those later.

Handing out briefing papers and endorsements issue by issue may be a good idea with people you are trying to convince; a single sheet aimed at an issue the member is concerned about is more likely to get read than a whole book. A complete book, on the other hand, may be helpful to people who are solid supporters but need help convincing others. Whatever tactic you use, try to hold written materials until the end of a visit, so that the member doesn't read while you are trying to talk.

17.10 Things to Do During Visits

Especially at your first meetings, it may not be a good idea to ask members directly to support your proposal. They'll usually dodge the question, often saying they need to study the proposal. You also are not likely to get very far by asking directly about what might convince a member to vote for the proposal. Most people won't answer because they don't want to be tied down. Even when people do answer, they tend to leave out important parts of the answer (like what political support is critical) when the question is that direct.

You should start by asking members what they think about the idea of a lesbian/gay civil rights or domestic partnership policy, and by drawing them gently out as much as you possibly can on what their concerns might be. This is more likely to give you information you need to begin building your argument for this member. Again, don't assume that you know a member's views because of past statements on similar issues or even earlier bills

Never leave a member's office on terms that make it difficult to go back. If a member raises objections, respond to the substance, but don't get into a fight. If a member sticks to an objection and refuses to listen to your response or engage in a discussion, ask to get back to him or her with more information later, and put the point aside.

On the other hand, don't let members off the hook either. Members who do not have a strong view on the proposal, and who are being lobbied by both sides, will often try to get one side to give them "permission" to vote for the other. For example, a member may tell proponents that although he finds their arguments convincing, it is not politically practical to support them "this time." You should of course give the member all the political reassurance you can (your endorsements, support in the district, etc.). But you should subtly make it clear that as you see it, leaders do not sacrifice important principles to expediency.

You should always treat people with respect. Never mislead anyone about anything; if you are discovered you will have no credibility. Don't make commitments on which you can't deliver.

If a member tells you that he or she will support your proposal, make sure that you can tell others. Ask if she or he will join as a sponsor (providing you have checked that with your chief sponsor), or if he or she will help you approach other legislators.

Finally (and this may sound like obvious advice, but a lot of people don't follow it), don't try to be somebody else when you meet with members. If you are down-home, stay that way. Don't be folksy if you are not, etc.

17.11 Convincing Members to Support You

Most of the things you need to do to convince members to support you are covered in other chapters. (See especially chapter 8, "Building a Case for the Policy"; chapters 27 and 28 on civil rights cases; chapters 34 and 35 on domestic partnerships; chapters 15, 29, and 36 on opposition arguments; chapter 9 on endorsements; and chapter 11 on election politics.) Here are a few additional points.

As you learn more about what matters to a member, adjust your plans. For example, as you find out more about who a member's political allies are and what groups the member thinks most important, target them for endorsements.

> **Often, the most important tactic is finding the right person to ask the member to support the policy. Chicago organizers are fond of telling about the member who equivocated almost until the final vote, and then said that he needed a rabbi, an important rabbi, to tell him that it**

> was **OK** to vote for the proposal. The night before the
> vote, organizers, with the mayor's help, got an important
> rabbi to call the member from his car phone and tell the
> member that he should vote for the ordinance. He did.

You need to think about how to disarm members' fears that if they vote for your proposal, it will cost them support and perhaps reelection or political advancement. One good way to do that is with convincing examples of politicians with similar constituencies in similar towns who supported similar proposals and did not suffer. Also, remember that just being able to say that the other politician did not lose may not be enough. If a politician's vote total dropped significantly, that may be enough to cause your member concern.

Opinion polls showing widespread public support for extending basic civil rights to lesbians and gay men may also help. Again, be careful. Look at the breakdowns in the polls and make sure it does not look like the members' constituents (as opposed to the population as a whole) are a group that opposes civil rights for gay men and lesbians. Perhaps the best reassurance for a worried member is evidence that there are supporters of the proposal in his district, and that they are organized and ready to support the member in a political campaign. Constituent visits are one way to do that. The mass and direct action tactics described in the next section can do it also.

17.12 Debriefing

Every visitor needs to be debriefed. You need to find out just what the member said about the bill. Most important, you need to find out what questions the member asked, and what promises the visitors made about getting the member more information, etc. Make sure someone from the campaign follows up on each.

A good way to keep track of your lobbying is to keep a binder or a notebook for each board member. You should record the date of every visit, who visited, and the results of your debriefing. Keep track of visits and drop-ins by the campaign worker assigned to that member (if you have one) as well. The book should include every promise to deliver more information or follow up on a question that the campaign makes and any deadlines that go with them. You should have space to check off when things get done.

18. MASS ACTION: TURNING OUT CARDS, CALLS, AND BODIES

18.1 The Point of It

One way to convince policymakers that they won't be hurt if they support your proposal—or even that they might be hurt if they do not support it—is to show widespread support for the proposal from constituents. This is most important if your board is a political body, like a city council or a state legislature. There are two ways to show constituent support: by having people present at public events in support of the proposal, or by having people contact the members to say they support the proposal.

18.2 Why You Need to Get People to Come to Hearings and Rallies

In most situations, you can't get a significant number of voters into a hearing room. Although more people can come to an outdoor rally, most of the time rally turnouts are not large enough to swing elections, either. Nonetheless, getting supporters to come to both rallies and hearings is important.

Elected officials know that most people never go to hearings or rallies of any kind, and that those who do usually represent a small proportion of people who support something. They also know that people who come to hearings and rallies are often people who care enough to help people who support them and to remember people who do not. In addition, especially with hearings, having a significant number of supporters in the room can make it feel like the tide is going your way. If it feels like you are winning, some board members may drift your way.

18.3 Turning Out the Bodies: How to Get in Contact with People

One way to get people to rallies and hearings is to use the usual techniques for communicating with the lesbian and gay community. Put notices of the event in the gay press and try to get stories about how important a good turnout will be. Send notices to the alternative press as well. If local papers or radio stations have community calendars or other listings of upcoming events, get the notices to them as well.

Print flyers or posters and distribute them to gay and gay-friendly businesses. Identify gay or politically supportive neighborhoods and put your flyers on bulletin boards, etc. Check to see if there are local laws about where you can post flyers. For example, some places forbid posting on utility poles, while others allow it. If you have enough help, shove copies under people's doors. Find out if local colleges and universities have lesbian/gay student groups. Make sure to send them event notices.

If your organization has a phone tree (see section 7.8), use it. Ask each volunteer who receives a call to call three friends who are not members of the organization and urge them to come. You can also use phone banks. Ask lesbian and gay organizations and supportive organizations if you can have membership lists with phone numbers. Find a friendly organization or business with multiple lines and have volunteers call.

Put together a notebook listing all the organizations, both inside and outside the gay community, that either support your proposal or are at least somewhat sympathetic. Find out if each organization has regular meetings or a newsletter or a phone tree, who is in charge of each, and how one gets on meeting agendas or puts announcements in the newsletter, etc. Find out what the access and scheduling deadlines are. Put everything in your notebook. As soon as you know the date for a

18.3

hearing or rally, try to place announcements in as many newsletters as you can and send speakers to as many meetings as you can. If you can't get into a newsletter or to a meeting, at least call some of the organization's leaders. Ask them to come and bring a few supporters.

> **Chicago organizers decided that they needed to stage a mass rally to convince local politicians there was a sizable, politically aware gay community, and that it supported the ordinance. They also felt a rally might increase support for the bill. They spoke to the owners of the city's best-known gay bars and asked them to agree to close their bars during the time set aside for the rally. They also asked the owners to contribute to the cost of buses to go from bar to bar and pick people up, and return to the bars after. The owners agreed.**
>
> **The organizers rented buses from the city's transit authority and staged the rally in the heart of downtown. As one organizer put it, the feeling as the city-owned buses pulled up and emptied hundreds of lesbians and gay men into the central downtown plaza was electric.**

If you have a gay neighborhood or a politically supportive neighborhood, set up information tables at busy corners. If you are feeling bolder, do a small march through the neighborhood at a time when it is likely to be crowded and pass out leaflets as you go. Ask the owners of gay bars and restaurants to stop the music and let someone from the organization stand up and briefly explain the upcoming event and why people need to go. Be brief, and be sure to give the time and place.

18.4   Scheduling and Preparation

If you want people to come to an event, do your best to schedule it at a time that will be convenient for as many people as possible. Saturday can be good day for rallies since many people have weekends off; there won't be many people at city hall, but it is a slow news day so coverage is often good. If you want to do a rally on a weekday, noon is usually the best time. You can often convince boards to hold hearings at night so people who work during the day can come.

If you are turning people out for a hearing, and there is a possibility of public testimony at hearing, try to prepare people who may come. (See chapter 22.)

18.5 Cards, Letters, and Calls

Nothing impresses board members more than contact from constituents. After personal visits (see chapter 17), the best kind of contact is an individually written note, followed in rough order by notes with "canned text" (messages made up by a campaign organization), phone calls, signed preprinted cards, and petitions.

Individual notes are most impressive partly because they are the hardest thing to get people to do. That, of course, is the problem with them. Most organizers think that the resistance to writing is so great, and that so few people follow up and make phone calls, that preprinted cards are the best choice. Petitions, though they are not much different than preprinted cards, seem not to impress board members as much as cards do.

You can use all of the devices for encouraging people to come to meetings described in section 18.3 to get people to make contact. If you use flyers or ads in papers, you can include a suggested text or a coupon for people to send in, and that may help overcome some resistance. Many more people will act if you make personal contact and have something for them to sign when you ask. You can do this door to door, but the most effective tactic is probably to set up tables at fairs, public events, or busy street corners and at shopping centers. Have preprinted cards ready for people to sign.

Some campaigns have been successful with blank cards that people personalize at booths, etc. Since these are still obviously part of an orchestrated effort, they may not have much advantage over the easier preprinted card. More nongay supporters may sign if you have a card that explicitly identifies the writer as a straight supporter of lesbian and gay rights. Chicago organizers made up a special card for people who were afraid to be identified as gay. It said: "I live in your ward and I want you to support the gay rights ordinance. Because of discrimination, I can't tell you my name." It increased the number of cards and reinforced the point that people are really afraid of discrimination.

The chance that the card will actually get mailed will go up if you have postage ready and you handle the mailing. Usually, people will contribute the cost of the postage if you ask.

If you handle the mailing, you may want to keep the cards undated, and hold them until the best strategic moment. Send in all the cards from one district if the board member representing it tells you he doesn't have any constituents who care about the issue. Some organizers like to send the cards in near the final vote.

> **There was a major effort to get cards supporting a state antidiscrimination law at San Francisco's lesbian/gay pride parade. Organizers printed up small "I signed" stickers and put them on each person who signed. The stickers identified people who had already signed to the signature gatherers. People who hadn't been asked to sign saw the stickers and asked what they were about.**

18.5

The toughest problem with constituent contact campaigns is that most people don't know who their representatives are. If the representatives are chosen "at large" (i.e., if all members on a city council represent the whole city), any constituent can contact any member. Under the more typical district systems, you need to be able to tell people who represents them. You can either get a map or directory from the city that will tell you this, or put one together. (See section 17.7.) If you use flyers, print the map. If you set up tables, have a map or directory at the table so that the cards can be correctly addressed. If you do phone banks, make sure your callers either have maps or directories or know how to tell people how to find out who their representatives are.

> **New York City organizers put out a weekly one-page flyer on contacting council members. On the front of it, there were instructions on how to find out who your council member was, how to write, and how to call. On the back, it had a weekly tally sheet showing where each council member stood and which were in particular need of calls, etc.**

18.6 Lobbying Days

One effective way to get people in contact with board members is to hold "lobbying days," in which you get as many people as you can to come to members' offices and meet with them. You should have everyone who is coming meet together at the start for a basic training in lobbying techniques. (See chapter 17.)

Lobbying days tend to work best on boards that provide offices for their members in one or two buildings. Before you schedule a lobbying day, make sure you pick a date when most board members, particularly those who need persuading or hand-holding, will be available to meet. Your campaign organization should make appointments for groups of constituents with each member. If you are reasonably sure you will have too many people for one appointment, make two. It is better to have a few too many people in a meeting than it is to have too few. Nothing is worse than a constituent meeting in which no one shows up.

The best way to organize a lobbying day is to pick a day when most members will be available, get commitments from people who are willing to come, and then schedule the appointments, always making each visiting group a tad larger than is comfortable for the office. Make sure to book groups in to see other influential city officials like mayors, city managers, city attorneys, etc.

19.1

19. PROTESTS AND CIVIL DISOBEDIENCE

19.1 Protests and Civil Disobedience: Defining Terms

Both protests and civil disobedience (c.d.) involve people getting together in public to express an opinion about something. *Protest* is used here to mean an event at which people obey whatever laws a city or a campus might have for demonstrations. For example, most places have laws about obstructing sidewalks or getting permits. C.d. is used to mean events at which people disregard those laws or others.

19.2   Do Protests and Disobedience Do Any Good?

Every movement for change seems to have a raging debate about whether protests and civil disobedience are useful or are counterproductive.

> **In both Connecticut and Massachusetts, some lesbians and gay men grew upset at how slow the legislative process was, broke away from lobbying groups, and began to use more confrontational tactics. Those who stayed lobbying inside say the confrontation tactics made the process take longer. The protestors say the bills would still be in committee if they hadn't begun visible public protests.**

People who are against protest and c.d. say that most of the time they persuade no one and alienate some. They also point out that protests take considerable effort, which they think could be better spent working inside the political process.

People who favor protest and c.d. say these street tactics can get public attention for your issue, public attention that in turn brings the attention of policymakers. They also argue that street protest sometimes makes people working inside the process look more like moderates—people who share a basic commitment to working in the system with the policymakers they are trying to persuade.

As usual, there is some truth in both views. Some protests surely do alienate people who might otherwise support your proposal.

> **Connecticut organizers are convinced that they lost votes when protestors lined up in a corridor through which legislators walked, hissed, and catcalled major opponents. They said many legislators were frightened and that some as a result turned against their bill.**

On the other hand, we should have learned from the protests over the war in Vietnam that protests can make both voters and policymakers pay attention.

> **Many people thought the tactics that ACT-UP used to protest how long it took to get new anti-HIV drugs were counterproductive. Those tactics included disrupting pub-**

> lic meetings by catcalling and having protesters burst into
> private meetings and chain themselves to furniture. Few
> today, however, would say **ACT-UP** was not an important
> part of speeding up the drug-approval process.

You may not have a choice about whether protest will be a part of your campaign. Some people may decide to protest even if the campaign organization does not want that to happen. You must decide, then, if you will work with the protesters.

If you think protest should be a part of your campaign, or if you think it is unavoidable, you should plan to make the most of it. Decide what kinds of protest will have the greatest favorable impact, and try to persuade people to do these things and avoid things you think could truly hurt.

19.3   Getting Noticed

Protests usually need to be noticed to have much effect. You need to get the word out—to the media and to your supporters. (See sections 6.5 and 13.5.) But simply scheduling a protest and telling the media won't guarantee coverage. Holding a protest in a busy part of town where a lot of people will see it often helps. Holding a protest at the same time as another event that is tied to your issue and is likely to attract media attention is an even better idea.

> For weeks after California governor Pete Wilson vetoed a
> law that would have outlawed employment discrimination
> based on sexual orientation, protesters were present vir-
> tually every time he appeared in public. All but a few of
> the protests were peaceful, and all received considerable
> media coverage. The veto and the protests brought
> scores of new activists into the campaign for the law,
> which kept going after the veto. Wilson later signed a dif-
> ferent version of the law the next year.

Clever protests, especially ones that illustrate one of the problems you are trying to get at or one of your arguments, are more likely to get attention.

The New York City Taxi Commission required applicants for cab licenses to take a psychological test that asked about sexual orientation and disqualified people who said they were gay men and lesbians. Protesters dressed in overalls and, posing as movers, carried a "psychiatrist's" couch into the office of the Taxi Commission and conducted a sit-in at the office with the couch for several hours. It got noticed.

19.4 Focusing on Individual Board Members

Protests aimed at individual members of the board can be effective in some situations. Focused protests can often get you meetings with members who are not die-hard opponents, but who are avoiding you because they do not want to deal with the issue. The best tactic here may be low-key persistence. If you have nonviolent picketers at as many of the members' public appearances as you can, and if you make sure that the member is asked about the bill at every meeting that allows public questions, there is a good chance the member will decide that it is easier to deal with you than it is to ignore you.

"Politicians hate potential confrontation and will go to great lengths to avoid it," says one New York activist who worked for the city's mayor for a time. "That means you can almost run their schedules if you show up to protest at public events. No politician can afford that kind of scheduling disruption. They will be forced to deal with you."

Focused protests can work with members who probably think the proposal is the right thing to do but are reluctant to support it because of heavy pressure from the other side (the classic "this is not the time" type of position), or with members who need to be convinced that there may be serious consequences to not supporting the proposal.

Chicago organizers aimed a picket at one alderman who they described as "gutless," but who was aware there were lots of gay men and lesbians and that a civil rights law was right. Lobbyists could not get a commitment from the alderman. The picketers, mostly people from the alderman's district, marched in front of his office and carried signs stating: "You are too good to vote against this." Organizers showed up at his office to lobby while the march was going on. He met with them and later voted for the ordinance.

19.5 Some Practical Tips on Protests

Always lowball your estimates of how many people will come; that is, predict that fewer people will show up than you are reasonably certain will appear. If you think you'll have fifteen picketers in front of a member's office, you always look better if you predict ten and get a few more than if you predict twenty and get a few less.

Protests that involve violence, threats, or intimidation are almost always counterproductive, at least if you are still trying to persuade people to support your proposal. Most Americans consider violence and threats to be outside the rules of the game.

The effect of strong language is less clear. Most insiders say it is counterproductive as well. However, most people who say they decided to oppose a policy because supporters used vehement language were looking for a reason to oppose it anyway. Sometimes strong words may help people to see that your commitment to the proposal is deep, and that you will not quit if defeated once.

19.6 Protest and Free Speech: A Brief Introduction

Find out about local and state laws on demonstrations well before you stage any protest. You need to know when permits are required, if there are limits on the amount of noise, if there are limits on the hours when protest is permitted, and what the laws are on obstructing sidewalks, marching in streets, etc.

Most cities allow sidewalk pickets without permits, but require that they don't block sidewalks or access to buildings. Most insist on permits for street marches.

If you can, get a lawyer with some knowledge of the First Amendment to help you find out about all the local laws. The single most common mistake that people make with protests is not finding out about permit requirements early enough. Organizers often announce marches publicly, only to find out that they don't have time to get a permit, or that after the route has been announced, the city legitimately insists on changing it to accommodate traffic, etc.

The First Amendment says that you can't be denied a permit or subjected to special conditions because of your message. It also states that to minimize the possibility that hostility to your message will infect the process, permit laws must have "neutral criteria" for deciding when permits will be refused or marches limited.

However, a surprising number of cities still have laws that appear to give officials almost arbitrary power to limit protests or deny permits altogether. Even if a permit law is invalid, you generally must apply for the permit and follow the process through to challenge it later.

Finally, remember that the First Amendment will not protect you if you are arrested for civil disobedience (sit-ins, demonstrating on private property or on government property not intended for speech, etc.).

19.7   Working with Direct Action Groups

No matter how you feel about protest and c.d., you will probably be better off if you have a working relationship with groups that will use either as a tactic. If there are going to be protests, it will probably be better if you can help aim them at people who might be swayed in the right direction or at issues that need dramatic illustration. On the other hand, if the protest groups are planning on violent or threatening actions, you may want to disassociate yourself from them.

Working relationships with direct action groups require mutual respect. Too often, direct action groups suspect that when mainstream organizers propose working together, they really want at a minimum to tell the direct action groups what to do, or set out to get the direct action group to abandon protest and work inside the system. Too often, the suspicions are well founded.

One way to begin building a good relationship is to have someone from the campaign attend meetings of the action group and participate in some of their activities. And reciprocate—ask the group to send someone to the campaign's meetings and to take part in some of its activities. Make sure the direct action group understands the campaign's plan. When the campaign suggests that the group not conduct particular types of protest or asks that it consider protesting, bring representatives of the group into the process and make sure they understand the campaign's thinking. Listen to their advice. And get used to the idea that your advice won't always be accepted.

20. WORKING WITH BOARDS

20.1 Basic Research on the Process

Your basic research (chapter 4) should include getting information on how the board operates. You need to find out about the structure of the process and its rules, both written and unwritten. With legislatures and most other boards, it is particularly worthwhile to sit in on a few meetings at the start. The advice you get from observers will make more sense when you can put it into context, and you are likely to pick up some of the subtle dynamics yourself. Friendly members of the body are apt to be your best sources for practical information about who would make a good sponsor, which members are likely to support you, which are effective as committee chairs, etc.

The next nine sections cover most of the areas you should research by following some of the more typical processes used by legislatures, start to finish. Most city councils, county commissions, and other boards have simpler processes, although most use some of the processes described here. The chapter ends with four sections of tips for working with boards.

20.1

20.2 How to Get the Process Started

There are three main possibilities. Most typically, policy proposals are introduced by a member of the board. In some places, policy can also be proposed by an executive or administrator, like a mayor, the president of a university, or a department head. Sometimes these proposals need the sponsorship of a board member as well. In some systems, commissions that are not subgroups of the board, such as local human rights commissions or faculty committees, are allowed to send policy proposals to the board as well. Like executive proposals, these may also need the support of a board member.

If commissions or committees that are not a part of the board can recommend policy, you should think about whether you can use the commission's process to your advantage. Find out what the possible commissions are and who the members are of each. You may want to use a commission recommendation to build support for your proposal before you get to your board. (See section 10.3.) If the commission holds hearings and it or its chair looks particularly open to your proposal, a commission hearing may give you a better opportunity to make sure that the hearing presents the information you want to get out. It also may give you the chance for a hearing on the problem instead of the policy, which can be helpful. (See section 21.3.)

20.3 Where Policy Comes From

Not the stork. Once again, there are three main possibilities. The most typical pattern until recently was that the person (again, usually a board member) who "introduced" the policy would start with a fairly general idea about what the policy should cover. He or she would ask the city attorney or the board's lawyer to write a specific proposal. Sometimes, this would happen before the proposal was introduced; sometimes, the board member would actually introduce the proposal with a general sentence or two, and then send it to the lawyers to be written up. Sometimes, a board member or more frequently a commission will present the board with a detailed report that calls for a policy. The report usually will not have a draft of the policy itself, but it will have detailed recommendations about what the policy should say. Reports like this also usually get sent to an attorney to be translated into a specific proposal.

More and more frequently, those who have organized to campaign for the proposal will present the member who is going to introduce it with a complete draft. The draft will then go to the board's attorney for review. If you can get your sponsor to accept a draft from you, this is by far the best way to start. The advantage of starting with a draft is simple: Your draft is likely to be stronger than anything a city attorney comes up with, and you will have a much easier time negotiating about the proposal if you start strong.

Your draft is likely to be stronger than any board lawyer's draft, because even board lawyers with the best of intentions usually begin writing using a policy adopted by another body as a model. But other policies are usually the end result of a process of negotiation and compromise, so they are usually far from ideal. In addition, few lawyers can resist the temptation to resolve some of the hard questions themselves. As they write, they will often make some compromises for you. Of course, if the board's lawyer is hostile to your proposal, he or she may use the opportunity to "write the idea up" to make it as narrow or useless as possible.

20.3

> In Flint, Michigan, the city attorney wrote amendments to the city's ordinance against discrimination to add sexual orientation. But his draft also made the sexual orientation parts of the ordinance unenforceable. The city attorney took out a section that would have given his office the power to seek court orders enforcing the law. He added an obscure, seemingly innocuous section defining what kind of "wrong" a violation of the ordinance was. It did not say a violation was a crime. But, as the city attorney knew, in Michigan if a violation wasn't a crime and the city attorney wasn't given the power to ask for a court order, the ordinance couldn't be enforced at all. Only after the ordinance had passed did its supporters find out what the city attorney had done. Supporters have had a tough time trying to amend the ordinance since.

You need to start strong. It is true, of course, that after you have a proposal, board members can amend it to make it stronger as well as to compromise. But when there is a concrete proposal, board members tend to treat it as the starting point in negotiations with opponents. It is much more difficult to toughen a weak proposal when there is active opposition than it is to weaken a tough proposal.

The drawback to having the member introduce a complete draft is that some board lawyers dislike it. In part, they correctly see it as "horning in" on what has traditionally been part of their job. It also takes a lot of policy-making power away from the lawyers, and like other people, they don't like losing power. While you'll do better if you can stay friendly with the lawyers, don't give up shaping influence over the first draft to do it.

20.4 On to the Departments

As explained in the last section, proposals typically go first to an attorney to be put into a draft. Find out if they go to other departments for comment or input as well. If they do, you may want to contact some of the important department heads and begin lobbying them before they respond.

If the proposals go to selected departments for comment, find out which ones. If, as is often the case, the selection depends on the content of the proposal, you may want to think about steps you might be able to take to get the proposal to good departments or keep it away from bad ones. For example, in some towns, all city employment policies go to personnel, and all policies on people who do business with the city go to a contracting department. If personnel looks sympathetic and contracting looks hostile and influential, maybe you should begin with a nondiscrimination policy that covers employment by the city but not discrimination by those who do business with the city.

20.5 "In Committee"

Once policy proposals come back in draft from the attorney, they usually go to a subcommittee of the board for a hearing. A few boards send proposals out to independent commissions, like human rights commissions, and a few have the whole board consider and hold hearings on them.

If your board has a committee process, you need to find out what the committees are, how the board decides which committee gets the proposal, and whether it may go to more than one committee. (Do the same thing if the board sends the proposal to an independent commission). If there is more than one committee or commission that could get the proposal, figure out which would be best and then see if you can do anything to get the proposal before the best committee.

To decide which committee is likely to be the best, find out who chairs each committee and which board members sit on each. Obviously, your first consideration should be the committee that is most likely to recommend that the board adopt the proposal. But the final recommendation isn't the only thing to consider. Find out about the committee's internal processes. How do proposals come to a vote? Sometimes the sponsor can insist, sometimes the committee chair must agree to schedule a vote. Often, committee chairs decide whether or not hearings will be held. If the committee is required to hold a hearing before taking a vote, the chair may effectively control whether there is a vote at all. Find out who controls how the hearing is structured, etc. If the committee chair can control the progress of the proposal or the hearings, a committee with fewer supporters but a sympathetic chair may be best. If there are ways to get the proposal out of committee without a favorable recommendation from the committee, a committee with a good chair but without a majority in favor of the proposal could be best.

Since committees are often organized around certain subjects (finance, health, etc.), you may be able to change the proposal to make it more likely that it will go to one particular committee than another. Obviously, you shouldn't make changes that significantly alter the proposal unless you think you have much to gain by influencing the assignment.

20.5

> **Hawaii organizers felt they had significantly more support
> on the labor committee in the state Senate than they did
> on the judiciary committee. Since comprehensive civil
> rights bills were usually assigned to the judiciary commit-
> tee, they scaled back their proposal to a bill that only
> covered employment discrimination based on sexual ori-
> entation. The committee reported it out favorably, and the
> legislature passed it.**

If the president of the board or some other person decides which
committee gets a bill, and if she or he has a lot of discretion in making
the decision, think about getting a sponsor for the proposal who may
help steer it to a favorable committee. For example, bills are often sent
to committees chaired by their sponsors as long as they have some
connection to the committee's function.

20.6 Getting Out of Committee

Find out if your proposal needs a favorable recommendation from the committee to get back to the board. This is customary,
but there are frequently more obscure procedures that may allow you
to place the proposal in front of the whole board without a favorable
committee recommendation. For example, boards can often call proposals out of committee with a discharge motion.

> **Milwaukee city council rules allow a proposal to be sent
> from committee to the full council with no recommenda-
> tion. Although the committee that had the bill in
> Milwaukee had more supporters than opponents, many of
> them were uneasy about it and didn't want to take a pub-
> lic stand until the final vote.**

20.7 At the Board

Find out how many times the board must vote on the proposal. City councils are often required to pass proposals twice, occasionally even three times. Final votes by bodies that vote more than

once are often viewed as formalities, but you should never count on that with a potentially controversial proposal. Keep your lobbying program in place until the end.

Like most cities, San Francisco had a tradition that second readings on proposed legislation were a formality. Debate was unheard of. That is, it was unheard of until the lesbian/gay civil rights law came up for a second reading. A vigorous, silly debate arose about whether the law would apply to "unattractive" cross-dressers. The proponents' chief writer was out of town, having been assured he was no longer needed. The legislation was passed, without a foolish amendment, but it was a near thing.

Find out if some types of proposals require "supermajorities" (i.e., a two-thirds vote), which occur most often with spending proposals. You may be able to adjust the proposal to avoid a supermajority requirement. For example, you might want to think about dropping a requirement that the city post nondiscrimination notices in its offices if spending bills require a supermajority, but other policies do not.

20.8   At the Executive

Although all federal and state laws require some participation from an executive (the president or a governor), this is not always true with city councils or other boards, and you should find out. If you do need executive approval (typically from the mayor), he or she needs to be a prime target for your lobbying.

An executive who strongly supports your proposal can be a powerful lobbyist. Sometimes board members who agree with a policy (or say they do) will be reluctant to support a proposal if they think it will not be approved; they don't want to risk losing support if the campaign is not going to succeed. Strong support from the executive may be critical to getting the support of these members; the prospect of a veto may be enough to keep them from voting for a policy.

An executive's effectiveness depends at least partly on the extent to which she or he is willing to make the policy an important part of his or her agenda. Members on the fence will be more willing to vote favorably to please the executive if they think their vote will be remembered when they have something important to them that the executive needs to approve.

If you need executive approval, find out what happens if the executive "pockets" the proposal and neither signs nor vetoes it. In some systems this is a "pocket approval" (i.e., the law takes effect without explicit approval); in some, this is a "pocket veto" (i.e., the law does not go into effect, despite the absence of an explicit veto). In some systems, the effect of neither signing nor vetoing a proposal depends on when the proposal reaches the executive. If the timing matters, you may want to make sure that an executive who is on the fence has the option of a pocket approval, but does not have the option of a pocket veto.

20.9 Knowing the Written Rules

You need to know all of the body's written rules as well as the structure. If the body has its own written rules, get a copy.

> Not knowing the rules may have cost New York City organizers years of effort. The very first time the bill was introduced, in 1971, it was approved by the committee and sent to the floor of the council. However, since a small change had been made in the text while the bill was in committee, local rules required that the council not act on it for thirty days after the committee report. This gave opponents, who were taken by surprise by the quick approval, time to mobilize and narrowly defeat the bill on the floor. It didn't make it out of committee again until 1986, the year it finally passed.

Someone in your organization needs to know *Robert's Rules of Order*. *Robert's Rules* is a set of rules for boards and committees and is available in any bookstore. There are actually several versions, but all are very similar to each other. Many bodies rely completely on *Robert's Rules of Order,* and most others use *Robert's* to answer questions their own rules don't.

Knowing the rules may have saved Milwaukee's law. Supporters on the committee that had the bill wanted to send it to the council without a recommendation. When the bill came up, a member who was not expected to support the bill moved that it be sent to council with a favorable recommendation. That motion failed. Though unclear as to why this happened, it may have been a clever ploy by opponents, because the city attorney then said that the rules did not allow the bill to be sent to the council with no recommendation after a vote to recommend favorably had failed.

The chair of the committee bettered the clever ploy by one. He moved that the bill be filed, and since that is usually how legislation is killed he apparently went along. The chair knew that under Milwaukee's rules, when the chair reports to the council, she or he can ask that the council itself take bills out of the "file" and act on them without any vote from the committee. The chair knew the majority of the council supported the bill, and at its next meeting, on recommendation from the chair, the council took the bill out of the file and passed it.

Sometimes, knowing the rules isn't enough. You can't push a board to stick to them. For example, in New York, all proposed laws are supposed to receive committee hearings. For years, the chair of the committee handling the lesbian/gay rights bill simply refused to schedule any. He was influential enough that no one dared to challenge him on it.

20.10 Knowing the Unwritten Rules

Every board has unwritten rules and structures that exist only in practice and tradition. These you can find out by talking to people who are part of the process, or people who have been watching it, or by observing it closely yourself. Here are some of the things you should look for:

* *Are the body's committees dominated by their chairs?* Often, chairs technically have little power, but actively control committees by controlling resources (staff, etc.) or simply through a tradition of deference. Obviously, the more committees are effectively controlled by chairs, the more important it is to try to steer the bill to a committee with a chair who is not hostile.

* *What traditions of deference does the body have?* With some boards, votes are close to a formality, since virtually every proposal that is voted out of committee is approved. The real approval process is in committee, and members who are not on the committee frequently participate informally in various ways. On the other hand, with some boards anything brought to the committee by its chair is approved, and committee vote is essentially meaningless.

* *To what extent is the body as a whole dominated by its leadership?* With some bodies, strong support from a speaker or a chair is a virtual guarantee of passage, opposition a virtual guarantee of defeat. Where this is true, the leadership must be the dominant focus of your lobbying.

Finally, as with written rules, unwritten rules are sometimes broken when people feel strongly enough about an issue. Know the unwritten rules, but never rely on them totally.

20.11 A Word About Timing

Some activists try to avoid bringing lesbian/gay proposals up near elections. The idea is that politicians who are worried about losing support will be most skittish at election time, and most willing to take risks when they think it possible that the vote will fade in voters' memories before the next election. While elections may not be a good time to take a vote on a policy, they are frequently a great time to begin or be in the process of a policy campaign. Candidates' nights are a great way to begin public discussion of the issue and a good way to find out where the members you'll be dealing with stand. Moreover, if you can get policy supporters visibly involved in the electoral process, you may be able to use the election to get commitments for support from members. (See chapter 11.)

Some activists try to avoid bringing policies up when budgets are under consideration. They fear that the policy will become an item for trading in the tough budget process, which is the most important function of many boards. However, if you have the support of an important budget player, this can work the other way.

Lining up what proved to the critical votes in favor of Chicago's gay rights policy, the mayor kept a copy of his proposed budget open on his desk. He made no explicit deals, but he did select budget items important to wavering members and told them that just as increased sanitation, or new clinics, etc., were important to them, the lesbian/gay civil rights bill was important to him. He got the critical votes.

For similar reasons, some activists try to avoid having policies voted on at the end of a legislative session with bodies that have sessions (some bodies meet for a session during a certain time of the year, others meet throughout the year). Again, whether "end of session" horse-trading is a drawback or an advantage probably depends most on how important the policy is to your major supporters. Finally, timing the vote can be very important if referendum or initiative is a possibility. (See chapter 24.)

20.12 Sponsors

Your sponsor should be committed to the policy. You want the sponsor to be effective at lobbying other members, to treat the policy as important, when he or she is trading with other members, and to use any formal or informal prerogatives she or he may have as a committee member, chair, etc., to help the policy along.

But being a supporter is not enough. Try to avoid members who are isolated; they won't be effective at lobbying other members. If you've got two (or more) parties, try to get members who can work with members of both. Senior members or moderates, if they are truly committed, may be more effective at bringing others over than someone with a stronger ideological commitment might be. Look for committee chairs or leaders who might be able to use their positions to move the proposal along.

Look out for members who might sponsor your proposal to exploit it. A member who can easily afford support for lesbian and gay civil rights or domestic partnership (either because she or he has a liberal district or a safe position) might be willing to sponsor to make points with and maybe pick up financial support from lesbians and gay men and others who support civil rights. There isn't anything wrong with that if the member is willing to truly sponsor and work for the bill. Sometimes prospective sponsors plan to give nothing other than their names.

20.13 When to Ask for a Vote

"Never ask for a vote," an experienced southern organizer says, "unless you are going to win. A losing vote makes it tougher the next time."

"Never let a session go by without demanding a vote," a widely respected New York organizer advises. "You've to hold their feet to the fire and make them understand they are going to have to take a stand every year until it passes."

There is something to be said for both theories. If a campaign is long (more than a year, or more than a session with bodies that have them), it is very important to make members take a stand on the policy every year or every session.

It is much easier for politicians, worried about the political risk involved in supporting a policy, to vote against you if they think it will only have to be done once, or perhaps not at all if you don't press for a vote unless you can win it. They assume (all too often correctly) that one bad vote will be forgotten soon enough, and that if they are otherwise somewhat supportive of lesbians and gay men, they will get our support back. Actual votes are also often the best barometer of where you stand, and they can tell you on whom you need to work.

On the other hand, a vote tends to end a chapter in a campaign. Once a body has voted on a policy, it is likely to want to be finished with it for a time. You will usually have to wait until the next year or the next session to begin lobbying the body again in earnest, so you shouldn't call for votes at every opportunity. (Never go away completely, though; let members know casually that you and your issue are still around.) Ask for a vote when you think it is time to bring a stage of the campaign to an end.

In addition, losing votes can demoralize the community. Although it is probably never a good idea to predict a loss, you should try to prepare the community, for example, by making one of the campaign themes that it could be a long battle and that the campaign, like the community, is here to stay.

20.14 Counting Votes

Not many things are more important than accurately counting votes. Never count a member's vote until the member personally tells that campaign that she or he will vote for the proposal. "Their mouths to your ears are the only real commitments," advises a Chicago organizer.

And don't count a promise unless the commitment is made either to a vote counter or someone deeply involved in the campaign. Listen carefully to exactly what the member says. Members who are not opposed in principle, but who do not want to support you for other reasons, will often try to get you to leave them alone by giving you the impression they will support you without actually promising to do so. Don't accept vague assurances of support; ask explicitly if the member will vote yes on the proposal.

No commitment is forever. Even if a member has explicitly promised you support, keep up contact periodically to learn whether they have new questions or concerns, and ask them to renew their commitment. Try to have at least two people in the organization keeping track of the vote count. You are more likely to flush out ambiguous promises if two people are tracking.

21. PUBLIC HEARINGS

21.1 Introduction: What this Chapter Covers

This chapter covers how to organize public hearings. The next chapter covers picking and preparing witnesses.

21.2 The Three Kinds of Hearings

There are three kinds of public hearings, and you may have more than one during the course of a campaign.

Most boards hold hearings on a proposed policy before they decide whether to pass it. (See section 20.5.) These "official hearings" are often required by law.

Special boards and commissions (such as a local human rights commission) and occasionally subcommittees of the board, often hold hearings before proposed policies are considered by the board. They also frequently hold hearings on community problems. Commissions and subcommittees sometimes hold hearings at the request of the board or a board member. Sometimes "commission hearings" are held in response to requests from community groups.

Public hearings with no real official status ("community hearings") are sometimes called by community groups, churches, and similar organizations to air local problems and possible solutions. (See chapter 10.)

21.3 The Audience

Despite the differences, any hearing is a chance to communicate with the public and persuade people that your proposed policy is a good idea. When you think about what to present and how to present it, the public, and in particular the board's constituency, is one of your primary audiences. When the board, or a group which makes recommendations to it, holds a hearing, the board or the group is also a primary audience. Public hearings have changed votes on city councils, usually with vivid testimony showing that discrimination exists and that people get hurt by it.

For the most part, you'll want to do the same kind of preparation and present similar testimony for both audiences. But if you have a hearing on a specific proposal, don't let the chance to address the specific concerns and questions of the board get away. Find out what they are (through research and lobbying visits; see chapters 4 and 17) and make sure your testimony deals with them. For example, if you know that a member of a policy-making group is an advocate for small business and is likely to be worried that the law may be costly, make sure that some of those who testify for the law are small business owners. If possible, get endorsement letters from small business groups in other cities that have laws.

21.4 What Should Be Said—The General Idea

In general, your first aim should be to support your major arguments with proof that they are correct and supply evidence that community leaders and groups support them. Your second aim should be to show that the arguments of the opposition are wrong. Begin planning any hearing by reviewing your case for the policy and your answers to the opposition. Think about what kind of testimony will make your points clearly and forcibly. When you evaluate what kind of evidence is likely to work, keep your audience in mind. Don't use testimony that relies on assumptions or a level of understanding that your audience may not have.

> **Organizers in Greensboro, North Carolina, had a good story from a man who was not hired because he was not married, and therefore, the employer said, "not reliable." They did not use it because they felt it would be too hard**

during the hearing to explain that decisions based on marital status discriminate against lesbians and gay men, and that unmarried employees, including lesbians and gay men, are not unreliable.

You also need to make sure that you expose any mistaken assumption your audience may have about gay people which could affect their views about the policy. For example, organizers in a place like Greensboro would want to make sure that the board or its constituents did not share the assumption that gay people are unreliable. If in doubt, you should, like the Greensboro organizers did, present evidence that lesbians and gay men make good employees (and perhaps that we have families as well).

If you are proposing a civil rights policy, probably the single most important thing you need to do at any hearing is show people that lesbians and gay men are in need of it. Stories are an important way to show that, but they are not the only way to do it. (See chapter 28).

More than one person should be involved in planning the testimony; this ensures that you won't miss drawbacks to some testimony and that you'll get a better range of ideas. If possible, you should have one or two people pivotal in planning whose perspectives on the policy will be similar to those of your audience.

21.5 Setting the Agenda for the Hearing

Two of the most important things to do in planning a public hearing is to decide on the precise subject for the hearing and set the agenda. Your ability to influence the agenda at a public hearing depends on the kind of hearing it is. If the hearing is an "official" hearing on a proposed policy, the policy itself will be the subject, and the board will usually have rules about who may speak, in what order, etc.

If the hearing is a "community hearing" and you have called it yourself, you have virtually complete control over the subject, how speakers are selected, etc. Community hearings are usually more credible if sponsored by mainstream organizations, which means you lose absolute control. However, if you suggest the hearing, both community groups and commissions and subcommittees are frequently willing to take suggestions on both the subjects to be covered and the process.

> **Activists in Greensboro, North Carolina, started their campaign by sending a written set of complaints to the city's human relations commission. The commission, at the suggestion of the group that drew up the complaints, used them as an outline for hearings sponsored by the commission. All or a part of each session of hearings was devoted to the general subject covered in one of the complaints.**

If there is more than one local commission or subcommittee that could hold a hearing, you should find out in advance which one has a more friendly person in charge of setting agendas and try to get your first hearing before that one.

You can use public hearings, typically "commission" or "community" hearings to begin building support for a policy. (See section 10.3.) This kind of a hearing should focus on the problem of discrimination and not any specific possible solution. The best way to avoid debates over the details of specific proposals is simply to make the purpose and focus of the hearing —to examine the problem—very clear and very public when you announce it. One of the ground rules people generally accept is that anyone who wants to speak at a hearing must agree to stick to the topic on the agenda. People who want to make speeches about specifics or opposition to nondiscrimination policies can be politely told that later hearings or board hearings will give them the opportunity to do that.

On the other hand, no matter who calls a hearing, never attempt to avoid a debate by preventing certain people from speaking altogether. Most Americans are committed to the idea that, in public meetings, everyone should be permitted his or her say as long as everyone follows the ground rules.

21.6   Structuring the Hearing

You need to think about the structure of the hearing if whoever is holding it does not have processes that are set.

There is no single right way to run a hearing, but in general, it is usually a good idea to have an organized presentation from witnesses who will make all of your main points before taking public testimony.

At hearings on specific policies, there usually will be opposition speakers. At hearings on community problems, there often is not. If there are opposition speakers, the group holding the hearing will sometimes ask people to alternate. Try to convince whomever is holding the hearing to let each side make its basic presentation without interruption and to alternate only with public testimony. The testimony is much more coherent that way.

21.7 Presenting Stories of Discrimination

People with compelling stories about discrimination make very effective witnesses. (See section 28.2 on how to get good stories.) Since policymakers everywhere like to view their institutions as more enlightened than others, the stories should come from your own institution or area if possible. If the hearing is about a specific proposal, stories about incidents that would have been covered by the policy are especially good. So, for example, if your policy covers employment discrimination by a city, look for someone who lost a city job or promotion because of sexual orientation.

On the other hand, you shouldn`t reject compelling testimony about events, especially discrimination, just because the incident might not have been covered by your proposed policy. Evidence of violence against lesbians and gay men has often been effective, even though few nondiscrimination policies cover it.

> **During the 1978 hearing on San Francisco's lesbian/gay civil rights law, the story of a lesbian who was not allowed to be in a hospital intensive care unit with her lover who had just been hit by a truck made a strong impression on the human rights commission. As it turned out, she might not have been helped by the proposal the city eventually adopted.**
>
> **In Greensboro, North Carolina, the human relations**

commission was deeply offended to learn that the local
Metropolitan Community Church was ejected from the
church building it rented when the denomination that
owned it found out most of the parishioners were gay.
Many civil rights laws, including the one the city adopted,
would not have applied.

The key to effectively using testimony about things that might not
be directly covered by your proposal is being able to tie the story to
one of your arguments for the policy. So, for example, testimony about
violence tends to be more effective if you are also offering evidence
that nondiscrimination laws help create an atmosphere in which hate
violence is less likely to occur. (See chapter 28 on ways to do this.)
Testimony about any act of discrimination almost always at a minimum
helps to prove that prejudice exists in your community.

Many people don't understand why verbal assaults are so unnerving
and psychologically damaging. Unless you can provide convincing,
quick perspective on why verbal assaults are not just name-calling, you
may want to avoid it. Testimony about anti-gay violence is often dis-
missed with the advice that gay victims of violent crimes should just go
to the police. This really misses the point, since police complaints don't
do anything to reduce hate or prevent assaults. Nevertheless, if the
local police do not take violent crime against gay people seriously, it
doesn't hurt to obtain evidence. Look for instances of police not
responding, arresting victims, etc. This can be powerful evidence of the
need for a civil rights law by itself.

21.7

The "take it to the police" objection to testimony about
violence was pretty thoroughly discredited in Raleigh,
North Carolina. A gay man testified that he had gone to
the police to complain about an assault and had been told
that he should drop it because he would probably lose
his job if the complaint were pursued and made public.
The man said he was not worried since he worked in a gay
bar. He finally gave up, however, when the police threatened to prosecute him for sodomy if he persisted with his
complaint.

If an incident needs to be explained to make the discrimination clear, think about how you might be able to do that quickly; if it can not be done quickly, think about not using it.

21.8 Other Kinds of Testimony

It is a good idea to illustrate the breadth of your support by getting at least some of the nongay organizations and individuals that have endorsed your effort to testify briefly about why they support you. Written endorsements from all the others should be presented to the group holding the hearing. (See chapter 9.) In most parts of the country, it is very important to present testimony from established churches that support nondiscrimination. (See chapter 16.)

Depending on how sophisticated your audience is, it may be a good idea to present testimony that being gay is not a sign of mental instability. Both the American Psychological Association and the American Psychiatric Association have good statements on this. You should also be able to get a local psychologist or psychiatrist to testify about the statements and what they mean. You may also want to present evidence refuting some common myths about lesbians and gay men if you think the board or its constituents may share them. (See chapter 15.)

You may need to have evidence about "choice" and sexual orientation. This is a difficult area because it is easy to get trapped in unhelpful arguments about the origins of sexual orientation. They somewhat miss the point about choice, are often very emotional, and ultimately can't be resolved since no one really knows what creates sexual orientation. Nonetheless, testimony may be important if you have decision makers who think that sexual orientation may be an adult choice and who think that has a bearing on civil rights protection. (See chapter 29.30.)

A good way to come up with unusual testimony is to think about how discrimination or the failure to recognize relationships hurts gay people and then to think about tangible things that reflect that harm. For example, social scientists can provide useful testimony about the costs of discrimination. (See chapter 28 for more examples.)

> At public hearings in San Francisco, a local economist
> presented an estimate of the dollar cost, in terms of lost
> productivity and government relief, of employment discrim-
> ination based on sexual orientation.

Don't get carried away with trying to do something out of the ordinary. Again, your aim should be to make your basic points clearly.

> The first proposal for a New York City gay rights law was
> introduced in 1971. A law was finally passed in 1986. One
> year later, tired of the annual parade of horror stories,
> organizers decided to have a "taxpayers" hearing, at
> which successful lesbians and gay men from around the
> city would testify about how much gay people contribute
> to the city. The hearing was, according to one of the
> organizers, a "disaster." The council was bored by the
> testimony, and the hearing reinforced the misconception
> that most gay men are wealthy and successful.

21.9 Public Testimony

Although official hearings often have set policies on
whether to allow public testimony, other types of hearings often do
not. The drawback to public testimony is that you have no control
over the messages and no opportunity to fully prepare people who
testify for your side. You can be surprised by both your friends and
your opponents. The advantage is that some of the most powerful
evidence about the need for the law comes from open public testimony, both from powerful stories you didn't discover, and from
unbridled opponents.

> In both New York and Chicago, activists believe they got
> significant additional support on the city council as a
> result of public hearings in which opponents were open
> about their violent hatred of lesbians and gay men. This
> kind of visceral opposition convinced several African-
> American and Puerto Rican members of the New York
> City council that there were parallels between race dis-

> crimination and sexual-orientation discrimination in a way
> lesbian or gay witnesses could never have done.

If your hearing will have public testimony, you can minimize some of the risks by having one or two strong "clean-up" speakers (see the next section). And you can minimize some of the risk of unprepared speakers for your side by trying to make sure that people who might come know a few basic ground rules. (See section 22.10.)

If the group holding the hearing has witnesses give names and addresses, arrange to get the list, or, if they don't make one up, have one of your supporters take down the names as people testify. This can be a good source of new supporters. Have someone from the campaign organization ready to talk to particularly good witnesses whom you did not know about, so that you are sure to get their stories, formal endorsements, etc.

21.10 Clean-up Speakers

A "clean-up speaker" is someone who is on standby to speak late at the public hearing in case you need to respond to something said by public speakers or by the other side. However, be careful about how you use "cleanups." Generally, they should just reply to things that appear to have impressed your audience in a way that is not helpful.

If you think an opposition speaker has said something that hurt the opposition, it may be best to refer to it briefly and gently or to leave it alone completely. For example, if someone claims that the Old Testament says gay people should be put to death, and the audience is shocked, it is probably not a good idea to respond indignantly. The stronger your attack, the more you risk creating some sympathy for the person who said it. And it is unlikely that you will increase the audience's dismay at the remark.

On the other hand, you want to be sure everybody understood the significance of something the opposition said that is likely to help you. If you are not sure, a quiet reminder will usually do the trick. In response to the example in the paragraph above, you might refer to some of the everyday things that the Old Testament also condemns. But keep in mind that you shouldn't respond at all to things that you are confident haven't moved your audience at all.

If you can, get an experienced speaker for the cleanup. He or she will have to put together quickly what is going to be said, and he or she will have to be ready to give very short, impressive replies.

21.11 Who Goes First, (Etc.)

Once you have decided on the points you want to make and who will make them (see section 22.2), you need to think about order. Some organizers think it is best to leave your strongest witness for last. The problem with that is that attention spans are shortest at the end. Sometimes many people are no longer listening at all. Perhaps most important, the media usually will not stay much longer than the first half hour or so. The other school of thought is that it is best to lead with strength, and hold a clean-up speaker or two for the end. Whichever school you accept, the strongest speakers will be those who:

* command the attention of the group holding the hearing because members of the group respect (or need the support of) the speaker; for example, a prominent politician or community leader;

* effectively summarize the campaign's major themes and arguments and do it in a way the media can use;

* silence (or at least mute) some of the major opposition or counter some of the myths on which the opposition may rely.

Rabbis, nuns, ministers, and priests frequently make good "tone setting" witnesses early in a hearing because, as a Wisconsin organizer put it, it is difficult to accuse a sixty-eight-year-old nun of being insensitive to religion.

In Chicago, the African-American community is the largest progressive political group. Support from its political leaders was crucial to passage of the civil rights laws. Chicago organizers also felt that neutralizing fundamentalist

> religious opposition was vital. **For the first speaker at the public hearing, organizers chose the head of Operation Push, a very important African-American direct action organization with strong ties to the church. The speaker told an intensely personal story about her son, who had recently died of AIDS, and of her refusal to accept the fact that he was gay until the hearing, and of the need to pass civil rights laws to begin changing attitudes.**
>
> **The chamber was silent as she spoke, and ministers who had waved Bibles at supportive speakers in past hearings sat quietly. Organizers felt that more than anything else, she set the tone for the hearing that followed, keeping the focus away from religion and instead on civil rights.**

You need to be flexible. If you have someone you particularly want the press to see and hear, be ready to move him or her back in the order if the press is late, while making sure that you still have a strong opening.

21.12

21.12 Written Statements

Although it is not a good idea to have witnesses write out their testimony (see section 22.5), it may be useful to have them write statements that will cover much of the same ground. You can submit the written statements to whomever holds the hearing so that there is a written record in case the hearing is not transcribed (most hearings are recorded, some are taken down by court reporters, but written transcripts are rarely prepared). With commission or community hearings, written statements submitted at the hearing can later be presented to the board.

Written statements are also helpful if time gets short. Witnesses can be encouraged not to repeat earlier testimony and instead to simply give their names and submit the statements for the record. Finally, you can use the written statements in media packets, either for the hearing or at any other point in the campaign.

21.13 Preparing the Group Holding the Hearing

You should think about preparing the group that holds the hearing. If you think its members may need either background information or greater detail on points that will be covered at the hearing, you may want to do fact sheets. (See section 12.4.)

You may want to talk with friendly members about questions. Some organizers like to have their own witnesses questioned because it gives them an opportunity to respond to members' particular concerns and to emphasize critical points. Questions can be a problem, however, if the witness is not well prepared or if the time spent responding comes out of the time allowed for the witness's presentation. Some organizers don't like to have the other side questioned because it may give them an opportunity to explain points that may be unclear. On the other hand, a few well-placed questions can slow your opposition down. For example, a group of fundamentalists argued against a nondiscrimination law to the city council in Chicago on the basis that lesbians and gay men are sinners. They were left groping for words when a council member, prompted by proponents, asked if unwed mothers should be denied jobs and housing as well.

You might want to provide members of the group holding the hearing with questions that emphasize your points and that, like the unwed mother question and all good polemical questions, help you no matter how they are answered.

21.14 Getting the Right People to Come

Unless this is an official hearing and you are trying to keep the policy quiet, you almost certainly want to get as much media as possible. (See chapter 13.)

You want to get supporters to come. First, your witnesses will feel more assured if they know there are supporters in the room. Second, you want the group holding the hearing to know that many of those in the room support you. It does not matter that those in the room represent a tiny fraction of the local electorate, or that every member of the policy-making body knows that you made an organized effort to turn out supporters. You look and feel stronger if you have a large number of supporters in the room. (See chapter 18, on ways to get people to come.)

Finally, if this hearing is not before the board, you want to get as many members of the board there as you can. You want to get allies and potential allies to the hearing because it is likely to provide them with information that will help convince them and that they can use to convince others. You want to get uncommitted members there so you can use the hearing to help begin the process of persuading them. You also want to get board members into the process as early as possible so that they feel like a part of it. Find out who in the group sponsoring the hearing is closest to each person whom you want to attend and get them to ask. You can have political allies and personal friends do the same.

21.15 Responding to the Other Side

Although this topic is covered elsewhere (see sections 7.10 and 22.8), it is so important that this section recaps the basic guidelines.

Never attack your opponents. It may build sympathy for them and it cannot help you. *Don't respond to their rhetoric or to emotional appeals they may make.* The crazier they get, the better we look if we stay calm. If they make claims about the policy or arguments against it, *respond to the merits only,* in a way as matter-of-fact as possible. Try to respond only to things you think may have moved or raised questions with one of the audiences.

21.16 The Outcome

If the hearing is being held by the board on a proposed policy, the desired outcome is easy: You want the board to adopt the policy. Typically, the goal of a commission or a community hearing is to move the process along. At a minimum, if you have a specific proposal, you'll want the group that held the hearing to endorse it and to tell the board in writing about the endorsement. If you do not have a specific policy, you will want the group to endorse the idea of one (for example, endorse the adoption of a nondiscrimination ordinance).

Especially if you've been able to make your case thoroughly, you may want the group that sponsored the hearing to make a report to the board with findings and recommendations. The report should briefly describe the hearings, perhaps attaching a list of witnesses, find that there is a problem and describe the facts that show it (the findings), and then make recommendations about what the policy-making body should do to remedy the problem. The report need not be long. You should talk to the group holding the hearing informally in advance and urge that this kind of document is important to give their work in holding the hearing maximum impact. You should always offer to prepare a draft or an outline.

22. WITNESSES AND TESTIMONY

22.1 Introduction: What this Chapter Covers

This chapter covers how to select and prepare witnesses. Although written specifically for public hearings, much of it applies to getting people ready for all types of public appearances.

22.2 Picking Your Witnesses

Here are a few considerations to help you decide which witness to use if you have more than one witness who can support one of your important messages. Try for diversity. There are lesbians and gay men of every color, religion, political view, etc., and we are disabled, poor, and wealthy. Illustrating that truth with a diverse group of witnesses is the best way to break down the stereotype that gay means successful white man. Diversity can also be a way to build bridges to other communities. It may be possible to have witnesses who have experienced other types of discrimination draw some important parallels, something other witnesses might not be able to do credibly. Since parallels can easily offend other minorities, they must be drawn with care. (See section 27.4).

Think about who will matter most to your audience. For the board, the best person is likely to be someone from whom members of the board think they will need help in the future. With the public, someone widely respected can give your campaign credibility.

People who are employed by the organization being asked to adopt the policy can be very effective witnesses. In Berkeley, California, the city council was visibly moved by a man who talked about his fears of being discovered and losing his job because he had an intensely homophobic supervisor. The council was stunned when, after recounting incidents illustrating the supervisor's anti-gay attitudes, the witness revealed that he worked for the city.

This is a risky tactic. The Berkeley council promised on the spot to protect the witness. Less friendly boards may not. If the policy does not pass, the witness may be out of a job. Even if the policy passes, the witness may have a hostile supervisor with a new focus for his or her hostility.

22.2

Some organizers are fond of using parents of lesbians and gay men. The advantage is that most parents who testify have made the intellectual and emotional adjustment you are asking the board to make. On the other hand, the validity of parents' perspective can easily be discussed because they *are* parents and want to see the best in their children. Another advantage to using parents is that even the most hostile opponents are reluctant to attack them. The difficulty is that one reason parents of lesbians and gay men are treated respectfully is that people feel sorry for them. Left alone, that can be a significant, if subtle, reinforcement of the idea that being gay is an unfortunate thing. The best parent testimony is usually testimony about what made the parent realize that discrimination is wrong and harmful.

22.3 Whom to Avoid

You probably should avoid people who are unwilling to focus on the aim of your campaign, people who are consumed with a desire to tell their story their way, or to present a political perspective that doesn't necessarily have anything to do with your policy proposal.

Some organizers recommend avoiding persons in "hot button" jobs, which might remind people of some basic fears about gay people. These might include teachers or day-care workers. You need to think carefully about this. Frequently, opponents will suggest at some point that certain jobs be exempted from civil rights policies. Often, solid testimony from or about a gay person in one of those jobs is the best answer to that.

> In a small **Marin County, California,** community, the school board was deeply moved by testimony of both students and parents about an inspirational gay high school teacher. **The boardroom was absolutely silent when two sixteen-year-olds testified about how well he had taught the need to understand differences among people.**

Other organizers suggest avoiding people who are too "flamboyant." This too needs careful thought. It is certainly fair to say to the community that unless a hearing is purely confrontational, it makes sense to plan the process of persuasion and not to assault on all fronts at once. On the other hand, it can be a mistake to portray the gay community as homogenized and indistinguishable from those who live in the stereotypical suburban tract. The lesbian/gay community includes both men and women who seem very "masculine" and others who seem very "feminine." You can combat stereotypes more effectively and more honestly by showing range and not just counterexamples. For example, as in San Jose, California, some powerful testimony about sexual-orientation discrimination came from a heterosexual man who had frequently been mistaken for a gay man because people thought he conformed to some stereotypes about gay men.

22.3

22.4 Preparing Your Witnesses: Introduction

Some organizers put a lot of time into reviewing testimony and role-playing with witnesses. Although both these techniques are valuable, the most important things you can do to prepare witnesses is to explain the process and tell them how to plan their testimony.

22.5 Planning Testimony

The point of a public hearing is to persuade the audience, not to tell it what you think. You may have a striking theory that civil rights or domestic partnership policies are essential for democratic institutions, though it is not likely to matter much with most boards.

Every witness should begin planning testimony by deciding what he or she can say that will reinforce one of the basic messages of the campaign. The idea is to help the audience understand why the policy is needed, either by making the arguments for it plainer or by recounting incidents that clearly illustrate one or more of those arguments.

Planning testimony does not mean writing out what you intend to say word for word. Most listeners get bored very quickly when people read prepared statements; memorized statements usually sound like statements being read.

A witness needs a speaking plan, a sheet of paper that has words or phrases that will flag each thing to be covered, in the right order. Writing the words and phrases in large letters with a bold pen makes it easier to refer to them while speaking.

22.6 The Formal Rules

Every witness needs to know the formal rules for the hearing, or for any other structured appearance. Witnesses need to know if there are limits on how long they may speak, on what they can say, whether there is an order of witnesses and if so, when they will be called. Witnesses need to know if they have to sign up to testify and if they will be asked for their names and addresses. They need to know when the hearing will start and how much time they may need to set aside to be present while waiting to testify.

If members of the group holding the hearing are allowed to ask questions, the witnesses need to be told that in advance. Tell them which members of the group are friendly, which may be hostile, and a little about the perspectives of each. Witnesses should know about the themes the campaign has decided on, and, if questions are a possibility, the answers the campaign has for hard questions.

22.7 Informal Rules — Time

Witnesses need to know that no matter what the formal rules say, they do not have much time. A witness who is part of a formal presentation, who has got the testimony organized and sharply focused, who is making a point that has not been made at the hearing yet and is not something that people hear day in and day out, who is either explaining well or telling a good story, may have as long as five to six minutes before he or she loses the attention of the audience.

Witnesses who appear early in the hearing generally have a little more time than those who appear later. Most witnesses will have three to four minutes at the most to work with. This means testimony must be stripped to its essential points. You cannot repeat yourself, and you should not repeat what other speakers say. Tell every witness this: If you really don't have anything new to say, give your name, your address (if local), state your position, give a one-sentence explanation of why you hold it, and sit down.

22.8 Informal Rules — Emotion

Strong emotion should be used sparingly and strategically. Most Americans think the process of adopting policy should be rational, and for most, rational means unemotional.

This does not mean emotion has no place in a hearing. But most of the time, strong emotion can be effectively conveyed by carefully describing what happened in a discrimination story far better than by reenactment of the emotions the incident caused.

While one or two speakers who do become emotional can rivet the audience if it identifies with the consequences to the speaker, if many more get emotional the audience is likely to think your side is simply unwilling to play by the rules and engage in a rational, deliberative process.

Witnesses should never allow themselves to react with raw anger. It will usually hurt the speaker's credibility, and it can create sympathy for an opponent if it takes the form of an attack. A good way to respond to an attack is calmly, by describing why the attack was unfair and showing just a trace of anger.

If it is plain that you are going to lose an effort to pass a policy, it may make strategic sense to make sure that the board knows that you and your supporters are angry. You may want to make sure they know people will not forget, that there will be political consequences, and that you will be back. Even then, an unbridled attack is likely to make the board member forget his or her own interests and simply return the anger.

22.9 Style and Appearance

Witnesses should not try to be anyone other than who they are. They should speak normally, using everyday language (remembering that public talk is always a bit more polite than private talk) and avoid formality, elegance, even poetry if it is not part of their usual manner. Witnesses should avoid jargon, whether political or professional, even if it is part of their usual style.

There is no particular right way to dress for a hearing. Be a neat version of yourself. One early Chicago coalition was almost destroyed when a hearing organizer insisted that all the men wear ties and all the women wear dresses. Putting aside the needless dissension it caused, this was a bad idea because part of the point of the hearing is to be natural and show people what we are really like.

22.10 Witness Preparation

If you can, go over all these guidelines individually with witnesses who will be part of a formal presentation. Ask each witness to run you through his or her testimony. Insist that the witness cover all points, major and minor, even if the review is not quite a dry run. This way you can make sure there are no unexpected bombs—statements that contradict your major themes—and that the witness is not making assumptions the people holding the hearing may not understand. You can help the witness stay focused and brief.

While you can't sit down and prepare all the witnesses who might testify if the hearing is open to public testimony, there are still a few things you can do to help public witnesses get ready. Hold a public meeting, ask people who plan to testify to come. Go over the campaign themes and these guidelines. Distill the themes and guidelines. Put them in a short sheet, and ask the local gay press, or alternate place to print it. Distribute your distillation in flyers at the hearing. There are no secret tricks here, so there should be nothing in a flyer which your opponents should not see.

22.11 Finding and Protecting Witnesses

Chapter 28 explains how to get the stories you need, chapter 3 explains how to get experts, and chapters 9 and 10 explain how to get other supporters.

Individual witnesses with stories of discrimination can present a special problem. Frequently, they will be unwilling to testify for fear of losing their jobs and homes, fear of violence, or fear of the reactions of family and friends. Organizers in Greensboro, North Carolina, dealt with this by closing portions of the hearing to the press and public. This certainly impressed commission members with how serious was the fear of reprisals. The problem with that tactic, of course, is that you cut out a primary audience.

In a number of cities, organizers have read statements from individuals who were afraid to testify. If you do this, make sure that your readers have some training so that they don't bore the audience. An experienced courtroom lawyer, a good actor, or a professional reader should be able to do the training. Try to alternate readings with live testimony.

In some cities, witness have testified as "Jane Doe" or "John Doe" and taken their chances on being recognized. Some people have worn masks. Organizers in Raleigh, North Carolina, came up with a particularly effective way of dealing with fear. They videotaped the statements of those who were afraid to testify and obscured their faces. They then played the tape at the hearing. The commission members saw and heard the real witnesses, and obscuring the faces really brought the depth of the fear home.

---

23. WRITING AND NEGOTIATING POLICY

23.1 Introduction: What this Chapter Covers

This chapter covers the process of writing policy. It will explain how to decide what type of proposal you want to offer and how to negotiate changes as you go through the process of getting it adopted.

23.2 Basic Principles

Most of the important things you need to know about the philosophy of policy writing have to do with negotiating changes. (They are covered below in sections 23.5 and 23.6.) But there are two important things you need to know at the start. First, every draft of a policy matters, even when it is clear that adoption of a policy is years away.

The first draft to be introduced is likely to be the version of the proposal the board will work with, perhaps until adoption. It will be difficult for you to change something to your own advantage in that draft. People will tend to see it as the most you are asking for, something you should negotiate down from. It may even be difficult to improve drafts once the board or your opposition has seen them, even if they haven't been introduced. So it is important to make the first draft as strong as you can. It is hard to undo mistakes.

In a campaign that lasts several years or sessions, you can try to make a "fresh start" with a completely new draft. Even if you do, board members and opponents are likely to remember features of the old one you'd like to forget. They may resurrect those features with the tough-to-answer question: "If it was OK last year, what's wrong with it now?"

> **Just before California's lesbian/gay civil rights law was adopted, a well-meaning moderate legislator inserted an "anti-quota" section from a previous draft. The old section had a serious flaw that could have drastically reduced the effectiveness of the remedies. Only a quick, very clear explanation of what was wrong, accompanied by a replacement that looked similar, averted a potential disaster.**

23.2

Second, words matter—but not always. Sometimes the use of particular words can be very important legally, even though the difference between two words might not seem important. Sometimes cases or other laws create a kind of tradition, giving a word a special legal meaning.

> **Like most civil rights laws, Oakland's proposal has a section that would allow discrimination if being gay or straight was really a job requirement. Organizers agreed to change the wording of their proposal, which used the common phrase "bona fide occupational qualification" to "contractual qualification." They didn't understand that court decisions have stated that laws that use the first phrase only allow discrimination if you can't operate the business without it. Since the change uses language no other law uses, no one can say whether it is as strict.**

Words can be important politically. If you agree to use the phrase "sexual preference" instead of "sexual orientation," you may find opponents later claiming that you agree sexual orientation is a choice. On the other hand, sometimes words that seem important are not, legally or politically.

> **Advocates in New York disagreed vehemently on the proposal to add a "disclaimer" that the civil rights law didn't endorse any particular life-style. The disclaimer was something of an insult at the time. But it has apparently no legal significance. And as an insult, it had little staying power. Within a few months, even those who work with the law regularly seemed to have forgotten that it was there.**

Together, these two things mean that every stage of writing needs to be taken seriously, and that at every stage you need a core group of writing advisers who can tell you about the legal and political consequences of any part of the proposal or any suggested change. Since the group may need to act quickly (see section 23.5, below), it should be small and its members should be easy to contact. The advisory group can be the core decision-making group (see section 5.7), but it can also be a special group of advisers to the core decision makers.

23.3 A Word About Style

With a "drop in" proposal (a proposal to "drop" the words "sexual orientation" into an existing notice) or a "duplicate freestanding" civil rights proposal (a proposal to create a new, separate policy on sexual orientation that is identical to an existing policy on another kind of discrimination; see chapter 30), style isn't a problem. You'll be using somebody else's. With other proposals, it's a major concern. Most civil rights and domestic partnership policies (like most other laws and policies) have become needlessly difficult to read, which means they are needlessly difficult to work with. They use words that people don't use in everyday life; they use sentences that go on too long to be understood in a single sweep; and they say things two and three times when once will do. For your campaign, and for everyone who'll try to use the policy later, you want to be as straightforward as you can be.

On the other hand, getting rid of language to which courts and enforcement agencies have given a special significance is dangerous. You not only lose the advantage of a developed meaning, you may well suggest to people that you used different words because you meant something different. Moreover, you need to make sure that you don't use words that courts and agencies have given special meanings you don't intend.

> **The writers of Berkeley, California's, domestic partnership registration law decided to have the partners promise to provide for each other's "common welfare." They didn't define that term, but in another part of the law, they said the partners would "share the common necessities of life." They didn't realize that phrase was one letter away from a phrase courts use to mean all living expenses, including medical costs. Without meaning to, the writers may have made everyone who signs up responsible for each other's medical costs, even though the law is a simple registration system with no financial advantages.**

The best solution may be to build a dialogue into your writing process. Make sure you have one writer or reviewer who knows about special language and is familiar with the traditions of policy writing (your lawyer would be the best candidate). Be sure to have a writer or reviewer who writes well and is committed to simplicity.

23.4 Input and Refinement

Getting suggestions from people who are familiar with civil rights policies and who share your ultimate goal will almost always make your proposal stronger. Talk to people who work with other kinds of civil rights policies. Contact lawyers at local, state, and national civil rights groups, especially lesbian and gay rights groups, and ask them to look over your proposal and give you comments. If you can, try to get input from lawyers or others who enforce policies or represent people with claims (like members of human rights or personnel departments and union representatives). Their practical perspective will be invaluable.

You can build support for your proposal by circulating it in the lesbian/gay community. If you can, schedule a public meeting or two at which you explain the proposal and ask for public comment. Chicago organizers got the local gay newspaper to print their entire civil rights proposal, and to solicit reader comments in writing and at later public meetings.

23.5 Negotiation—Basic Principles

If most of the members of the board and most of their constituents take it for granted that the policy is a good idea, you may not have to do a lot of negotiating. Most of the time you will.

The most difficult part of negotiating is deciding when to compromise on what things and when to hold firm. There aren't any hard and fast rules. The process is likely to be more satisfactory if you analyze each round of negotiations as a balancing process. For each alteration over which you negotiate, you should decide how much you think you will really gain and how much you think you will really lose by making a change.

How much you gain is a function of two things. First, what support will making the change really get you, and how much do you need that support to get the policy passed. Second, how much sooner will you get the policy if you make the change (this second factor is based on the assumption that if you wait long enough, you'll be able to get almost any policy passed; concede something if you think the policy could never be adopted without the concession).

> **In California, organizers decided to accept a mild anti-affirmative action clause in their statewide civil rights policy because they needed it to get the vote of the only Republican assembly member who voted for the law. They believed that the Republican governor would never sign the law if it didn't have some Republican support. The governor had at least three more years in office, and it looked like he could well be elected to a second term.**

> **No other Republican assembly member was likely to vote for the law under any circumstances.**

How much you lose depends on the likely legal effect of the change and its impact—how many fewer people will be covered, how much harder will it be to show discrimination or qualify for a benefit. It also depends on the political impact of the change.

> **The California organizers decided that mild anti-affirmative action provision wasn't much of a loss. It probably allowed outreach programs. It clearly did not allow quotas or tough timetables, but they didn't think a court would ever order quotas or tough goals and timetables. On the other hand, they think they probably made a mistake by including housing in one bill and then later giving it up during negotiations because housing discrimination based on sexual orientation was already covered by another obscure state law. The lesbian/gay community thought it had lost something important, and the organizers were never really able to make people understand it hadn't.**

Part of assessing the time factor is estimating how long you might have to live with a change that does some real harm if you accept it. Some policies, once passed, are very difficult to change; passing it establishes a precedent. With other policies, acceptance of the idea is the tough battle, and improvements later are sometimes easier to achieve.

> **During the campaign for the 1964 U.S. Civil Rights bill, proponents were forced to accept very narrow enforcement rules for the section on public accommodations. Despite causing some real, unfair hardships, that section of the law was unchanged thirty years later and had served as the model for laws protecting other groups.**

Even under the most quiet, deliberative conditions, it is tough to figure out the legal and political impact of a change, predict its effects on future cases and the community, calculate how the change will affect your support, and estimate when the policy could be passed without the change. But many of your most important negotiations

23.5

won't happen under those kinds of circumstances. They'll happen instead in heated moments shortly before a vote, after you've been working frantically on the campaign for months. In those situations, two very common reactions tend to make it even harder to balance all the considerations.

The first reaction is the sometimes overwhelming desire to have something to show for all your months or years of work. When a change looks like it could make the difference, people sometimes agree when they should not.

The second reaction, as negotiations drag on, is the common problem of blowing things out of proportion and treating them as if they were more important than they are; digging in your heals because you are tired, feel beat up, and a proposal sounds insulting, even though it really isn't very important.

The person (or small group) who makes your decisions in negotiations will need a legal adviser and a political adviser available to make the judgments you need to balance gain and loss. Those judgments are less likely to be skewed by the heat of the moment if one or both of those advisers are not actually negotiating and are able to bring an outside perspective. If, for example, your regular legal adviser is the prime negotiator, try to have another on call during the process.

23.6 A Couple of Negotiation Tips

Don't actually make a change, especially an important change, to gain someone's support without an ironclad commitment. If you can get an endorsement card signed, do so. Board members and politicians usually won't sign endorsement cards. But getting a board member's promise made to or in the presence of someone whose support the member needs, who is willing to go public if they try to back out, is just as good. This is the place to use politicians or other important supporters.

Don't waste your time negotiating with diehards. Sometimes, diehard opponents will try to negotiate with you, usually with board members or important moderate forces present. Their aim is to raise objections and persuade the moderates to pressure you to compromise. However, they will almost never support the bill after changes are made. If you can, try to convince the board members or moderates to "smoke out" the other side by testing their commitment to compromise. If you can't, insist on an ironclad commitment the first time you agree to a change before you make it. That will usually end the process.

Don't say things to people you are negotiating with that have nothing to do with the process. Don't abuse people, call them names, or get emotional. Don't make threats. Don't talk about your strategy or plans. And while a very rare strategic loss of patience can be useful, it should be carefully applied.

24. KEEPING IT

24.1 Introduction: It Ain't Over till ...

Any policy can be repealed or amended to the point where it becomes meaningless. The board that passed it can do either of those things. A board with superior powers can do them. For example, some states have system-wide university boards that can usually overrule the decision of a board that governs a single campus. State legislatures can usually overrule local governments. In many states, voters can repeal government policy with referendums and initiatives. There is no way to eliminate the possibility that any of these things might happen. However, there are a few things you can do to improve the odds.

24.2

24.2 Pay Attention to Timing

This is most important with boards whose actions can be overridden by either a *referendum* or an *initiative*, in which voters decide at an election if they want to keep a board policy. In most places, issues are put on the ballot either by petition (voters sign a petition demanding the question be voted on) or by the board. With a referendum, the policy is usually suspended (that is, it doesn't take effect) until after the vote. Petition signatures have to be gathered quickly after the policy is passed and the question goes on the next ballot.

Initiatives can be used to pass new policies or to get rid of existing ones. They don't have to be done immediately after a policy is passed, and the policy remains in effect until (and unless) the voters reject it. As a practical matter, the risk of a repeal by initiative is greatest soon after the policy is passed. The longer a policy is on the books after passage, the less threatening it is likely to seem. Opposition usually dissipates over time.

Some elections are much more likely to be better for policy proponents than others. In general, civil rights and domestic partnership policies do much better at presidential elections or at elections where a state governor is elected. They tend to do much less well at elections that are purely local. They do worst at elections that only involve issues or candidates for mundane offices.

24.2

> **Opponents of San Francisco's 1989 domestic partnership law mobilized quickly after its passage and obtained enough signatures for a referendum. The only other issue on the November 1989 ballot was whether to build a downtown baseball stadium. The only office up for election was an uncontested race for city treasurer. A few weeks before the election, the Loma Prieta earthquake rocked the city. Although supporters ran a vigorous campaign, the law lost by about half a percent of the vote.**
>
> **One year later, proponents put the domestic partnership law back on the ballot as an initiative. This time they ran a simple, bare-bones campaign. But this was an election for governor and all members of the city board of supervisors as well. The domestic partnership law won with a comfortable eight percent margin.**

Voters who tend to be more liberal, and thus will be more likely to support the policy, tend to vote in greater numbers in presidential and gubernatorial elections. More conservative voters tend to vote in every election, so they are a higher proportion of the voters in less exciting elections. (Trends could be different in your area, so check with local political pros.)

If your policy could be subject to an initiative or referendum, talk to someone who knows election laws. If your lawyer can't help you, try to find a lawyer who practices political law, or check with the local registrar of voters or the secretary of state.

Find out when a referendum can be placed on the ballot or when the first chance for an initiative after passage of the policy will be. Then, time the passage of your policy so that a referendum or the first chance for an initiative will arise at an election likely to be favorable to you. Delaying passage to get a better election could just save the policy.

Even if your policy is not subject to referendum or initiative, you should think about timing if your board is elected. An election campaign can provide opportunities to begin a policy campaign (see section 20.11). On the other hand, the risk that a civil rights or domestic partnership policy will become an issue in a board election goes up if it is adopted close to an election. Ask local political pros about how long before election campaigns typically begin. Time passage to reduce the likelihood that some candidate will decide to use the policy as an issue.

24.3 Keep the Possibility of Repeal in Mind

Although your campaign should focus on the board, you may be able to reduce the possibility of a repeal if you keep the board's constituency and any superior authority in mind during your campaign. (See section 7.2.)

Some organizers think that stealth campaigns run the greatest risk of repeal. A policy is most vulnerable to a demand for repeal by the public (either by pressure on the board or by referendum), they reason, if you've done nothing to sell the public on the policy during your campaign. They also think the public tends to view stealth campaigns as attempts to "sneak" something through. As persuasive as those arguments are, the truth is that policies resulting from both grass-roots and stealth campaigns have been repealed.

Whatever you decide about visibility, when you make basic decisions in your campaign for the policy about passages, endorsements, etc., keep the possibility of repeal in mind. Fighting a repeal will be easier if you use the passages you would use in a campaign against a repeal in your campaign for the policy. It will be easier if you get the endorsements you would want in an anti-repeal campaign during the campaign to get the policy adopted. For example, you may be able to pass a policy with the support of just one faction or party on a board. If board passage were your only goal, and you could pass it with Democratic votes alone, you might not bother with Republican endorsements or endorsements important to Republican board members.

If you are anticipating a repeal campaign, especially one that will go to voters or a higher power, those more conservative endorsements could prove critical.

24.4 Be Ready for Another Campaign

Once your policy is passed, opponents may try to launch a campaign to get the board to repeal it or to get a superior authority to override it. This is more likely if they were caught napping and didn't mount strenuous opposition during your campaign.

Be ready to campaign to keep the policy. Try to keep your lobbying, mass action, media, and endorsement groups from completely disbanding. Make sure people who worked together on those aspects of the campaign stay in touch and that they know about each other's address changes, phone changes, etc. If you can, keep whatever system you came up with for maintaining communications with the lesbian and gay community. (See section 6.5.)

If you lose people at the end to burnout or exhaustion, try to find replacements to have ready if the campaign needs to be restarted.

Have your lobbyists stay in occasional contact with the board members with whom they worked. Make an occasional "social" call just to keep in touch. Don't let your lobbying, communications, mass action, etc., systems get lost. Make notes about how they worked, put the notes together with all your written materials, and keep them with a campaign historian. It will be much easier to crank up the campaign again if you do.

24.5   Get Involved in Board Elections

If the policy becomes an issue in a board election campaign, be ready to defend the members who voted for you. Individuals from your campaign should get as involved as they possibly can in the members' campaigns. (See section 11.6.) Moreover, there isn't much reason for the campaign organization itself to stay neutral anymore. On the contrary, the campaign should help those who proved to be friends. If it is legal, endorse candidates and use whatever resources you've got to support the people who supported you.

24.6   Consider an Anti-petition Campaign

In some places, it is seems virtually impossible to keep determined opponents from gathering the signatures they need for a referendum or initiative. This is most likely to be true if the required number of signatures is low (for example, five percent of those who voted in the last election), and if your opponents can circulate petitions at places or events where large numbers of likely signers may be present. Churches and county fairs are prime locations.

On the other hand, sometimes anti-petition campaigns work. Anti-petition campaigns are most likely to work if you have endorsements from the moderate and more conservative groups and individuals that signers may likely respect. You've a much better chance of having them ready if you get them during your campaign.

24.6

> **Petitions for a constitutional amendment that would have prevented any town or the state itself from ever adopting a lesbian/gay civil rights policy were circulated in Arizona. The issue didn't go to the ballot because proponents didn't submit signatures to the secretary of state. Most observers think the opposition of the state Republican party and prominent Republican politicians was a major factor.**

"Don't sign" grass-roots campaigns have also sometimes been effective. Direct contact with potential signers seems crucial. If this means a precinct walking campaign, you are likely to need a large number of volunteers. You may be able to reduce this if you can find a creative way to target potential signers more exactly.

> The lesbian and gay community in Durham, North Carolina, mounted a "don't sign" campaign in opposition to a petition to recall a mayor who had supported a lesbian/ gay pride celebration. They quickly realized the petitions were being circulated at shopping centers. Each morning, they would send scouts out to find out which shopping centers the petition circulators were working. Then, they would set up counter, "don't sign" tables near the circulators.

If you attempt a tactic such as Durham's that brings your supporters nearby the circulators, you must take steps to avoid confrontation, especially the possibility of confrontation that escalates to violence. The potential for harm to your supporters is real. And any incident could reflect badly on your campaign. Be careful about whom you send out, and use people who are trained in minimizing confrontation.

24.6

III. *Civil Rights Policies*

---

25. FINDING OUT ABOUT EXISTING CIVIL RIGHTS POLICY

25.1 Why It's Important to Find Out What Exists

You have two critically important research tasks at the very start. You need to find out what policies on discrimination already exist, and what policies the institution you plan to focus on has the power to pass. This chapter will look at the first question, the next chapter will look at the second.

Existing policies are important for two reasons. First, they often play an important role in the debate about your proposal. Opponents are fond of making misleading claims about the extent to which lesbians and gay men are protected by existing policy. (See section 29.4; and see chapter 15.) Moreover, boards usually want to know the extent to which lesbians and gay men already have civil rights protection and how it compares to the protections given other groups.

Second, existing policies will significantly shape your options on the kind of policy you want to propose and the kind of campaign you will run. They will have an impact both on what you decide your proposal should cover and on whether you want to propose a policy focused on sexual-orientation discrimination or a comprehensive civil rights law.

25.2 What You Need to Know About What Exists

You need to get the big picture. You need to know what policies the institution you are working on has. You also need to know what policies superior institutions (those which either regulate yours or which regulate some of the same areas but are higher on the ladder of power) have.

Most of the time, the important superior institutions are the federal government, state government (if that isn't the institution you are aiming at), and, if you are working on a business or university policy, the local government. If you are working on the policies of a local branch of a regional or national organization, the regional or national is a superior institution as well.

Find out as much as you can about existing policies, but pay particular attention to these five things:

> ∗ First, what characteristics are protected by each policy? *What are the things, such as race, gender, etc., that the policy says cannot be used to discriminate?* Pay particular attention to whether any of the policies cover sexual orientation and whether any of them cover characteristics that are not usually thought of as innate, like marital status and religious beliefs.

> ∗ Second, *who may not discriminate under each policy?* Most policies cover one or more of three broad groups. Some policies apply just to the institution itself; the city or the business, etc., promises that it will not discriminate. Some policies apply to people who do business with the institution; the city or the school insists that those who do some types or any type of business with it promise that they will

not discriminate. Some policies apply to people who are governed by the institution; the city or the district says that all those who live in it may not discriminate. Governments are usually the only institutions that have the power to adopt this last type of policy.

* Third, *what acts does the policy cover?* What does it say may not be done? Some policies only apply to one aspect of how an institution operates. For example, the policy may say that the city or the school won't discriminate in employment. Some are much broader and say that the institution will not discriminate at all.

* Fourth, *how is the policy enforced?* Some policies are enforced internally; the institution says that if anyone has a complaint about discrimination, he or she should bring it to a certain office. The institution will investigate itself and correct the problem if it finds one. Some policies are enforced in court; you can sue if you are discriminated against. Some policies are enforced by special commissions, like human rights commissions. These last two types are usually only passed by governments. Often, policies do not say anything about enforcement at all. Sometimes, especially if the promise not to discriminate is in a personnel policy, the policy can be enforced in court even if it does not say anything about enforcement.

* Fifth, *what are the exceptions to and exemptions from the policy?* What are the circumstances in which people are allowed to discriminate? What persons or institutions are let out of the policy completely? Many employment laws let some small business out of the law; some housing laws let small rental units out. Some policies let religious groups discriminate on the basis of religion in some jobs or admissions; a few let religious groups out completely.

25.2

25.3 Some of the Ways Existing Policy May Affect Your Goal and Your Campaign

First, a word about terminology. The way existing policy affects your proposals will have a lot to do with whether the policies of your institution are "better" or "worse" than the policies of superior institutions (like the state and federal governments), and whether or not you want to "improve" your institution's policy. Your opinion about whether one policy is "better" or "worse" than another should be based on a comparison of who is told not to discriminate, what they are told not to do, how the policy is enforced, and who is exempt.

Often, deciding whether one policy could be "improved" or is "better" than another is an easy call. Policies that protect more people are usually better than those that protect fewer. So, for example, city laws that cover all employers in the city are usually thought of as better than those that just apply to city government itself.

The basic premise of this section is that you should always propose policies that provide protection as good as that which covers other groups protected by civil rights policies, but that, as a practical matter, you usually can't shoot for better. Trying to get a policy better than those that cover other groups will often draw you into odious arguments about what kind of discrimination is worse and may create a lot of hostility among other groups that rely on civil rights protections.

The basic premise means that if your institution has a nondiscrimination policy that does not cover sexual orientation, you have two campaign/drafting options. First, you can focus on sexual orientation and add it to the existing policy. That will probably lead you to use the "drop in" or the "piggyback" model. (See section 30.3.)

Second, you could try to improve your institution's policy while adding sexual orientation, for example, by covering more activities or telling more people not to discriminate, etc. If you want to do that, you should usually make the changes for all the groups covered by the policy. This may not always be possible. (See section 26.5.) You shouldn't try to change the whole policy unless you are working in coalition with other groups covered by it. That may or may not be possible or desirable. (See section 5.4.)

If your institution's policy already covers sexual orientation, improvement is usually your only option. However, there is another option if your institution's policy is not as good as one of the policies of a superior institution, and sexual orientation is not included in best superior institution policy. For example, you may be interested in a city with a policy that applies only to employment discrimination by the city itself. Both state and federal laws cover employment discrimination based on race or gender by most employers, and they also cover housing and business discrimination. At the time this was written, neither federal nor most state laws covered any type of sexual-orientation discrimination. In addition to either of the options described above, you could propose a local policy that would bring protection against discrimination based on sexual orientation up to the level of state or federal law, whichever is strongest.

This kind of proposal usually won't upset other covered groups, because you really are aiming for the same protection they already have from the superior institution. If you do this, you'll usually want to use one of the "stand alone" options described in chapter 30, taking care to tailor it to the best superior policy covering other groups.

> Between 1978 and 1992, seventeen cities in California passed civil rights laws against sexual-orientation discrimination. Although most of those cities had policies in which the cities themselves promised not to discriminate on the basis of race, gender, religion, or other characteristics, most passed laws banning sexual-orientation discrimination by all employers and in all forms of housing anywhere in the city. These laws generally were not opposed by other groups because state law prohibited religious, race, and gender discrimination in employment and housing.

25.3

If your institution has no discrimination policy at all, you can either propose a comprehensive policy or a policy that only applies to sexual orientation and brings protection to the level of either state or federal law, whichever is stronger. Again, people are not likely to object to a sexual-orientation-only policy that is aimed at "big picture" parity.

25.4   A Short Primer on What You Can Expect to Find

This is a short, general description of federal and state law (at the time of this writing). The idea is to give you a first look and help you get used to thinking about different laws and comparing them. Don't try to use it as a substitute for finding out what state and federal policy is when you begin your campaign.

There are many federal laws on discrimination. In general, they tend to prohibit discrimination based on race (and color), religion, gender, national origin, ancestry, age, and disability. Federal laws are the most comprehensive in terms of who is told not to discriminate. The federal government has rules for itself, for its contractors, for people who receive federal funding (aid, grants, and similar money), and for state and local governments and private persons and institutions as well.

The federal laws that cover people who receive federal funds are very broad and prohibit discrimination in anything the federally funded organization does. Other federal laws usually prohibit discrimination in specific activities, such as employment and housing and somewhat less extensively in education and services by businesses. The laws often overlap; for example, the employment practices of a county that receives federal aid will be covered by federal laws on people who take federal funds and by laws on employment discrimination.

At the time this was written, a few federal agencies had policies that said the agency could not discriminate against its own employees because of sexual orientation. With the exception of these policies, federal law did not apply to discrimination based on sexual orientation.

Most federal laws say that if you have been discriminated against by the federal government itself, you must complain to the offending federal agency. If you have been discriminated against by someone who receives federal funds, you may complain to the agency that dispensed the funds, although it may only have the power to cut off the money and not the order that you get your job or lost pay. You can usually go to court instead if you want to. In most other cases, you must file a complaint with a federal agency (or a state agency authorized to take the complaint by the federal government), but, again, you can later go to court if you want to.

While the laws against discrimination by those who receive federal funds usually don't have many exceptions, the other laws do. Most federal laws on employment discrimination only apply to employers with fifteen or more workers.

State laws often protect groups that are not protected by federal law. For example, many states prohibit discrimination based on marital status, and at present, eight states have laws against discrimination based on sexual orientation. Most state laws apply to private employers, landlords, home sellers, businesses, etc. Some have laws that apply to themselves and their contractors as well. Most state laws cover specific activities. They typically cover services by businesses and education more comprehensively than federal law does.

State laws usually set up agencies to investigate complaints of discrimination and most require that you file a complaint with the agency. Some permit you to go to court instead, after you have filed with the agency.

State laws often have fewer or smaller exemptions than federal law does. So, for example, state laws often apply to employers with five or more workers. On the other hand, some state laws completely exempt religious groups.

26. FINDING OUT WHAT KIND OF CIVIL RIGHTS POLICY IS POSSIBLE

26.1 Introduction: What You Need to Find Out

Two factors will have an important influence on the kind of policy you decide to propose: the kind of institution you want to have adopt it, and what superior law allows.

26.2 What Kind of Organization

Divide the organizations that could adopt policy into three

groups: first, businesses, nonprofit organizations, and social groups; second, governments; third, universities. Depending on which group an organization falls into, it will have an impact on who can be told not to discriminate (factor two in section 25.2) and how the policy is enforced (factor four in section 25.2).

26.3   Who Can Be Told Not to Discriminate

Businesses and clubs generally have power over themselves, but not over anyone else. This means that they can adopt policies saying they themselves will not discriminate. They can also probably adopt policies insisting that those with whom they do business agree not to discriminate as well.

> **Like a lot of organizations, Kaiser hospitals insisted in the late seventies during negotiations with its nurses that it could not adopt a policy promising that it would not discriminate against its own employees on the basis of sexual orientation. The reason, Kaiser said, was that neither state law nor federal law made discrimination based on sexual orientation illegal. Kaiser backed off and began negotiating when the nurses retained a lawyer. He made the employer admit that although state and federal laws did not make sexual-orientation discrimination illegal, they did not stop an employer from voluntarily agreeing not to discriminate either. It took a few more years of work, but eventually Kaiser adopted the policy.**

Unlike businesses, etc., a government generally has power over people and organizations located in its jurisdiction, as well as power over itself. State governments all have power to pass all three kinds of nondiscrimination policies; they can outlaw discrimination by themselves, insist that those who do business with them have nondiscrimination policies, and they can insist that employers, landlords, business, schools, etc., located in the government's area not discriminate.

Cities get their power to govern from the states, and states often limit what powers they pass on. Sometimes they do this for all cities in the state with a general law on city powers. Sometimes the state gives each city its own charter, spelling out its powers individually (some states do both).

The powers granted to cities are sometimes very specific, and while almost all can adopt nondiscrimination policies for themselves, some may not be able to insist on nondiscrimination by those who do business with them, and some may not be able to outlaw discrimination by business, etc., located in the city without special permission from the state. However, don't accept the argument that the city does not have the power to adopt a certain kind of policy without getting a lawyer to do some research for you. Claiming lack of power is a favorite way to deflect pressure for a more comprehensive policy. Many cities have some general "police power," which is what they need for nondiscrimination laws that cover everyone in the city.

Universities are something of a hybrid. They certainly can make policy for themselves, and they have the same right to insist on nondiscrimination by those who do business with them that business and clubs have. But universities have some government-like powers as well, particularly over campus clubs and associations, especially those which are sponsored or supported by the school. They also sometimes authorize student businesses. Universities probably can impose nondiscrimination policies on many of these. However, if a group is academically focused, and not a pure social club or a pure business, the university may be reluctant to impose nondiscrimination policies, on the theory that they interfere with academic freedom.

26.4

26.4 Enforcement

Policies that say the institution itself will not discriminate can always be enforced (and typically are) by some type of internal complaint to personnel, to an equal opportunity office, etc.

The problem with internal enforcement is that organizations find themselves at fault much less often than neutral outsiders do. If you can get a nondiscrimination policy into a union contract, this usually gives you a better remedy, because the grievance process usually leads at some point to a neutral arbitrator.

Virtually any organization has the power to adopt a policy about itself that will allow it to be sued in court if it violates the policy. Few are willing to do that in so many words. In some states, promises in some employer personnel policies or in club charters and by-laws can be enforced in court even if they don't say that. Ask your lawyer if that is possible.

Policies which say those who do business with the organization must agree not to discriminate are usually enforced by the organization that insisted on the promise. Typically, the remedy is to cancel the contract. In most states, the policy could say that all contractors must promise not to discriminate, that the promise is for the benefit of those covered by it, and that they can sue. Contractors may be reluctant to agree to this.

In addition to the kinds of enforcement businesses and clubs and associations use, governments sometimes create commissions and give them power to take complaints under all types of policies. Typically the commissions can mediate and try to settle the complaint. Cities can always give commissions the power to order the city itself to return someone to a job or pay damages (although this is not common), and they can always make contractors agree to that as a part of the deal.

Some cities have the power to create commissions that can order private employers, landlords, businesses, etc., to stop discriminating and to pay damages.

Most cities can make violation of a nondiscrimination policy a small crime (usually a misdemeanor). Some can say that anyone who is discriminated against may go to court.

26.5 Superior Law

The other major limit on what kind of policy you can have comes from "superior law." This is basically a problem with governments. The federal government is at the top of the power structure, followed by the states, and then by local government, which is often divided among relatively equal, separate agencies (you could have a city government, an independent transit district, and an independent school district all existing together at the same time without one having power over the other).

Generally, higher government can tell lower government not to make a policy in a certain area. This is usually called "preemption." Governments can either do this by saying so (which, unfortunately, is not all that common) or by regulating something so completely that they "take over the field." This is another explanation that is often used for not adopting policy even when it does not apply. If a city says your proposal is "preempted," get help from your lawyer.

Federal civil rights laws almost never preempt state or local laws. Congress often says that in so many words. If you are told that a policy proposal is preempted by federal law, be very suspicious.

State civil rights laws sometimes do preempt local laws that apply to private employers, landlords, etc. Although opponents sometimes claim they preempt even policies for the city itself, this is rare. Moreover, while state laws often preempt local laws which cover the same forms of discrimination the state law covers, they less often preempt different local laws. So it is less likely that a local policy on sexual-orientation discrimination will be preempted if state law does not cover sexual-orientation discrimination.

27. THE CASE FOR CIVIL RIGHTS

27.1 Introduction: What this Chapter Covers

This chapter reviews some of the most important arguments used to support civil rights policies at the time this chapter was written. Although these arguments haven't changed much over the last few years, they may have by the time you read this. Make sure you talk to others who've recently worked on similar policies, and take the time to develop your arguments in the way described in chapter 8.

27.2 Primary Arguments

If you trust polling data, when this was written, much of America continued to disapprove of lesbians and gay men. At the same time, more Americans believed that discrimination based on sexual orientation was wrong than approved of it.

In that apparent paradox lies the heart of the argument that has been most effective so far in persuading people to support nondiscrimination laws.

The argument focuses on what the policy would actually do if enacted—prohibit discrimination in jobs, housing, services, etc.—and calls on people to support it regardless of how they may feel about lesbians and gay men in general.

In a society where individuals must work to survive, the argument goes, for example, an employer cannot be allowed to fire someone who does a job well just because the employer disapproves of her or him as a person. Employment in a multicultural society has to be based on ability and willingness to work. If it isn't, given all the kinds of personal prejudice we have—racial, religious, etc.—people simply won't be able to take care of themselves.

The argument does not admit that any kind of intolerance is right, only that it is a pervasive fact of life, and that it cannot be allowed to dictate whether or not a person has a job.

> **Organizers in Irvine, California, are convinced that their campaign to retain their civil rights policy failed at least in part because it relied too heavily on the theme that lesbians and gay men ought to be accepted as part of society in Irvine. It didn't matter, they say, whether voters accepted that idea. Many of them wanted an explanation of why the policy was needed, since the campaign did not provide one.**

The argument goes on to say that the function of civil rights laws is to return the system to its focus on merit once it becomes clear that some people are losing their jobs for reasons that have nothing to do with merit. Similar arguments can be put together for housing policies, accommodations policies, etc.

This is a remedial argument. It says things are happening that should not happen, and the policy is designed to stop them. There is an important prevention/protection variation on it. In this form, the argument says that since it is wrong to take away a job for reasons unrelated to ability, the aim of the policy is to prevent discrimination regardless of whether it is happening. The prevention version is usually offered as a secondary theme. However, it can serve as a primary theme if resource limitations prevent you from showing that discrimination exists, and the institution is strongly committed to the idea that discrimination is wrong.

> **Organizers in Flint, Michigan, succeeded with a limited campaign that didn't involve hearings or proof of discrimination. They attribute that success in large part to their ability to tap into a deep commitment to nondiscrimination by the largely African-American city council.**

There may also be some institutions and places where all you need to succeed is a prevention argument. For example, Oakland, California, adopted a comprehensive lesbian/gay civil rights law in 1984. No opposition appeared at the hearings, so the leader of the city council thanked the proponents and then closed the hearing. At the full council vote that followed, he summed up the debate well when he said, "I can't believe we didn't do this years ago. This is embarrassing."

Still, even where approval seems a foregone conclusion, careful organizers would use the remedial argument as a secondary theme and be ready to support it with proof.

27.3 Secondary Arguments

Anti-lesbian/gay violence is probably the most important secondary theme today. For some board members, testimony about violence without more is enough, because it shows how serious homophobia is. For others, you'll need to draw a connection to the antidiscrimination policy. (See section 21.8.) You may be able to get law enforcement witnesses to help.

Connecticut's civil rights policy got a big boost the year
before it passed when the legislature considered and then
enacted a hate crimes law. The hearings on that law
showed that anti-gay violence was a serious problem.
Some legislators who had not been supportive of the
nondiscrimination law before those hearings changed their
view because, they said, they had not understood the high
cost people paid for being gay.

You can use testimony about anti-gay violence at hearings on a
nondiscrimination policy. You may want to consider making a hate
crimes policy part of your effort, or a first step. (See section 10.2.)

Showing that nondiscrimination policy is a trend is another useful
secondary theme. Check with one of the national lesbian/gay organizations to see if you can get a list of similar institutions that have
adopted nondiscrimination policies.

Diversity is also an important secondary theme. Boards often
assume that most gay people are white men, and that white men are
least likely to need protection from discrimination. While proof, for
example, that white men can lose their jobs for being gay is one answer
to that, proof of diversity is also very helpful.

27.4 Themes to Avoid

It is the almost universal experience of organizers that it is
a mistake to make analogies to discrimination based on race, religion,
and gender. That shouldn't be surprising, however. Making the comparison implies that you understand what race or gender discrimination
is like. People who have experienced it naturally resent that presump-
tion, just as most gay people resent it when heterosexuals claim they
know what it is like to grow up gay in America. Even when the anal-
ogy is drawn by someone who has experienced both kids of discrimination, racial and religious minorities are more apt to take offense than
be persuaded.

People are most apt to take exception to claims that not adopting a
nondiscrimination policy is somehow akin to the Holocaust or slavery.

Even putting aside the most outlandish claims, discrimination against different groups is just different in important ways.

There is also a difference between claiming that sexual-orientation discrimination is "the same" as race discrimination, and allowing people to see that some discriminatory policies and some of the motivations for discrimination are quite similar. Simply allowing similarities to appear can be one of the most powerful arguments for a policy.

> As it began to appear more likely that the New York City council would pass a lesbian/gay civil rights law, the attacks of it by opponents became more virulent. Some organizers are sure that at least one person of color on the council who was not sympathetic to lesbian and gay rights voted for it because of his visceral response to the opposition, which he connected to the kind of prejudice he had faced in his own life.

At most, you can gently point out similarities between specific discriminatory policies or arguments, but you should always be ready to disclaim the argument that one type of discrimination is the same as another. When you do point out this type of similarity, make sure you have the historical proof you need to make your point.

Finally, although this should be obvious by now, you should avoid arguments that aren't focused on what the policy would do.

28. PROVING THE NEED FOR CIVIL RIGHTS

28.1 Introduction: You've Got to Prove You Need It

Many people really think lesbians and gay men are not discriminated against. Again and again, organizers have found that the most effective way to change the minds of moderates who aren't enthusiastic about civil rights policies is to show them that discrimination is a real problem.

At one time, a popular reply to the objection that there is "no discrimination here" was to say that discrimination is wrong, employers and landlords shouldn't be allowed to do it, and that regardless of whether anyone is being hurt at the moment no one should even have to face the possibility of discrimination. Though this is never completely a satisfactory answer, this argument is least effective when an ordinance is hotly contested.

> **In Irvine, California, the vote on whether to repeal the civil rights law brought out strong emotions on both sides and divided many friends and family members. Organizers believe their failure to show that discrimination exists and people are hurt by it was the single most important factor in losing the election. They think moderates resented being confronted with the emotion and being forced to take a stand in the absence of proof the law was necessary.**

28.2 How to Get Stories of Discrimination

Although there are several ways to show that a law is necessary, presenting stories from people who have been discriminated against is one of the best. "Real" people with stories are often more convincing than experts, and compelling stories are difficult for even tough opposition to write off.

The first difficulty with proving discrimination is that since it is not illegal in most states, people who are affected usually don't come forward. There is no one to complain to. Yet, there are several ways to find people who have been discriminated against. One good tactic is to set up a phone number that people can call to tell their stories. Some campaigns have used a volunteer's phone, others have gotten a local lesbian and gay organization, a social service organization, or a sympathetic business to make a line available.

> **In Greensboro, North Carolina, organizers set up a discrimination hotline with an answering machine and had volunteers call people back to get details. A local bookstore agreed to pay for the phone line in exchange for a brief message on the tape saying that it was the sponsor.**

If you get a phone number, you need to get people to call. Typically, people post flyers in gay bars and in other gay or gay-friendly businesses. If there is any gay press in the area, you should be able to persuade it to print the flyer for free. Obviously, if you have a newsletter for your own organization, you should appeal for stories there.

> In Berkeley, California, organizers printed flyers asking for stories. The bottom of the flyer was cut into little tear-off tags with the hotline number. They posted the flyers on bulletin boards, telephone poles, etc., all over town.
>
> Durham, North Carolina, organizers distributed flyers with a hotline number for stories of discrimination to alternative bookstores throughout the region, trying to make sure they picked up people who might have moved out of town.

Most organizers call local advocacy groups, like the ACLU, and local lesbian and gay organizations, to see if they have received complaints and whether they can put the organizers in touch with those who complained. The more liberal churches, women's organizations, and counseling organizations are also good sources.

> Greensboro, North Carolina, organizers asked a local counseling hotline to tell callers with discrimination complaints about the campaign and ask them to call the discrimination hotline. Other organizers have done the same thing with advocacy organizations that have hotlines, such as the ACLU.

28.2

While most organizations will not give out the names of people who have called them, they will, with a little prodding, contact the people who called and ask them to get in touch with the campaign. Sometimes they will give you the stories in a way that does not reveal anyone's identity, and you can often only use these and just cite the organization as the source.

> In Chicago the person who answered the phones for one of the council members closely identified with the proposed law testified about who called. This paid a special dividend, because she could talk not only about people

**who had been discriminated against, but also about peo-
ple who called and said they wanted to discriminate and
would do so in the future.**

**Durham organizers called the district attorney to get
the names of witnesses in a recent locally famous gay-
bashing case. Since court hearings are public, you should
be able to get these names from court records if the D.A.
is uncooperative. You can often get the name and date of
a case through newspaper records (this may give you the
witnesses' names as well).**

Word of mouth is the single most important source of stories. Tell
your friends that you are looking, and think about stories you've heard
in the past. A Raleigh activist has a good word of advice: "We are so
accustomed to some of the things that make good stories," she says,
"that we overlook them."

28.3   Checking Out the Story and Protecting the Witness

Do a little checking, particularly if you plan to feature one
or two stories in a big way (for example, in press releases, or by making
the person with the story available for press interviews, or by featuring
one story at a hearing). Don't reject a story just because the employer
or the landlord has a different view of what happened. People who
have come into conflict usually have different ideas about what happened, and while some sexual-orientation discrimination is very blunt,
much of it is subtle. All you really need to do (perhaps all you can do)
is ask the person with the story if anyone else knows what happened,
then call a few of those persons named to learn whether they generally
think the person who gave you the story has a valid perspective.

When evaluating a story, remember that the essence of discrimination is different treatment. Suppose a lesbian, her lover, and their child
get evicted from a one-bedroom apartment because three people in
that kind of unit violate the city's occupancy rules. That is OK if the
landlord applies the rule to all three-person families; it is not OK if
heterosexual couples do not get evicted.

Finally, your witnesses and their stories do not need to be perfect. Real people rarely are.

One difficulty with discrimination stories is that people are often reluctant to tell their stories in public, because if they do, they risk further discrimination. Losing your apartment is bad enough; you could lose your job if you make a stink about it. Section 22.11 describes some of the ways in which you can limit the risks for people. Most of the techniques described there will work for media and public information as well as for public hearings.

28.4 Explaining the Stories

When you evaluate the stories to decide which ones you will use and which ones you will feature, remember the perspective of the audience. Merely relating how an injured woman's partner was kept out of an intensive care unit while blood relatives were allowed in may not be as powerful as it could be if your audience thinks that lesbian and gay relationships are similar to pleasant friendships. Having the person with the story describe a few of the things that reflect the deep commitment of the relationship may make the story much more effective.

However, there is a related audience perspective problem. People generally do not yet have a very sophisticated understanding of discrimination against lesbians and gay men, so they often think the only stories that show discrimination are stories that involve "smoking guns"; that is, stories in which the motive is obvious ("You're fired because we don't want queers working here.").

A lot of discrimination is more subtle, and, with more familiar types of discrimination, most people understand that. If an employer says it has hired no African Americans because it could find none who were qualified, or if it places almost all the women it hires in clerical positions, most people today become suspicious.

If your stories involve anything but the most blatant kind of discrimination, make sure you tell the audience what it needs to know to understand. You may have to explain some common myths about lesbians and gay men (for example, that we are more emotionally unstable or more apt to assault children) and show convincingly that they are untrue; you may have to explain that some policies that don't mention lesbians and gay men hurt them (for example, a policy that says you must be married to be promoted beyond middle management).

One good way to make sure that you understand the perspective of the audience and provide any needed explanation is to have a couple of people who are close to that perspective helping to evaluate the stories.

28.5 The Big Picture

One drawback to stories is that they don't really tell your audience how pervasive discrimination is. A compelling story or two may make the question of pervasiveness go away; if someone has been seriously hurt by discrimination, people are more inclined to accept the idea that it should not be allowed even if you can't show that it is an everyday occurrence. On the other hand, you strengthen your position if you can show that discrimination is more than an occasional aberration. And if you are unable to provide many individual stories, "big picture" proof that discrimination is not uncommon may be important evidence of the need for your proposal.

One way to get information on discrimination is to call the doubter's bluff. Ask the board to ask the local human rights agency to keep track of discrimination complaints.

> **In New York, quite a few members of the city council did not believe discrimination was a problem, and they said they were unimpressed by the argument that the backers of the bill couldn't produce statistics because discrimination was not illegal. Organizers got a grant for the city human rights department that allowed it to keep track of all the calls it received complaining of sexual-orientation discrimination. After a year, the department published a report that silenced most of the claims that there was no discrimination.**

This tactic has to be used carefully. If the city does not have a clearly identified human rights agency, people may not think to call. Even if it does, you'll need to get word out in the community (through the gay press, with flyers in bars and businesses) so that as many complaints as possible are called in. If the agency's staff is hostile to your proposal, it may be better not to try this at all. They may ignore calls, lose them, discourage callers with indifference, or scare them with hostility, etc. Even if you are not sure the staff is hostile, you should check on it periodically with a few test calls.

Distributing questionnaires in the lesbian/gay community is another way to get information about discrimination. You can publish them in the press, distribute them at events like gay pride rallies or in bars and other businesses. The information you gather is likely to be more useful if you hire someone trained in surveys to help write the questions. Many social scientists have training in writing survey questions, and you can often receive help at local universities or from local psychologists or social workers. If you prepare a questionnaire, think about what you might want to ask people in addition to whether they have been discriminated against. For example, in Connecticut, a discrimination survey asked if people were "out" and if not, why not. Organizers felt they gathered good evidence to refute the claim that you cannot be discriminated against if you are not "out," and some good evidence about how widespread fear of discrimination and reprisal is.

You might ask a professional to train a small group of volunteers to interview people at events or in bars, etc., to be sure you receive a decent number of responses. You might be able to persuade an academic or a graduate student to do a small study of individuals in depth to try to see how discrimination has had an impact on their lives.

To minimize the chances the questionnaire will discourage people afraid to come forward, you should include a statement on the front explaining that you will not reveal the details of any set of answers, but will instead provide a summary totaling all the responses. However, both questionnaires and interviews can also be a good source of stories. After the promise not to reveal details, you can ask people who are willing to give their telephone numbers, so that you can follow up on particular stories you think may be interesting.

28.5

Neither questionnaires nor small-scale studies will give you reliable statistics on discrimination. But the point really is to show that discrimination is more than an occasional problem, and they will do that. Opponents sometimes attack surveys or studies as "collections of unproven allegations." But, of course, there is never a way to prove or disprove any kind of discrimination claim unless you have a policy-making discrimination illegal and a way to enforce it.

North Carolina has an ambitious documentation project. Every major city in the state has a local documentation project with a hotline. The number and the project are advertised in the gay press, the alternative press, and with flyers in bars, businesses, etc. Each local project "clips" the area press looking for every use of the words "homosexual," "lesbian," or "gay." The data is then sent to the statewide project, which puts together an annual report, categorizing all the reports it received. In the early 1990s, the project was recording 600 to 700 incidents per year. At the time, it was an all-volunteer organization.

Finally, you can use testers to document some forms of discrimination. For example, in Chicago one year, teams of same-sex couples applied to rent one-bedroom apartments together. Some couples told the prospective landlords that they were gay, others did not. The testers then prepared reports and testified at hearings.

While this tactic often gets good evidence of housing discrimination, it has its problems. Although this is an accepted way of proving housing discrimination (most fair housing agencies use it), it involves deception. You can also alienate fair-minded landlords who are willing to rent to you when you explain that you don't really want the apartment.

28.6 Showing the Damage Discrimination Does

Once you show that discrimination occurs, you've shown that the law is necessary if the audience you are aiming at agrees that discrimination is wrong. However, you may also want to provide some evidence of the harm that it does. There are two obvious ways to do that.

First, you can show how discrimination harms the whole community. For example, most economists agree that employment discrimination costs business and government money because able, productive workers are fired, not hired or promoted. You should be able to get an economist or other social scientist associated with a university to explain why discrimination costs.

Second, you can try to show how discrimination damages individuals. Although some of the economic damage that goes with a lost job is obvious, some consequences (foreclosures on homes of people who can't pay their mortgages, long-term career damage) are not. If you use a social scientist to show harm to the community, he or she should be able to testify about this as well. You can also illustrate the points with your stories, for example, by having people who lost entire careers describe what happened to them after the incident.

You may also want to talk about the psychological damage that discrimination inflicts on individuals. This can be tricky. Most people have never been fired or evicted, and they don't understand how traumatic it can be. Even those who have lost their jobs, for example, usually lost them because of a dispute about job performance or misconduct, or because a company downsized or went out of business. They don't understand the special psychological shock that accompanies losing a job because of something central to who you are that has nothing to do with your ability to work. If you try to make people understand by having people with stories describe what they went through, you run the risk that you will inadvertently reinforce the old stereotype about gay people being emotionally weak. And most people are simply not very good at describing emotions and psychological trauma.

28.6

If you want to try to overcome these hurdles, you should get an expert who can talk about the effects of employment discrimination based on race, gender, disability, etc., as well as discrimination based on sexual orientation. Try to have the expert to be as vivid and direct as possible.

You probably need to back any expert with at least one or two accounts from individuals with stories. If possible, try to have your witnesses work with a professional, such as a trial lawyer, to figure out how to describe what happened in a way that will make people understand the emotional trauma.

28.7 Showing the Other Good Things a Law Will Do

You may also want to provide proof about other things a policy can do that will be helpful to the community. There are two obvious possibilities.

First, by making a strong statement that discrimination is not acceptable, nondiscrimination policies help to reduce prejudice and make hate violence less likely. There are studies on prejudice and hate violence, and you should be able to convince someone from a local university to testify about what the studies say. Police officers, especially high-ranking officials, are often very good witnesses on this point and are willing to testify more often than you would expect. If all else fails, you should be able to gather written materials from some of the national lesbian and gay organizations.

Second, antidiscrimination policies allow many lesbians and gay men to lead easier lives by reducing (if not eliminating) the need to keep a central part of their personalities secret. This may be the most important thing nondiscrimination policies do, but it is difficult to make many people understand it. A lot of people think that lesbians and gay men should keep quiet about their lives, and they don't understand how difficult that is, or that it frequently requires outright deception. Experts can be useful, but you need a few good stories that will make people understand at a gut level.

In the Berkeley, California, hearings, an individual who described his vociferously homophobic supervisor was able to make people see why his partner could not call him at work, or pick him up in front of the office, and why he had to be on guard constantly so that he did not inadvertently refer to his partner in a way that all of us refer to family members day in and day out. At another hearing, a quiet man explained how he began to stand out as odd to his coworkers because he never spoke of a wife or girl-

friend, as all of them did, and how that led to offers to get him dates, etc., which eventually led him to create a fictional girlfriend.

28.8 What to Do with the Testimony Once You Have It

It is a good idea to have people with stories prepare short written versions and to have your other witnesses write up short reports, summaries, or statements. You can use these in press packets, with individual policymakers when you lobby them, with editorial boards, and with groups from which you seek support. You may also want to submit the written statements at public hearings if the witness cannot attend, or if you have enough other live witnesses.

Have the most impressive witnesses testify at public hearings. You may also want to make them available for press interviews, visits with policymakers and editorial boards, and at appearances before other groups whose support you are seeking.

Be careful from the start not to release all of your evidence in every medium. If the media has all your stories, it may discontinue coverage. Most policymakers won't listen to the same story more than once if they can help it.

29. ARGUMENTS AGAINST CIVIL RIGHTS

29.1

29.1 Introduction: How to Use this Chapter

This chapter will cover some of the typical present-day arguments against civil rights policies. Although this chapter should help with your response if you encounter any of these arguments, take each response through the process described in chapter 15. The arguments may have changed, and you will need to tailor your response to your audience.

29.2 "No Special Rights"

This is the current favorite opposition rallying cry. It has frustrated advocates for lesbian and gay rights. Most of the time it has been merely a slogan, which makes it hard to refute, and it seems to be both effective and resistant to counterslogans. Part of its apparent effectiveness is a reflection of its popularity with people who are opposed to the policy anyway and who want a handy phrase that seems to justify their opposition. Pay them no mind; a good response won't help with committed opponents.

With potentially uncommitted members and constituents, a counter-slogan may not work well because the vague idea the "no special rights" slogan invokes probably connects to more background political feelings than similarly vague counterslogans like "equal rights." Dislike of special interests runs deep these days, and there is something of a subterranean backlash against civil rights laws as "special" laws. The best strategy may be to show, quickly, clearly, and as often as you can that the slogan isn't really an argument, and stick to your affirmative rallying cries.

The "no special rights" position could mean two things: First, it could be a suggestion that the policy only protects lesbians, gay men, and bisexuals. This simply is not so. The policy protects anyone from discrimination on the basis of sexual orientation. A respected legal expert may be your best backup for this point, although a simply worded policy that you can read out or give to people with a definition that includes heterosexuals can be a big help.

Second, the slogan could be a strategy of claiming that sexual orientation is the only characteristic that employers and landlords are legally not allowed to use. Again, this is simply not so. Whenever our society has found that some personal characteristic other than ability and merit is being used in employment or housing, it has passed laws to restore the basic "merit" system, so we have federal, state, and local laws against race, religions, ethnic, or gender discrimination. Your best backup here may be your coalition allies—women's groups and other minority groups. A respected legal expert could help as well.

This last argument is usually the best response to the claim, occasionally made as an explanation of the slogan, that lesbians and gay men should have the same rights as everyone else. The response to this is that the policy does just that, by making merit the issue. This works especially well if you've gathered good case stories to illustrate the need for the law. (See chapter 28.)

If the "no special rights" cry appears to be making real headway with the uncommitted, you might want to organize an event using both coalition partners and legal experts to explain the two points affirmatively, and condense their statements into a short handout. Again, make sure to use your affirmative messages.

29.3 It's a Choice, So Civil Rights Protection Isn't Appropriate

This is the opponents' favorite backup when the "no special rights" argument begins to falter. It has two parts. First, it says that being lesbian, gay, or bisexual is a choice. Second, it says that civil rights laws only provide protection against discrimination based on things that are innate, not chosen. Both parts are factually wrong.

But there is the danger that responding to the first point will lead you into a quagmire of arguing about the causes of sexual orientation (never talk about what causes you or anyone else to be gay; instead, talk about what causes anyone to have the sexual orientation he or she has). The truth, at least right now, is that nobody knows why an individual has a particular sexual orientation, so there is no way to settle an argument about it. Moreover, many people have very strong emotional commitments to their personal views about the origins of sexual orientation. That means if you get into such a discussion, it is likely to be long and passionate. That's a problem, because discussions about whether the causes of sexual orientation are genetic or environmental miss the real point of what is wrong with the opponents' argument.

If you feel you need to take on this first part of the argument, point out that almost all respected experts and people who think about the issue in terms of their own sexual orientation agree that sexual orientation is not a simple choice. The emotional and sexual

29.3

attraction we call sexual orientation is difficult, perhaps impossible, to change. You will need respected psychological authority for this. It should be easy to get, because this is the overwhelming view. If you can't get a respected local source, call one of the national psychiatric or psychological associations.

This may prompt opponents to respond that if emotional attraction is not a choice, the decision to live in accordance with it is. This leads directly to the second point. We have an extensive body of civil rights law that protects people from discrimination based on decisions that stem from important elements of who they are. For example, we prohibit discrimination based on religion, and in most states we prohibit discrimination based on marital status, both of which typically involve a lot more change and a lot more choice than sexual orientation does. Coalition partners and religious supporters may be the best backup here.

29.4 Federal and State Laws Already Protect

At present, there is no federal protection against sexual-orientation discrimination, and only nine states have it (Wisconsin, Massachusetts, Hawaii, Connecticut, Vermont, New Jersey, California, Minnesota, and Rhode Island). If you are not in one of those states, it should be simple to get a respected legal source to help you expose this. If you are in a state that has a lesbian/gay civil rights law, you most likely are doing the campaign for one of three reasons:

* to pass a better policy at your institution for many groups;
* because your state has a weak law or one that is not comprehensive, so that the point of your proposal is protection against sexual-orientation discrimination that will be equivalent to the protection that, for example, federal law gives other types of discrimination (see section 25.3);
* to simply add lesbians or gay men to the existing policy of your institution, which already includes other groups.

The first two reasons answer this argument; you are either trying to get better policy for all, or you are trying to achieve "parity" for sexual-orientation discrimination. (See section 25.3.) With the third reason, you might, in addition, say that you want to get the institution itself on record. If the other groups covered by its policy are also covered by state or federal law, duplication should be no objection to adding lesbians and gay men.

29.5 Discrimination Is No Problem as Long as You Keep Your Sexual Orientation Private

This is an increasingly popular argument. We don't need these policies, it says, because lesbians and gay men won't be discriminated against if they keep their sexual orientation private. There are two answers to this. First, most discrimination is the result of employers and landlords assuming or being told by someone else that a person is gay. The best way to show this is with local stories you get to prove the need. (See chapter 28.) If that isn't possible, contact one of the national lesbian/gay civil rights organizations and ask for some illustrative stories.

Perhaps a better answer is to focus on what it means to keep your sexual orientation private. When opponents make this argument, they usually argue that all we need to do is refrain from lurid descriptions of bedroom acrobatics while at work. The truth is that to keep your sexual orientation "private," you have to keep yourself from ever referring to the person with whom you are closest, and the persons with whom you spend most of your time; the people, in short, you love. You may also have to keep from referring to most of the civic and social organizations to which you belong. Ask your board members how well they think they would do trying to get through a week never referring to spouses or partners. Keep a list one week of how many times coworkers refer to them. Ask board members to try it. They'll get the point.

29.6

29.6 The Policy Is Not Fair to Others Who Think Being Gay Is Wrong

It's unfair, this argument goes, to make us hire, work with, rent to, live near or serve, people whom we disapprove of. Often this is put in a religious framework; it is unfair to make people who think lesbians and gay men are sinners to do these things.

Start by pointing out what the policy does: it doesn't say that people have to change their views or that they have to ask lesbians and gay men over to dinner. It says gay people shouldn't lose their jobs, (homes, etc., whatever is appropriate for your policy) because you disapprove. Then point out what would happen if a coworker's disapproval, even if based on a deeply held conviction about sin, could be used to take away someone's job. Lots of sincere mainstream people think all non-Christians are sinful and condemned. Should you lose your job if you are not a Christian but work next to one who believes that? Historically, many Americans believed that men were superior to women, whites superior to Asians and African Americans. These beliefs were usually based on either religion or "science." Many people still have beliefs like that. And don't forget people who disapprove of dancing or working on the Sabbath. Your religious allies should be helpful here, both on tolerance and on the consequences of the argument.

You can finish this by returning to the policy. Like all civil rights policies, its idea is that in a nation as diverse as ours, in which people need to work to live, a person's job cannot be made to depend on another person's dislike or disapproval.

29.7 It Will Be Unfair to Business

Often this argument begins with the claim that compliance will be expensive. Since there is virtually nothing business must do except not discriminate, there really are no compliance costs. The next variation is to claim that business will be forced to hire lesbians and gay men to avoid getting sued. This is an adaptation of a conservative argument used against race and gender discrimination laws. It focuses on the fact that in race and gender lawsuits, you can sometimes use the fact that an employer has, for example, very few women employees in comparison to the number of qualified women in the local workforce as evidence suggesting discrimination. The notion that an employer could face that kind of an argument in a sexual-orientation case is silly. We don't know how many of anyone's employees are gay, and we don't know how many qualified lesbians and gay men there are in the local workforce.

The best answer to this argument may be simply to point out that in places where there are policies, businesses haven't been forced to recruit lesbians and gay men to avoid claims. Check with cities and states that have laws. Try to persuade business associations in those cities and states to confirm what you say.

Finally, opponents may argue that defending false claims is expensive. Tailor your answer to the policy's enforcement mechanism. If the law is enforced outside of court, it probably isn't expensive anyway. If it is enforced through court, you can probably get a civil rights expert to confirm that it is very difficult to get lawyers to take discrimination cases, so that most cases that do go to court are not meritless. Finally, you should be ready to acknowledge that virtually every policy generates some false claims—that is the price of restoring a merit system. The alternative is to make those who suffer discrimination pay, which is an alternative we should not accept.

29.8 Being Gay Is an Illness

This is just wrong. Contact the American Psychiatric Association and the American Psychological Association for their statements on this. Try to persuade a respected local authority to make the point for you. Again, make it affirmatively. For example, "Lesbians and gay men are as healthy and well adjusted as any other group in society."

29.9

29.9 Sodomy Is Illegal: *Bowers v. Hardwick*

This is another claim that is usually more of a slogan than an argument. The point seems to be either that a sodomy law represents some type of official condemnation of lesbians and gay men or that a rights policy will encourage violations of the sodomy law. First, find out if your state has a sodomy law, and if it does, whether it applies (as only a few do) only to same-sex couples. If sodomy isn't illegal, or if it is as illegal for heterosexual couples as for lesbian and gay couples, start by pointing that out. In either situation, the "condemnation" and "encouragement" arguments are beside the point. If your state has no sodomy law, nothing is condemned or discouraged. If it does but applies to anyone, there is no condemnation of gay people. Use your respected legal expert if you need to.

If you have a same-sex-only sodomy law (or need to carry the response on for some other reason), you'll need to make people understand that being gay and committing sodomy are not the same thing. Be thoughtful about distinctions between "status" and "conduct." When carelessly made, they often reinforce two very problematic myths. The first is that any outward expression of being lesbian or gay —any "gay" conduct—is sexual. Lesbian/gay attraction is no more just about sex than is heterosexual attraction. Being gay is about companionship, love, sharing lives in every dimension, from hanging around on the stoop on Friday night through building a committed relationship; it's about friendship; it's about living day in and day out. Sex shouldn't be swept under the rug; however, far too many people assume it is the only thing significant about being lesbian or gay. If you need to make this point, simple stories of people's lives—from lesbians and gay men and from their families and neighbors—is the best way to put this across.

The second dangerous myth is that any sexual expression between lesbians and gay men is illegal in states with sodomy laws. This just isn't true. Although a few states like Missouri have tried to cover everything, it did not succeed. And in most states, most sexual expression between lesbians and gay men is not illegal. Use your legal expert if you need to.

Your point should be that while you think sodomy laws, especially ones that single out lesbians and gay men, are wrong, there is no reason to assume that lesbians and gay men who live with and love other lesbians and gay men violate them.

It is usually as part of a "sodomy" argument that opponents will bring up the "Bowers thing"—a loose collection of claims based on the Supreme Court's 1986 decision in *Bowers v. Hardwick*. They may say the court said sodomy was illegal, or ought to be, or that lesbians and gay men were not a true minority.

You need to know two things about *Bowers*. First, that it says none of these things. The court ruled that the Constitution does not stop states from making sodomy illegal if they want to. The court specifically said it was not saying whether or not the states ought to do that, and it specifically said it was not considering any discrimination arguments, since none had been made in the case. Second, the law the court upheld applies to sodomy when committed by a heterosexual couple as well, even if the members are married.

Your legal expert should be able to provide you with two or three examples of things that the court has said states may do, yet which most members of your board are apt to think should not be done. Making the examples vivid should take care of the *Bowers* argument.

29.10 This Will Be Harmful to Children

Three claims come under this heading. The first is that gays molest children. This isn't right. Most adults who sexually abuse children are so fixated on them that they don't really have an adult sexual orientation, so they can't really be called "gay" or "straight." It's age, not gender, that is important. The characteristic that reliably distinguishes adults who are child abusers is that most of them are men. Yet we wouldn't use this fact to justify discrimination against men. Turn to your local psychological expert if you can, or call one of the national psychological or lesbian/gay organizations if you need to.

The next claim is that gay people shouldn't be allowed to be role models for children. Sometimes this argument is offered against the whole law, sometimes as an argument to exempt child-care workers or teachers. There is no evidence that children or adults exercise much conscious choice over sexual orientation, so the fear that kids will try to be gay to emulate a fine teacher is groundless. You can use your psychological experts here. Better still is testimony from people who have had gay teachers and from parents of kids who have or had gay teachers.

29.10

Finally, the claim is sometimes made that child molesting is a sexual orientation, so that your policy protects those who abuse children directly. A clear definition should take care of this. (See section 30.7.)

29.11 AIDS Is a Threat to Public Health

This is another slogan that takes some unraveling to understand. The claim appears to be either that gay people get AIDS more often than others do, or that gay people are transmitting HIV to others who are not gay. Thus, the argument continues, you shouldn't have a policy either because not having one will encourage gay people to be heterosexual or, at least, encourage them to stay away from your town or institution.

This argument is so unattractive that it will often bring you supporters if it is just left alone. If you need to respond, have a public health official tell the board that while gay men in the United States originally were more likely than heterosexuals to become infected with HIV, time and the rest of the world have shown us that this was the result of chance, not a reflection of some flaw in lesbians and gay men. He or she should also be able to talk about transmission. (See section 29.3 on deciding to be heterosexual.) The "get out of town" argument is its own response.

29.12 Military Arguments

Occasionally, you'll get arguments based on those used by the U.S. military at various times, that lesbians and gay men are unreliable under pressure or that others won't work with them. Most often, these come from fire and police departments. Meet the argument of unreliability with the response to the "sick" argument (section 29.8); meet the "won't work with" argument with the response to the "it's unfair to those who disapprove" argument (section 29.6). Often, letters, or better yet, testimony from police and fire departments that have openly gay members is most powerful here.

29.13 This Will Hurt Other Minorities by Diverting Resources

People often respond to this by pointing out that state and city agencies that enforce nondiscrimination policies haven't been overwhelmed by sexual-orientation claims. You many want to check with a few and obtain supportive letters. The truth is that if people resist any policy, enforcement will take some resources. If a board thinks a policy is worth having, it ought to be worth enforcing. Endorsers from other minority groups may be the best people to make this point.

29.14 Other Insane Scenarios

Spinning what Tom Stoddard used to call "insane scenarios" is a favorite way of objecting to a civil rights proposal. Opponents used to be fond of warning that the policy would permit men with beards to wear skirts to work, or that it would allow teachers to "recruit" in schools. Your legal expert can usually field these. One neat way to respond to insane scenarios is to have someone from a similar town or institution to verify that passage of the policy didn't cause an outbreak of bearded men in chiffon or teachers lecturing on how to be gay. If an insane scenario catches hold of your board, think about amending the policy to be rid of it. (See section 31.13.)

29.15 A Couple of Others

To respond to the argument that the policy is unnecessary because there is no discrimination, see chapter 28. To respond to the argument that your board doesn't have the power, see chapter 26.

29.15

30. WRITING CIVIL RIGHTS POLICIES— BASIC STRUCTURE

30.1 Introduction: What this Chapter Covers

This chapter covers the basic structure of a civil rights policy. The next section reviews some important features of civil rights policies. Appendix A has models for most kinds of discrimination policies. While they were "up to date" when this was written, policy writing evolves every time a new policy is written. You should check with national lesbian/gay organizations and with others who have recently passed policies to get the latest thinking.

You begin by finding out what kind of a policy the board has the authority to adopt (chapter 26) and what kinds of policies it has already (chapter 25). Your basic structure options depend on whether the board already has some type of civil rights policy or policies.

30.2 Basic Structure If Your Board Has Existing Policies

If your board has a civil rights policy, you can:

* "drop in"—simply add a definition of sexual orientation to the policy and drop the phrase "sexual orientation" in to the list or lists of groups whom the policy protects (see Appendix A, model A);

* "piggyback"—adopt a short policy that makes the existing policy apply to discrimination based on sexual orientation (see Appendix A, model B);

* adopt a new policy (usually identical or very similar to existing policies) for sexual-orientation discrimination and any other categories you may be covering in your campaign (often called a "freestanding" policy; see Appendix A, models C and D).

The "drop in" option is the one people use most. It neatly creates parity—the same rights for all, the same policy. (See chapter 25.) It is also very simple to write. The drawback to the "drop in" is that if the existing policy is detailed, your proposal, which basically restates the whole policy, will be long. You can keep it short by referring to the parts of the policy to which sexual orientation will be added instead of reproducing the whole thing. But to show anyone what your proposal does, you need to show them the entire existing policy.

The "piggyback" has the same effect as the drop in—the same rights, the same policy. But a piggyback achieves this through one or two short paragraphs that directly say that the new policy will ban sexual-orientation discrimination in the same way the existing policy covers other types of discrimination. If you want to use the text of your proposal in the campaign, either with board members or the public, a piggyback is much more likely to be useful if the existing policy is longer than a paragraph or two. If you are trying to improve the existing policy as well as add sexual orientation to it (see sections 25.3 and 5.4), the piggyback won't help much, because you'll have to show the entire existing policy to explain it.

Most of the time, the freestanding approach has little to recommend it. It will generate a long policy if the existing policy is long, and it won't show as vividly as the piggyback that the new policy does for sexual orientation the same thing the old one does for other groups. However, groups covered by existing policies occasionally do not want sexual orientation added to them. Typically, they say they are afraid that whoever enforces the policy will weaken it by interpreting it to be as weak as possible in instances of sexual-orientation discrimination. Obnoxious as this argument is, sometimes you need to accommodate it to obtain critical endorsements. If you do use the "freestanding" option, you must decide whether to duplicate the existing policy or adopt a better one.

30.2

Freestanding policy makes it possible to improve a bit on exisitng policy; nothing says it has to be identical. Other groups are somewhat less likely to complain about differences in your proposal if they've forced you to propose a separate policy. On the other hand, if your proposal isn't a duplicate, you lose the sometimes powerful "same rights, same policy" appeal, and your opponents may have an easier time forcing you to accept something worse.

No matter which structure you adopt, if your board has more than one existing civil rights policy (i.e., several policies covering different subjects; for example, one for housing and one for employment), you must decide if your goal will be to add sexual orientation to all of them or just some.

> **For what proved to be the next to final round of California's campaign for a policy, organizers prepared a new proposal. First, they surveyed all California laws and found over twenty-five separate civil rights laws. Then, after concluding that many duplicated each other and that a few others were comparatively trivial, they decided to just add sexual orientation to the state's major civil rights law.**

Keep two things in mind as you decide. First, be thoughtful. It may not make sense to add sexual orientation to some policies (a policy, for example, on pregnancy leave as a form of gender discrimination). Second, it may make sense politically and legally to narrow the focus of your campaign.

30.3 Basic Structure If Your Board Doesn't Already Have Some Civil Rights Policy

If your board doesn't have any civil rights policies, you'll have to propose a new "freestanding" policy. You have two basic options.

First, you can propose a simple, direct nondiscrimination statement. With private institutions such as universities and businesses, this is what people typically use. (See Appendix A, model C.) The advantage of the simple statement, like the piggyback, is that you can use the text itself to help convince board members. It is especially valuable in disarming extravagant opposition claims about what the policy will do. If you think the text will be valuable in convincing the board or the public, a simple statement is essential.

> The policy eventually adopted by the New York City council was a simple statement/piggyback type. Shortly before the vote, *The New York Times* printed the whole proposal. Organizers think that reassured many influential people in the city who had been concerned about things the opposition was saying about the bill. They also think it hurt the opposition's credibility.

Most cities, on the other hand, adopt comprehensive policies that spell out how they work in detail. This is especially true if the policy is going to apply to contractors or private employers or landlords. The advantages of a comprehensive model are that it gives people a detailed idea of just what they may or may not do, and that it can (somewhat) prevent people who are covered or who enforce it from creating ways to get around it. However, no policy can completely prevent attempts at evasion, and a carefully worded simple statement can be almost as effective at this as can a detailed law. (See Appendix A, models C and D.)

30.4 Changing Structure for Tactical Reasons

No matter which basic structure you choose, in a long campaign, be open to the idea of changing. Sometimes change for its own sake is a smart tactic.

> It took fifteen years to get a policy passed in New York City. In the year it passed, its proponents switched from a "drop in" proposal to a "piggyback" proposal. There were several reasons for the change. First, the opponents had succeeded in distorting what sections of the old bill did. The new proposal at least started without those distortions. The proponents believed the new proposal was harder to distort and that they were more ready to meet and deal with distortions than they had been in the past. Second, the new draft made it easier for board members who had voted against the old proposal over the years to move. They could say this was not the proposal they had opposed. Finally, the proponents felt that after years of

30.4

> claims and counterclaims about what the proposal would do, no one was actually reading the bill anymore. They felt they'd have a better chance at convincing people if they could get them reading the proposal again.

30.5 Language

Policies should cover discrimination based on "sexual orientation," not "sexual preference" or "affectional orientation." "Sexual orientation" has become the most common term, so using something else could be taken as a suggestion that you mean something else. In addition, the term "preference" suggests you think sexuality is a matter of an ongoing adult choice. "Orientation" implies an established part of personality.

If possible, policies should refer to lesbians, gay men, bisexuals, and heterosexuals, not to "homosexuals," a clinical term that most lesbians and gay men find alienating when used by others, and almost never use themselves. It is no more exact or precise than "lesbians and gay men." (See Appendix A.) On the other hand, policies that use the terms "lesbian" and "gay," for purely grammatical reasons, tend to be awkward. (Don't let this become a big deal.)

30.6 Who Will Be Protected and Who Will Be Regulated?

Decisions about who should be protected by the policy will largely depend on who is protected by current policies and by what other groups want to participate in a campaign. (See sections 5.4 and 25.3.) Decisions about who will be regulated will largely depend on what kind of institution you are asking to adopt the policy. (See chapter 26.)

30.5

30.7 Defining Sexual Orientation

Like race and, to a lesser extent, religion, sexual orientation is a difficult thing to define. It is tempting to simply leave the term undefined, as most civil rights laws do with race and religion. The problem with that approach is that if you don't define the term, opponents are likely to claim that the policy will protect people who have sex with animals, adults who have sex with children, etc. The best way to head off this argument is with a definition that says that the term "sexual orientation" covers lesbians, gay men, bisexuals and heterosexuals. (See Appendix A, models H-1 and H-2.)

Including a definition of sexual orientation often brings up the question of whether the law should apply to people who are changing their gender. While gender change is not a sexual orientation, individuals who change gender certainly do experience discrimination and deserve legal protection. Whether you can negotiate to get that protection at the same time as you get a policy on sexual-orientation discrimination could be another matter. If you do decide to include coverage for people changing gender, you should probably do that by including them as an additional protected category, and not by artificially putting gender change into the definition of sexual orientation.

30.8 Actual or Perceived Sexual Orientation

It ought to be obvious that in terms of impact and fairness, it doesn't much matter whether a person loses a job because she is a lesbian or because her employer incorrectly thinks she is a lesbian. Unfortunately, it isn't obvious to everyone. Employers try to argue that it is the employee's actual sexual orientation, not the employer's motivation, that counts. A few agencies and courts have agreed. To preempt this bit of nonsense, the policy should apply to "actual or perceived" sexual orientation, which you can do by either including it in the definition of sexual orientation or in the ban on discrimination. (See Appendix A, models A, B, C, D, and H.)

30.8

31. WRITING CIVIL RIGHTS POLICY — IMPORTANT DETAILS

31.1 Introduction: What this Chapter Covers

This chapter covers some of the important sections that you'll find in the models in Appendix A (and in most policies). You need to understand them so that you can explain them and deal with proposed changes in negotiation. Like the models, parts of the chapter might be outdated by the time you get to work. Most of the sections in this chapter cover details that only apply to the detailed policies that governments enact as laws and ordinances.

31.2 Findings and Arguments

Many policies contain short summaries of the policy's goals, along with a capsule version of the case for the policy—a few short statements summarizing the proof that the policy is needed and the arguments for it. These can be valuable, especially if you are going to be involved in a campaign where you hope to publish the policy or use it to help persuade the public. However, you've got to keep them short and simple.

Findings can also be helpful if the policy is challenged in court. Opponents have grown fond of arguing in court that some types of nondiscrimination policies are not really very important. Summarizing evidence developed at hearings could be helpful in meeting those arguments, especially if your board keeps incomplete official records of its hearings (as most do). (Appendix A, model D has an example. Make sure to tailor your draft to your case and to the evidence developed at your hearings.

31.3 Enforcement

See sections 25.2 and 26.3. They explain the best enforcement options.

31.4 Notices

This little provision may be the most important part of any policy. Nondiscrimination laws don't do much good unless people know they exist. Notices are most important in the workplace. Federal and most state laws require nondiscrimination signs at many job sites. Since those signs don't mention sexual-orientation discrimination, some people are apt to think that it is legal even after you pass a policy.

People often fail to post notices simply because they don't know about the requirements. Appendix A, model D calls for a small fine and only for willful violations (those that occur after an employer knows the rules).

31.5 Exceptions: An Introduction

An *exception* is a special section of a law or policy that says that the policy won't be applied to something that it otherwise would cover. For example, a policy that generally bans discrimination in renting housing might have an exception for someone who is renting a room in his or her apartment. Exceptions are sometimes called *exemptions*. The purpose is to take into account some of the competing interests that the board members think are legitimate. In the housing example above, the board might think that people ought to be allowed more leeway about whom they actually live with.

Policy negotiations tend to focus on exceptions. If you are trying to add sexual orientation to an existing policy or achieve parity with a different policy that covers other kinds of discrimination, you'll probably have to accept most of the exceptions that exist for other groups. (See, sections 25.2 and 30.2.)

In general, you should fight against attempts to create special exceptions for sexual-orientation discrimination. In a few instances they can be a response to differences in various types of discrimination. For example, one can argue that legally mandated systems of segregation in the past make a special case for affirmative action with race and sex discrimination. One might also argue that domestic partnership pre-

31.5

sents a unique concern for lesbian and gay couples (since they are not allowed to marry).

However, most of the time, special exceptions for sexual orientation reflect the most obnoxious stereotypes about lesbians and gay men. It is important to fight this so that your policy doesn't legitimize those stereotypes.

Typically, the two best arguments against special exceptions are proof that the exception is based on an inaccurate stereotype, and evidence that the arguments for the exception could apply to other types of discrimination as well.

The next seven sections focus on some areas where negotiations over exemptions are common. The first section comes up with most policies; the remainder usually arise with government policies that regulate others (employers, landlords, etc.).

31.6 Domestic Partnership Exceptions

If your policy applies to any situation, which could involve couples, questions about domestic partners are likely to come up. For example, if you are proposing a nondiscrimination policy for a business, and the business usually pays moving expenses for spouses or it provides bereavement leave if a spouse dies, someone is apt to ask if the policy will require payment of expenses or leave for the domestic partners of lesbian and gay employees.

The answer depends on what you say in the policy. If you say nothing, a nondiscrimination policy probably will not require any recognition of domestic partners. Although policies that recognize married couples discriminate against lesbians and gay men, they do so because states don't let lesbians and gay men marry. Courts that have considered these policies have usually said that they discriminate on the basis of marital status, not sexual orientation.

If you want the policy to include recognition of domestic partners, you should adopt a domestic partnership policy. (See Part IV.) Especially if health benefits are involved, domestic partnership can be one of the more hotly contested questions. Be careful about wording if you decide to treat domestic partnership as a separate issue or to compromise by excluding recognition of domestic partnerships from your nondiscrimination policy. You don't want to allow someone to recognize unmarried heterosexual couples but not unmarried lesbian or gay couples. Exceptions that say that the law won't be interpreted to require any recognition of the domestic partners of lesbians and gay men may do that. You also don't want to allow employers or others to use martial status in making most decisions, such as hiring, firing, renting, etc. Some exceptions that say the law doesn't prevent policies based on marital status may do that. The solution is probably an exception to the law for marital status classifications in health plans, or benefit plans generally. (See Appendix A, model E-1, for a term which should work.)

31.7   Quotas and Affirmative Action Exceptions

Affirmative action is probably the least popular area of civil rights these days. People often demand that new policies exclude it by saying that affirmative action is not required. The danger with that is that older federal civil rights laws use the term "affirmative action" to include almost every remedy for a victim of discrimination, including things such as being rehired or receiving lost pay. If you just say the policy doesn't require affirmative action, you could be taking away most of its remedies.

One solution is to ban the use of quotas. (See Appendix A, model E-2.) This is what most people are really worried about. You don't give up much because, for example, nobody knows either the percentage of the workforce that is lesbian/gay or the extent to which a particular company's employees are lesbian/gay, so you couldn't put together a sexual-orientation quota system even if you asked to do that. (See section 29.7.) If need be, you can extend the section to cover "quota-like" devices. (See Appendix A, model E-3.)

Opponents, borrowing from arguments used against other civil rights laws (see section 29.7), often argue that the law should say that affirmative action clauses are neither required nor permitted. If the

31.7

section is limited to quotas or quota-like devices, that should be agreeable since they aren't practical. But if an anti-affirmative action section goes beyond quotas, be careful. Many institutions (police and fire departments, for example) have a history of excluding lesbians and gay men. They should be allowed to conduct outreach such as advertising in the gay press to attract lesbian and gay applicants. An anti-affirmative action clause that goes beyond quotas and quota-like devices and prohibits voluntary action might pass though.

In some cases, it may be appropriate to require an employer with an egregious history of discrimination to do outreach. This will only be possible if an anti-affirmative action provision is limited to quotas and quota-like devices.

31.8 Exceptions for Religion

No matter what your policy says, if it is a government policy, it won't apply to those operations of a religious group that pertain to belief. For example, employment laws don't apply to hiring ministers or religion teachers; public accommodations laws don't apply to membership in a church. They don't apply because the First Amendment to the federal Constitution exempts the core operations of religious groups from government control.

Even though it doesn't matter what the policy says, sometimes board members will want this exemption restated in the policy, at least in part to mollify religious opposition. Appendix A, model E gives two possible religious exceptions. The first, which restates the idea that federal laws control, is better because it is flexible; if the federal law changes, it changes with it. Some board members prefer the second, which explains the exception.

Some laws also say that church-operated schools, camps, etc., may prefer members of the church. Although a policy like that will effectively discriminate if the church excludes lesbians and gay men from membership, the federal Constitution may require that preferences like these be allowed anyway.

Occasionally, churches will argue they should not be covered by a nondiscrimination policy at all. A few states have laws that completely exempt religious organizations from civil rights laws. A complete exception probably makes sense if you are adding sexual orientation to an existing policy that doesn't cover religious groups at all. However, you should fight any religious exception from the policy on sexual-orientation discrimination that is broader than the religious exception from policies on race, gender, and other types of discrimination. (See section 29.6.)

31.9 Housing Exceptions

Many people feel that in close quarters, people ought to be allowed to be more arbitrary. Appendix A, models E-6 and E-7, offer "small housing" exceptions for policies that apply to housing. One applies to roommates, and the second applies to an owner-occupied small-unit exception.

Occasionally, boards want assurance that the policy doesn't somehow override the city's zoning or occupancy rules. While that in itself isn't a problem, avoid exceptions that say broadly that the policy doesn't require any occupancy not allowed by law. Many states have arcane laws that make it illegal for people to live together if they are not married. Any "zoning" exception should be carefully tied to zoning and occupancy rules.

31.10 Small Employer Exceptions

Most people work for small businesses, so "small employer" exceptions greatly reduce the coverage of a law. If you are adding sexual orientation to a policy with a small employer exception or seeking parity with one, you'll probably have to accept one, though the case for them is weak. Working with someone is not like living with someone. Since everyone needs to work to live, it is fair to insist on greater tolerance of difference in the workplace. Most "small employer" exceptions define a small employer according to the number of employees. If you had to accept a small employer exception, make

31.10

sure that management and supervisors are included in deciding if an employer has the minimum number.

31.11 Exceptions for Teachers, Day-Care Workers, (Etc.)

Don't accept them unless you are absolutely convinced you can't get the policy for a very long time without them and that there is much to be gained by getting the policy now. These exemptions reinforce the worst stereotypes about lesbians and gay men.

31.12 Miscellaneous Employment Exceptions

The exception for "bona fide occupational qualifications" or "bfoq" (Appendix A, model D) allows discrimination if an employer really needs someone of a particular sexual orientation to do a job. These originally appeared in laws on gender discrimination.

It is hard to think of a situation in which an employer might legitimately need an employee of a particular sexual orientation, so it is difficult to make a good argument for this exception. Moreover, the existence of the exception gives employers an opportunity to invoke stereotypes about lesbians and gay men. For example, a school might claim that because students emulate teachers, being heterosexual is a bona fide occupational qualification. Avoid this exception if you can, although it may be tough since it appears in many laws. You might want to use it as a compromise. A general "bfoq" exception probably is better than a specific exception for some occupations, like teachers or day-care workers, since it leaves it to whomever will enforce the policy and decide if, for example, you need to be straight to teach.

Seniority system exceptions were designed for institutions with a history of explicit race discrimination. Again, it is hard to see how the exception could apply to sexual-orientation discrimination, but it is probably harmless. (See Appendix A, model D.)

31.10

31.13 Denials—An Explanation

A denial is a special section saying the policy won't apply to something that it wouldn't cover anyway. For example, New York City's law says that it doesn't legalize anything that state law says is illegal. New York City couldn't do that anyway.

The purpose of denials is to remove arguments from the opposition that prove hard to overcome even though they are wrong. They give the campaign and members of the board the ability to answer "insane scenarios" by pointing to the policy and saying, "See, that won't happen." They can be a potent tool, and they can give board members cover with constituents. Since they cover things that won't happen anyway, typically they have no legal effect and are forgotten shortly after the law is passed. Legally, they are relatively harmless.

On the other hand, denials are also often insulting; they often include statements such as, for example, the board isn't endorsing any particular life-style. Why would you need that on a sexual-orientation discrimination law but not on a religious discrimination law? Denials can be more harmful if they perpetuate stereotypes. For example, a denial which says that the law doesn't permit criminal acts implies that lesbians and gay men are more prone than others to break the law. These are not just a political problem. Some could certainly be used by courts to narrow the effect of the law in some circumstances. If you are faced with proposals for denials that perpetuate stereotypes, enlist a lawyer to help you minimize any damage.

(Appendix A, sections F-1—F-3, contains a few typical denials. Denials are also called *disclaimers*.)

31.14 Impact Cases

Most discrimination is intentional; the different treatment is motivated by the fact that a person is male or female, Asian or Latino, lesbian or bisexual, etc.

There is one kind of discrimination to which civil rights policies sometimes apply where the different treatment may or may not be intentional. These are called "impact" cases. Impact cases typically

31.14

surface in situations where some rule or test excludes a much higher percentage of a group protected by a civil rights law than others. For example, minimum height and weight rules for jobs often exclude many more qualified women than men.

Courts and agencies interpreting civil rights laws often say that if a rule has that kind of an impact—usually called a "disproportionate impact"—the employer or other institution has to justify the rule by showing it is, for example, related to ability to do the job.

For the most part, impact cases won't arise in sexual-orientation discrimination for a very practical reason. Since you never know how many gay applicants or gay employees there are, you can't show a disproportionate impact. But there are some rules that will obviously have an unfair impact on lesbians and gay men; for example, a promotion rule that requires employees to be married.

Because of some court decisions in the 1990s, it isn't clear that civil rights laws cover impact cases unless you say so explicitly. Appendix A, model G-1, includes language you could use and make it clear that a policy applies to impact cases generally. Model G-2 allows impact claims only when "mental status" is used to discriminate against lesbians, gay men and bisexuals. Model G-3 is the "business necessity" exception to laws that do allow impact claims.

This is a difficult area. If you need to enter into it, you'll need expert advice.

31.14

IV. *Domestic Partnership Policies*

32. DOMESTIC PARTNERSHIP – WHAT'S POSSIBLE

32.1 Introduction: What this Chapter Covers

This chapter is a basic introduction to a group of different kinds of policies, which are all loosely referred to as "domestic partnership." The next chapter goes over some of the things you should consider in deciding which type of domestic partnership policy to propose.

32.2 Three Kinds of Policies

Domestic partnership policies all involve an intimate relationship between two people who are not married and usually are not related by blood.

There are three kinds of domestic partnership policies. Some proposals mix two or all three together. First, there are *registration* systems. A registration system is an official system for creating and ending domestic partnerships. A pure registration system doesn't do anything else.

Second, there are *benefit* systems. A benefit system gives something to a person because she or he is a domestic partner of another person. There are benefit systems that are financially significant and those that are not. An employer-provided health plan that covers the domestic partners of employees is financially significant because it usually costs the employer something to insure the partners and is usually worth a good deal to the domestic partner. A bargain-rate domestic partnership membership at a gym or a museum, or an employer-provided funeral leave plan is usually not very financially significant. As explained below, financially significant benefit plans have special requirements that other plans don't have.

Third, there are *recognition* systems. These are systems that take account of a domestic partner because he or she is the closest person to someone else. Recognition systems are in some ways similar to benefit systems, but with recognition systems, the relationship, *not* the benefit, is the most important thing. Recognition systems also usually aren't very financially significant; for example, a policy allowing domestic partners to visit patients in intensive care units, or allowing employees to receive calls from domestic partners at work.

San Francisco's first domestic partnership proposal in 1981 had all three types of systems. It had a registration system run through the city clerk. Anyone who signed a declaration saying they had agreed to take on the basic obligations of domestic partners could sign up.

It had two specific limited recognition systems. One required hospitals in the city to allow domestic partners the right to visit people in intensive care units or, in other circumstances, with limited visitation. The other required the city jail to let domestic partners visit inmates.

It had a general nondiscrimination section, which would have had some recognition and some limited benefits consequences. It said the city had to treat domestic partners the same way it treated spouses. This would have affected health-care decisions in city hospitals and it

32.2

would have opened up family museum memberships. Because of a quirk in San Francisco's charter, the proposal wouldn't have affected the health or pension plans.

32.3 Basic Possibilities—Registration

Registration systems have two purposes. First, they give a form of official status to the relationship. For some people this is important in itself. For example, the voter-approved domestic partnership system adopted in San Francisco in 1990 was a "pure" registration system, with no benefits. Hundreds of couples registered on the day it took effect (Valentine's Day 1991). Moreover, the official status that goes with registration can be significant. If the registration system has people swear that they are in an intimate, committed relationship, it would be good evidence against a later claim that two people were just roommates or friends. This might have social and possibly legal consequences. (See section 34.4.)

Second, registration systems create a mechanism for institutions that want to voluntarily adopt benefit systems or recognition systems. They aren't essential; employers, hospitals, etc., can create their own definitions and documents if they want to. But institutions may be more willing to include domestic partners in benefit and particularly recognition systems if they don't have to create their own system or much paperwork. There is also some real value in having all institutions in an area using the same definition of domestic partnership; people who change jobs, for example, won't have to "reregister."

Since the idea of a registration system is that it creates an official record of the relationship, only a government can create one. State governments definitely have the power to do this. Special agencies, like transportation authorities or water districts, probably don't have the power to create registration systems, since they usually can only do things related to their special jobs. They often can have benefit plans and recognition systems. Some cities and counties can set up registration systems, others may not be able to do so. As explained in section 26.3, cities and counties get their power from the states, and sometimes

32.3

their powers are quite limited. Since pure registration systems don't really regulate anything, even some cities with limited powers to govern, which might not be able to pass broader civil rights policies, may be able to set up registration systems. On the other hand, cities that have very specific, limited grants of power may not. (See section 26.3.)

Since registration systems don't fit neatly into any of the existing legal rules about the powers of cities, you shouldn't accept the claim that the city doesn't have the power without further investigation. At present, the only challenge to the authority of a government to set up a registration system was rejected by the Georgia Supreme Court, which upheld Atlanta's system. Since there aren't clear answers, you may want to urge the city to take a broad view of its powers and take a chance. Because pure registration systems don't have direct legal consequences, there isn't a great deal to lose.

32.4 Basic Possibilities — Benefits Systems

Most institutions have the power to voluntarily adopt whatever benefit plans they want. However, if the institution uses insurance (as opposed to paying the costs itself, sometimes called "self insurance"), it may have trouble finding a company that will cover domestic partners. As health plans have become more regulated, some states have begun to pass laws about what they may and may not offer. If the federal government adopts a comprehensive health-care reform system, it may greatly regulate the terms of health plans.

Government agencies may be even more limited. They sometimes get their health and pension plans from the state government, and these often are not flexible about terms.

The City of Oakland, California, appeared ready to adopt a domestic partners health plan. But the city obtained its coverage from a plan run by the state. That plan was created by a law passed by the state legislature, which spelled out who could be covered by the plan. Domestic partners weren't included. To cover them, Oakland would have had to either leave the state plan, or persuade the

32.4

legislature to change the law. When this guide was written, the city was working hard to change the state law.

However, be wary of the claim that an institution can't adopt a domestic partnership benefit plan. The claim is made far more often than it's true. Have your lawyer look into it.

Moreover, most employers can provide at least some health care even if they can't add domestic partners into existing plans by buying roughly equilavent individual health plans for domestic partners (government agencies again may be a little more restricted here).

In the mid-eighties, the American Civil Liberties Union of Northern California decided to include domestic partners in all its benefit plans. Neither of its insurers would cover them, and the ACLU couldn't find an insurer who would. Ultimately, the organization told the partners of employees to get individual insurance, and it paid the premium. This was probably more expensive than including domestic partners in the group would have been, and the coverage wasn't as good. But it was a start.

At the time this was written, neither cities nor states had the power *to require* private employers to include domestic partners in health or pension plans. A federal law said they could not do that with any financially significant employment benefit plan. If you aren't sure whether a benefit you want to have a city or a state require is covered by this federal law, seek legal help.

32.5 Basic Possibilities—Recognition Systems

Most institutions can adopt whatever voluntary recognition systems they want to have. One exception is that an agency administering a federal or a state program may not be able to recognize a domestic partnership unless the federal or state government allows it. So, for example, a county social service agency probably can't recognize domestic partners as a family for food stamps (typically with social service programs, there aren't any advantages to that anyway).

32.5

Again, be skeptical about claims of powerlessness here. Most federal housing programs, for example, allow local agencies to recognize domestic partners as family if the agency wants to do that.

States have considerable power to require institutions to adopt recognition systems. So, for example, most states could tell doctors to consult domestic partners for health-care decisions for people who cannot make their own. Some cities and counties may be able to require recognition systems as well. It depends on the city's power to regulate and whether or not the state has taken over an area of regulation. (See sections 26.3 and 26.5.)

32.6 A Warning About "Extended Family" Proposals

There have been a couple of proposals for "extended family" registration systems. The idea is that a group of people who consider themselves family could register as such. There are two problems with the idea, the second of which is very serious.

The first problem has to do with logistics. These plans won't work at all for couples-focused benefit plans (like health or pension plans) or for recognition systems that are aimed at primary relationships. It is also difficult to make them work. What if two people have a falling out? Can the rest of the family expel one member? If one member decides to leave, does the family continue as such, or does it need to reregister?

Much more serious is the problem of adults and children. A few proposals have sought to address the problem of "co-parents," typically partners of biological parents who are actually involved in raising the biological parents' child but who are not legally recognized as parents. These proposals usually purport to make the adult responsible for the child, financially and otherwise, and to create a right for both the adult and the child of continuing contact even if the co-parents cease to consider themselves family.

Legally, domestic partnerships and alternative families are basically agreements among the members. While many states will allow an adult to make an agreement taking on financial responsibility for a child, few will permit an agreement to treat an adult who is not a parent as if he or she were. The result is that at best these provisions are meaningless. They are likely to prove a cruel disappointment if put to the test. Worse, they may result in binding the co-parent to financial responsibility without creating any other rights.

Perhaps worst of all, people may think that they don't need to take other steps to legally establish their co-parenting relationships.

33. DOMESTIC PARTNERSHIP – DECIDING WHAT KIND

33.1 Introduction: What this Chapter Covers

This chapter is designed to help you decide which kind of domestic partnership policy to adopt. The goals you want to achieve with a domestic partnership plan, and the systems you want to change, will have a profound influence on the terms of your proposal. This chapter explains some of the ways in which specific goals, and the desire to change specific systems, shape domestic partnership proposals.

33.2 The Goals of Domestic Partnership

Most domestic partnership policies are adopted with one or more of three goals in mind. While the goals themselves aren't contradictory, any one of them tends to have requirements that may make a policy serve one of the other goals less well. As you consider which kind of policy you want, you need to sort through your goals and decide, when they pull in different directions, which are most important.

One goal is equal treatment. The idea here is that couples who are not married deserve the same treatment as those who are. Domestic partnership can be a way to equalize treatment. (See section 34.3 for more details.)

33.2

A second goal is relationship finding. We have many legal systems designed to locate the person who is closest to another person when the second person can't tell us. These include everything from lists of who receives property if a person dies without a will through lists of who is allowed to visit in hospitals and jails. Domestic partnership can be a way to find the most important person for people in relationships who can't or don't decide to marry. (See section 34.4.)

A third goal is visibility for lesbian and gay relationships. They are less visible than heterosexual relationships, the argument goes, because society only notices marital relationships, and, in most places, lesbians and gay men can't marry each other. Since the invisibility reinforces stereotypes about lesbians and gay men, visibility is a good thing for its own sake. (See section 34.5.)

33.3 Ways in Which Goals and Systems Shape Policy Proposals

If a health benefit or a free-ride pension benefit for domestic partners is an important part of your plan, your proposal will have to have a detailed definition of domestic partnership. (A free-ride pension plan continues to pay at least part of a pension to the spouse of the person who earned the pension after he or she dies. It is a "free ride" because the payments to the person who earned the pension are not reduced to compensate for the continuing payments to the spouse. Those benefits need a relationship that can be objectively verified apart from what people say about themselves. (See section 38.3 for an explanation of why this is so.) So, proposals that include health and free-ride pension benefits usually have definitions of domestic partnership with significant requirements and obligations.

Health and free-ride pension benefits don't necessarily require a definition similar to the definition of marriage. But to the extent that equality is an important goal of your proposal, it will push you toward a very "marriagelike" definition of domestic partnership. When your case is that domestic partners should get treatment equal to that given married couples, people are apt to insist that the domestic partnership resemble marriage as much as possible. In some places, this has led to definitions that closely follow a state's legal definition of marriage; in others, it has led to definitions that require some or all of the things that married people typically do, even though they are not things that are legally required. For example, some definitions require pooled finances, as shown by things like joint checking accounts, even though married people can keep their finances separate if they want to. If equality is central to your arguments, it will push you toward a "marriagelike" definition even if health and free-ride pension benefits are not part of your plan.

The goal of relationship finding tends to pull proposals away from high definition and marriagelike definitions. If you want a system to locate a person's closest relationships, especially in times of crisis, definitions and requirements shouldn't be so important. As much as you can, you want to let people decide for themselves who they are closest to. Relationship finding as a primary goal tends to lead to policies in which people designate others in advance as domestic partners or closest relations, with little or no definition of what the terms mean. So, for example, a bereavement leave plan might require employees to simply tell the personnel office who their "domestic partners" are if they are unmarried, or even simply require all employees to name the five or ten people closest to them.

Simple designation tends to work best with recognition systems. They don't have the financial consequences of benefit systems, which require high definition.

The goal of making lesbian and gay relationships more visible often leads people to emphasize proposals with registration systems, since they involve official recognition of the relationship. Visibility as a goal tends to make proposals focus on couples and some definition, because designation proposals don't really make relationships very visible. On the other hand, visibility tends to pull away from the most marriagelike definitions since many lesbian and gay relationships don't take on all the typical aspects of a heterosexual marriage.

It is possible to design proposals that accommodate all three goals and that work for all three types of policies. (See, for example,

33.3

Appendix B) But these proposals typically involve some compromises on all three goals and some limitations on each system.

33.4   Ways in Which Health and Free-Ride Pension Plans Affect Proposals

If your proposal includes health or free-ride pension benefits for domestic partners, they are likely to become the most important part of your plan. Aside from the way they will shape your proposal by dictating a very defined relationship, they are the most expensive things you can do. (See section 38.3.)

Because they are expensive, health and free-ride proposals generate the toughest opposition. They often make opponents of moderates who have no problem with the idea of domestic partnership but are worried about cost and profits. They also lend themselves to lesbian/gay-only compromises as a way to control costs. The rationale is that lesbians and gay men only should get the benefit because unlike heterosexual couples, they cannot get married. This approach is likely to make the proposal's definition more marriagelike.

If you want to propose a comprehensive domestic partnership plan with some type of health benefit, and you think the cost of the health plan could be a serious issue, think about splitting the proposal.

> **The San Francisco charter required that the city's proposed registration system be a law separate from the proposal to extend its health plan to domestic partners. The separation proved to be a blessing, since any costs associated with the health plan were not an issue when the registration law was put on the ballot in a referendum.**

In one sense, expense shouldn't be an issue. Lesbians and gay men are no more expensive to cover than heterosexuals, so extending coverage to lesbian and gay couples seems only fair. (See section 36.3.) On the other hand, extending coverage to domestic partners simply increases the unfairness of giving financially valuable benefits to employees in couples that are unavailable to single employees.

One answer to this question of fairness and the problem of cost is to advocate "cafeteria" benefit plans and pension continuations based on adjustments with no free rides. In a cafeteria plan, the employer offers to spend the same amount on benefits for each employee, and the employee chooses which benefits to take, paying for selections that exceed the employer's agreed contribution. Adjusted pension continuations allow you to continue your pension, reducing the payments to you by the amount needed to keep it going for the other person after you die. With either of these approaches, a domestic partnership proposal would simply advocate putting domestic partners on the list of people for whom you can designate health coverage or a pension continuation.

The difficulty is that these proposals reduce the amount of benefits that are going to the people who get the most under the current system. For example, with health benefits, if the employer spends the same total amount on benefits, employees with big families, who are getting much more than single employees now, will get less. Both proposals are likely to draw very tough opposition from those who are getting the most from free rides and generous family/spouse health plans. Some of these opponents, often unions, will be allies if you move to extend the existing plans instead.

On the other hand, relationship-based health plans and pension free rides are dinosaurs. The rationale for spousal health and free-ride pension benefits has disappeared now that both partners in most couples work. If the federal government or your state adopts a universal-coverage health plan, the spousal health benefit will be mostly meaningless. How hard are you willing to fight to rearrange the deck chairs on the *Titanic*?

33.5   Other Considerations in Formulating a Proposal

A good way to begin deciding what kind of policy you want to propose is to survey your institution; find out all the ways in which the city, employer, business, or university uses or recognizes intimate relationships. Decide which issues present problems you want to tackle and what kind of proposal, or combination of proposals, best responds to the problems you are interested in.

If you decide to urge one of the three types of proposal instead of a combination of two or more, think about keeping your proposal adaptable. For example, if you decide to propose a pure registration system, think about whether you want to design it so that it can be used by employers, hospitals, etc., for recognition and/or benefits systems. (See sections 37.2 and 37.3.)

If you are proposing either benefits or recognition systems, think about whether to make them voluntary or mandatory. Some institutions, like hospitals, typically don't oppose mandatory recognition systems for things like visitation. Other types of institutions, like businesses, often adamantly oppose any type of mandatory recognition. Given the limited number of things you can require (see sections 32.4 and 32.5), it may be better to set up a registration system and then organize a campaign to get business and institutions to use it. This would be particularly advisable if you could pick up business support for a voluntary system.

34. THE CASE FOR DOMESTIC PARTNERSHIP

34.1 Introduction: What this Chapter Covers

This chapter reviews some of the most important present-day arguments used to support domestic partnership policies, which are still a relatively new phenomenon in the mid-nineties.

> **Although a few institutions included "significant others" in some miscellaneous policies starting in the late seventies, the *Village Voice* became the first to include partners in a health plan in 1982. The City of Berkeley, California, followed in 1985, and since then a number of cities and businesses with significant workforces have adopted various types of domestic partnership plans.**

The arguments reviewed here are current. They may not be when you begin your campaign. Make sure you talk to others who've recently worked on similar policies and take the time to develop your arguments in the way described in chapter 8.

34.2 Three Major Arguments

There are three major arguments for domestic partnership policies, which closely parallel the goals of domestic partnership. They are arguments for equal treatment, relationship recognition in crisis, and relationship acknowledgment generally. On the goals, see section 33.2. However, the goal that is most important to you shouldn't necessarily dictate which argument you use in making your case. Your resources and your audience should. (See section 8.4.)

These arguments also somewhat parallel the different kinds of domestic partnership policies. Equal treatment arguments, for example, seem to fit best with benefit systems, crisis recognition arguments with recognition systems, and acknowledgment arguments with registration systems. On the different kinds of policies, see section 32.2. Hence, the arguments parallel the three policies, each of the arguments working more or less with the other policies, so your policy choice doesn't necessarily dictate your decision about the main argument either. Moreover, if you propose a policy that combines two or all three types of domestic partnership policies, you'll have to decide which argument to emphasize.

34.3 Equality Arguments

This is the argument: Many policies of a government, workplace, or business use marriage to determine important things such as eligibility. This is unfair to unmarried couples. It is particularly unfair to lesbian and gay couples, since lesbians and gay men aren't allowed to marry their partners.

This argument works best with employment benefit plans. Since benefits are an important part of a person's pay (estimates vary from twenty percent to forty percent of the value of total compensation), the argument goes, giving benefits to employees with spouses and denying them to those with unmarried partners is simply not equal pay for

34.3

equal work. Outside the workplace, this argument not only carries less force, it is sometimes successfully exploited by the opposition.

> San Francisco's first domestic partnership registration law was passed in 1981 and vetoed by the mayor. The apparent problem with the law was a small section of it that stated that the city would give domestic partners the same treatment that it gave married couples. The difficulty wasn't money; because of San Francisco's unusual government structure, the law couldn't apply to the city's health or the pension plan. The problem was the wording. The section seemed to imply that domestic partnerships were the equivalent of marriages. That outraged religious leaders, and the city's moderate politicians were sympathetic to them.

Much of the opposition to domestic partnership focuses on the fact that implicit in the equality argument is the position that unmarried couples are equal to married couples. Opponents of domestic partnership generally don't accept that, and a surprising number of moderates, who are otherwise willing to recognize that nonmarital relationships are important, don't accept it either.

Actually, the argument only claims equality in terms of entitlement to a specific benefit or recognition; it says married and unmarried couples are "equal," in the sense that both should, for example, be on the list of people who can visit a patient in an intensive care unit. But that's a bit of logic that may be too subtle for many campaigns. The argument tends to work better in the workplace because there it focuses not so much on the couple as it does on the employee member of the couple; it is he or she who is not getting equal pay.

If instead of a benefit plan you propose a recognition or registration system, either consider one of the other fairness arguments, both of which don't emphasize equivalence, or prepare to meet the equality argument head on. You may be able to do this best with examples of deeply committed relationships that have received shabby treatment at the hands of some institution. (See section 35.2.)

34.3

34.4 Recognition in Crisis

This argument focuses on the injustice of society's failure to recognize unmarried couples. Society uses marriage and blood, the argument goes, to decide who a person's family is. Since nonmarital couples don't, and lesbian and gay couples can't, come within those definitions of family, we are often separated from our most intimate family members when we need them most.

To be made convincingly, this argument needs two things. First, it needs illustrations of the problem. Good stories that illustrate just how devastating nonrecognition can be are very powerful. (See section 35.2.) Second, the argument needs to be tied to your proposal. If your proposal has a recognition system (like a bereavement leave policy for an employee, or hospital visitation), the easiest way to do that is by presenting stories that would have come out differently had your policy been in place. But you can also use this argument with registration systems.

Karen Thompson has always insisted that her fight to maintain her relationship with Sharon Kowalski after Sharon's devastating injuries in a traffic accident would have gone differently if the two had been able to register as domestic partners. The domestic partnership wouldn't have given her any "rights" in the Minnesota guardianship proceeding. But, Thompson points out, it would have been powerful evidence against the claim of Kowalski's parents that the two women were nothing more than roommates.

34.5 Relationship Acknowledgment

Registration systems and, to a lesser extent, recognition systems and, benefit plans all amount to some form of acknowledgment that nonmarital relationships are important. This argument simply says they *are* important and deserve the minimal respect those systems give them. Similar to the previous argument, this one can also be powerfully supported by stories that illustrate the consequences of not acknowledging nonmarital relationships. It can also be helped by proof about how widespread nonmarital relationships are. (See section 35.3.)

However, this argument can and does draw the same opposition the equality argument draws; that is, it suggests equality with marriage. But the very modest or, in the case of pure registration, nonexistent practical consequences of domestic partnership make this easier to deflect, since equality isn't part of the argument. (See sections 36.6–36.8.)

34.6 Problematic Arguments

Acknowledgment and recognition arguments are occasionally recast, especially in light of AIDS, as arguments that society should give lesbian and gay relationships all the help it can. This version of those arguments makes some sense when it is used with illustrations of the harsh consequences visited on people taking care of partners who are seriously ill because their relationships are undefined. It needs to be handled with care because occasionally it becomes an argument that we should pass domestic partnership laws to encourage exclusive relationships. This of course makes a value judgment about coupling you may not want to make; worse, it beggingly invites reliance on old stereotypes about commitment being particularly difficult for lesbians and gay men.

All three of the main arguments have a strain that points out that because lesbians and gay men can't marry their partners, we are hurt more by society's failure to recognize nonmarital relationships than are heterosexuals. This sometimes becomes a justification for limiting a domestic partnership policy to lesbians and gay man. Occasionally, it becomes an argument in itself; that is, that lesbian and gay relationships ought to be recognized because lesbians and gay men cannot marry their partners.

This argument is problematic because it invites all the "equality" opposition described above, and, since it smacks of an attack on the limitation of marriage to heterosexuals, it often intensifies that opposition. At the same time, this argument jettisons two significant groups of supporters: unmarried heterosexual couples and others who think alternative models for intimate relationships are legitimate and deserve recognition.

35. PROVING THE CASE FOR DOMESTIC PARTNERSHIP

35.1 Introduction

Read chapter 28 on proving the need for civil rights policies. It will tell you much of what you need to know, especially about personal stories. Pay particular attention to section 28.2 on how to get stories, section 28.3 on checking them out, section 28.4 on how to explain them, and section 28.8 on written statements. Section 22.11 tells you how to protect vulnerable witnesses.

35.2 Personal Stories

Stories may be the most important kind of evidence of the need for domestic partnership policies. They work with all three types of domestic partnership policies and with all three arguments for domestic partnership. If you are proposing a benefits or recognition policy, the best stories are those about situations which the policy would directly cover.

> One of the most powerful witnesses at the first San Francisco hearing on domestic partnership described his wonderful, difficult eleven-year relationship with a depressed man with strong suicidal tendencies. The man eventually took his own life, and his partner described the painful job of claiming his body, arranging for cremation, and comforting an extended family. He concluded by saying that when he returned to work he found he'd been "absent without cause" and his pay was docked because domestic partners weren't covered by his employer's bereavement leave policy.

There is a possible exception to this general guideline. If you are proposing a policy to add domestic partners to a medical plan, testimony about persons with serious diseases who aren't covered is definitely a mixed bag. People often like to use this kind of testimony on

35.2

the theory that the hardships endured by a person with a serious illness who has no insurance is likely to create sympathy. They do, and they are also likely to remind listeners that illness can be very expensive and that adding domestic partners will increase cost, even though partners are not more expensive to cover than spouses (see section 36.4). Moreover, if the uncovered illness in your story is, say, like HIV, it may reinforce the incorrect notion that domestic partners are more expensive to cover. You'll probably need to confront the second idea with expert evidence (see section 36.4). But you may want to avoid anything that plays into either of these notions.

With health plans, you may be better off sticking to stories that emphasize the economic unfairness to the employee of not covering nonmarital partners.

> **One witness before the San Francisco health systems board explained in detail all the ways in which the individual plan she and her self-employed partner had bought for the partner was inferior to the city plan, which would have covered the partner if she were a spouse. At less than half the price. Another witness described the amazing lengths to which she had gone to piece together coverage for her partner's children, all of whom would have been covered had her partner been her spouse.**

Free-ride pension plans are just unlikely to generate sympathetic stories at all.

Particularly with "pure" registration systems, virtually any story of nonrecognition can be helpful. Limited though the acknowledgment of a registration system is, in most situations, it is likely to make some difference.

Stories about the indirect impact of domestic partnership—about social recognition of nonmarital relationships or about the use of domestic partnership to prove the nature of a relationship rather than to establish rights—can also be used to support proposals for recognition systems or benefit plans. A declaration on an employment form that two people are domestic partners may not be as convincing as a registration, but it is not insignificant.

Use a few positive recognition stories if you can. These can illustrate how your policy would solve some of the problems detailed in your stories. Some institutions in your area may have voluntarily recognized domestic partners, either formally or informally. If you can't find one, contact an institution elsewhere that has and gather the stories or information you need. One or two mundane stories can help as well. Tragedy generates empathy, but sometimes you can make people understand how important recognition is with everyday examples that are similar to things they experience.

35.3 Big Picture Evidence

Along with stories that illustrate why recognition is important to individuals, you should usually present evidence that recognition is important to a large number of people. Information from the 1990 census about the number of Americans living in households where the family includes persons who are not related by blood or marriage is helpful. Call cities that have pure registration systems and ask if they can tell you how many people have signed. Several cities, including Los Angeles and San Francisco, have done studies on alternative families as well. There is some academic writing on nonmarital couples. You can try the library yourself, ask one of your experts to help you, or, if they can't, try to recruit an academic expert on family matters. (See chapter 3.)

35.4 Cost Evidence

If you are proposing a plan with little or no cost, that fact ought to be obvious—but don't count on it.

If you are proposing a registration system with a filing fee, have someone from the office who will perform the filing or have the city's finance office explain that the fee will cover the cost (make sure it will when you write the policy). If you are proposing a policy that extends family memberships or discounts, have an economist or marketing

35.4

expert explain that those plans are thought to make money by bringing in additional business.

If you are proposing something that has real cost, like a health or free ride pension plan, you are apt to need three kinds of evidence. An economist or a management specialist can be very helpful in gathering all three and in evaluating any counterevidence. Try a local university as a source.

First, you'll want evidence of the economic value of the benefit to support your equal pay for equal work argument. You may be able to get that from the employer's human resources department. There are general estimates on the value of various fringe benefits in academic studies of the workplace. You can find very general information about the value of fringe benefits from management texts, etc. One secondary confirmation of the value and importance of fringe benefits is the prominent role they play in labor negotiations.

Second, you'll need evidence that domestic partners are not more expensive to cover than spouses. The best evidence here is the experiences of employers who have added domestic partners to their plans. You can simply call a few or have your expert advisers do that. Plan administrators are usually more than willing to talk.

> **Among the cities and businesses that had adopted domestic partners health plans when this was written were: the California cities of Berkeley, Santa Cruz, and San Francisco; Seattle (Washington) and New York City; Levi Strauss, Lotus Development, Apple Computers, Time Warner, Inc., Microsoft, the *Boston Globe*, the *Seattle Times*, Silicon Graphics, Ziff-Davis Publications, MCA/ Universal Studios, the *Village Voice*, National Public Radio, Stanford University, Montefiorre Medical Center, and the American Civil Liberties Union.**

35.4

Several employment consulting groups have conducted studies of domestic partnership. You should be able to get details from one of the national lesbian/gay civil rights organizations.

Be wary of these consultants' studies, however, especially studies conducted for the institution on which you are working. They tend to be based on very pessimistic assumptions about how the system will work. To analyze and respond to these studies, you'll need the help of an economics expert.

Some health plans try to exact special surcharges for covering domestic partners. The argument for the surcharge is that since the insurer doesn't have enough history with domestic partners, it needs a hedge against the possibility they will be more expensive to cover. Now that there is history with a number of significant domestic partnership plans, surcharges are unjustifiable. They've been dropped from most plans that originally accepted them, and several employers have negotiated plans without them. Gather details both from plans that dropped them and plans that avoided them to fight any surcharge proposal.

Finally, you'll probably need testimony estimating the real cost of adding domestic partners; that is, the increase that comes simply from putting more people on the plan. This testimony is likely to be critical if the institution is thinking about limiting costs by restricting the plan to lesbian/gay domestic partners. Again, the best information comes from existing plans, both those that include heterosexual domestic partners and those that don't.

36. ARGUMENTS AGAINST DOMESTIC PARTNERSHIP POLICIES

36.1 Introduction: Expense — Registration Systems

By far, the most common argument made against every domestic partnership plan is that it will be expensive. With pure registration policies, this is simply nonsense. The only cost associated with them is a bit of red tape. Nonetheless, since cost has become such a potent political argument, consider dispensing with it altogether by making the registration system self-sufficient. Have the policy set a registration fee so that it covers the costs. (See Appendix B, model A, section 5-d.) If you are setting up a registration for a government that

36.1

also issues marriage licenses, be wary of setting the same fee for both.

One of San Francisco's early domestic partnership registration proposals called for the filing fee to be the same as
the fee for marriage licenses. Opponents seized on the
provision as subtle proof that the real aim of the system
was to set up a parallel to marriage with "all its benefits
and none of its obligations." The argument was a persis-
tent enough nuisance that the provision was dropped
from all later versions.

36.2   Expense—Recognition Systems

With many recognition systems, such as jail and hospital
visitation plans, there simply is no expense at all. With others, such as
bereavement leave, the cost is both small and equal to that for other
relationships, which are often far less close (funeral leave plans, for
example, often cover in-laws).

With good illustrations of how unfair the failure to recognize nonmarital relationships can be, these minor cost arguments are usually not
very convincing. If cost is a hot-button issue, consider restricting the
policy to true no-cost items and making the issue go away.

36.3   Expense—Valuable Benefit Plans

It will cost money to add domestic partners to valuable
benefit plans, such as health plans and free-ride pension benefits. The
kind of additional cost is very important to responding to objections
based on cost.

If domestic partners were to use the benefits to the same extent that
spouses do, each domestic partner would cost the same as each spouse.
The additional cost of the domestic partnership plan then would be the
additional cost that would come from allowing more people, all costing
the same amount each, to participate in the plan.

The best answer to objections based on this kind of cost is that cost
has been artificially kept down by excluding nonmarital partners.

Suggest that you could control cost just as well by refusing to allow any new spouses to be added to the plan. Most people will say that would be unfair, and with employment benefits it would be a violation of equal pay for equal work.

There is a second type of cost that could pose more difficulty. If domestic partners used the benefit more than did spouses, they would cost more per person and would drive up the costs of the plan by more than an equal per-person amount. With benefit plans, this kind of cost is usually referred to as "adverse selection," which means the group you are bringing in uses the benefit more, so it costs more to cover each member.

Most adverse selection cost arguments used against domestic partnerships are based on the implicit claim that domestic partners are more likely to become ill than spouses (AIDS is usually the unstated premise here) or are more likely to "cheat" and use the benefit to cover not only partners but those who are ill and in need of coverage. The best answer to this argument is that we have considerable data to counter this argument. A number of cities and businesses have added domestic partners to health plans; the partners have not used the benefit more than others and costs have not gone up because of them.

Contact an institution similar to yours with an existing plan to back up your answer. If you don't know of one, contact one of the national lesbian/gay organizations for a referral. There aren't any studies about why domestic partners cost the same as spouses. People who work with the plans note that AIDS actually is far from the most expensive disease to treat and suggest that domestic partners have fewer prohibitively expensive childbirths and heart and lung cases. But there is no hard data.

As for cheating, domestic partners seem at least as honest as everyone else.

When Berkeley, California, opened its health plan to domestic partners in the mid-1980s, many of the first to sign up were heterosexual employees who had previously listed their partners as spouses. The city had never asked for verification of marriage.

36.3

Domestic partnership plans have the potential to create one type of adverse selection that has nothing to do with cheating or illness rates. Occasionally, health insurers will try to negotiate for a domestic partner's surcharge, a perhaps temporary increase in rates to give them a cushion against the possibility that domestic partners will cost more.

These were difficult to oppose when domestic partnership was new and no precedent existed, but there is no reason to accept them now that there is considerable evidence that domestic partners don't cost more. (See section 35.4.)

If your employer accepts a surcharge, and if employees pay all or a part of the cost of covering their spouses and partners, insist that the surcharge be added equally to the charge for all employees, not just those adding domestic partners. Here's why: domestic partnership will be artificially made more expensive than coverage for spouses by the surcharge. Because the cost for domestic partners will be higher, some may not decide to take it. Those who are healthy are more likely to do that than those who are not. So a higher proportion of domestic partners who are signed up could be people who already have health problems. If that happens, it really will be more expensive to cover domestic partners. The surcharge, in other words, may create an "adverse selection" if the only employees signing up are domestic partners who have to pay for it. (See section 33.4.)

36.4 "All the Benefits of Marriage"

This is the favorite rallying cry of opponents. Marriage has two kinds of "benefits." It has intangible social benefits: the respect people and institutions pay to, and the positive assumptions they make about people who are married (for example, that they are stable, loving, willing to take care of each other, etc.). Again, it may be tempting to argue that domestic partnerships deserve those same intangible benefits. But the fact is that giving a relationship a label and slight legal rights does not give it all the respect society gives marriage.

This argument is more with the second type of marriage benefit, that of tangible benefits and legal rights. Most of these are created by state and federal governments. They include the right to inherit if your spouse doesn't have a will; the right to make medical and other decisions for a disabled spouse; deductions from inheritance taxes if a spouse dies; property tax breaks if a spouse dies; continuing Social Security pensions, etc. Virtually none of these benefits are covered by most domestic partnership policies. Some of the "default" systems—things like inheritance and medical decisions—probably should include domestic partners. Be up front if that is your long-term goal. But the many state and federal benefits of marriage are tied to marriage. Local domestic partnership policies won't ever change that.

36.5 "None of the Obligations"

Legally, marriage has two kinds of obligations. First, married people are obligated to provide basic support to each other. In most states, this means that if one spouse can't provide for his or her own basic needs, the other has to. Basic needs usually includes food, shelter, clothing, medical care. It usually requires support at the level at which the couple has lived, if possible.

The obligations of domestic partnership depend on what your proposal says. In a pure registration system that isn't designed to be used for benefit plans, there may be no obligations. You can explain that by saying there aren't any rights either. More typical systems will include a basic general support obligation somewhat more limited than the one that accompanies marriage. The idea is that the system is supposed to be set up for committed couples, hence the obligation, but that it seems unfair to attach extensive legal obligations to a relationship that carries few or no legal benefits.

This argument is particularly effective if the obligations increase when the relationship is recognized, as with plans where the partners are responsible for each other's medical expenses if they get covered on each other's medical plans. (See section 38.9.)

A few plans have the same obligations. While this is problematic, (see sections 38.6–38.9), it allows you to say that domestic partnership has all of the obligations and few or none of the benefits.

36.5

> In Berkeley, California, some of the proponents of its unusual registration law say they deliberately gave domestic partners the same support obligations that married people have, even though they don't get the comparable help of health and government benefit plans. "We wanted to show we were responsible by taking on all the obligations first," they say.

The second obligation is "marital property," which isn't really an obligation at all. In most states, married people have a legal right to share in each other's earnings. Since the obligation to share comes with a right to share, "marital property" or "community property" is really an even swap of rights and obligations (at least in the abstract). Although domestic partnership plans could have similar rights, most states have very differing rules (as in marital property) duplicating this would greatly duplicate your proposal; just referring to them won't really tell people who sign what they are getting into.

36.6 All the Drawbacks and None of the Benefits of Marriage

This critique typically comes from people who favor non-marital relationships. It comes a bit closer to the truth, especially on the benefits side, as domestic partnership has few of the tangible or intangible benefits of marriage.

The question of obligations is determined by how you define domestic partnership. The most important thing you can do is simply be clear about what the obligations are and how they compare to marriage.

Sometimes this argument surfaces from advocates for persons with AIDS or other serious disabilities and those who worry about the effect domestic partnership will have on benefit eligibility. Some government benefit plans—SSI, some Medicaid, and some food stamps—make eligibility depend on your income. Many of those plans assume that a spouse's income above a certain base amount is available to you, and include it in figuring your income to decide on eligibility for benefits ("imputed income").

"Imputed income" works like this: Suppose the Medicaid rules were to say that you can get Medicaid if you make less than $500 per month. Suppose they were to say you get all your medical bills paid if you make less than $250 per month, and half paid if you make between $250 and $500. If you make only $200 a month, you'll receive the full benefit. An important income rule would say, for example, that anything your spouse makes over $500 a month is "available" and will be counted as yours, regardless of whether you actually get any of it. So if your spouse makes $700 per month, $200 will be counted as yours, and you'll receive half the benefit. If your spouse makes $800 a month, you won't be eligible at all.

You may need to consult an expert, but, generally speaking, all federal programs only impute the income of "spouses," and define as "spouses" those who are married under state law. Domestic partnership is not considered a marriage.

Occasionally opponents will seize on the fact that domestic partnership is not likely to be a disqualifying factor in benefit programs as further evidence of the "all the benefits, none of the obligations" argument. The answer to this is that most of these programs have special benefits for marriage as well; Social Security continues pensions for spouses; Medicaid lets one spouse keep a jointly owned home even though the other is receiving benefits on the basis of poverty. Domestic partners don't get these benefits.

36.7 An Attack on Marriage and the Family

There are two related, very strange, ideas here. The first is that if society recognizes any form of relationship other than marriage, marriage will collapse. For example, the person responsible for blocking San Francisco's first domestic partnership plan told a stunned group of lesbian and gay supporters that if it took effect, women would no longer be able to get men to marry them.

Probably all you need to do to answer this is to point out the faulty assumption; people get married because of its legal consequences.

36.7

Add to that the fact that even if they did, something with as little to offer as domestic partnership would be unlikely to draw many away. Opponents who make this argument probably have less faith in marriage than most people.

The other idea is that recognizing the existence of any other form of relationship somehow demeans marriage. The idea seems to be that personal commitment and love are characteristic of marriage and that admitting that they exist outside of it makes marriage less special.

The best answer to this argument is to point out again that committed relationships exist outside of marriage, and that the failure to recognize them is unjust. Recognizing the dignity of one relationship does not demean the dignity of another.

36.8 Special Benefits for a Small Group

With valuable benefit plans, opponents occasionally argue that the money should be spent on additional benefits for all employees rather than for the small group of employees with domestic partners. For example, when adding domestic partners to San Francisco's health plan was proposed, the system's actuaries proposed a new vision plan instead. The virtue of the plan, the actuaries said, was that it would benefit all employees.

The answer to this is to return to the argument of equal pay for equal work. The point of the domestic partnership proposal is not to give a new special benefit to some, but to equalize the pay of employees who've long been excluded from an important benefit.

36.8

37. WRITING DOMESTIC PARTNERSHIP POLICIES — THE RELATIONSHIP

37.1 Introduction: What this Chapter Covers

This chapter covers the crucial core of domestic partnership policies—the definition of the relationship.

37.2 The Relationship: An Introduction

The heart of any domestic partnership policy is its description of the relationship the partners have created. Four kinds of descriptions are used (some policies use just one, some use all four). First, some policies have very general descriptions of the kind of emotional commitment the partners have to each other; a "hearts and flowers" declaration. (See section 37.4.)

Second, some policies say domestic partners must meet the basic requirements, like age and consent, for marriage; the "marriage requirements." (See section 37.5.)

Third, some policies describe some tangible things many people who live together do (for example, having joint checking accounts or rent receipts in both names), and say two people must have some or all of them to be partners; the "couple's requirements." (See sections 37.6–37.8.)

Finally, some policies have the partners make promises to each other that they will provide for each other in some way; the "obligations." (See section 37.9.)

Some policies, particularly a few pure registration policies, have almost no definition beyond the hearts and flowers declaration. The theory behind them is that since the registration has no legal significance, people should be free to design whatever relationship they wish. However, three forces usually require some requirements and some obligations.

First, the arguments being made for the policy will usually recommend some requirements and obligations. Equality arguments, for

37.2

example, often lead to policies that require that the relationship have characteristics people think typical of marriage and obligations like those that married people assume. (See section 34.3.)

Second, the politics of your campaign may dictate some requirements and obligations, both to gain supporters and to respond to the opposition. (See section 35.2.) Don't underestimate the importance of real obligations to convince people that relationships need recognition. (See section 36.5.)

Finally, and most important, if you have a valuable benefit like a health plan or a free-ride pension, you'll need to have requirements and obligations to make it work.

37.3 Relationship Definitions and Health and Pension Plans

Here is why health and free-ride pension plans need obligations and requirements (free-ride pension plans are explained in section 33.3.)

With perhaps a few rare exceptions, people don't marry so that they can get their partners coverage under health plans or free-ride pension continuations. There are two reasons for this: First, the legal consequences of marriage are considerable. For example, married people are usually responsible for each other's medical expenses; so while your partner gets coverage, you are on the hook for any deductibles, co-payments, expenses not covered, etc. Married people generally have a right to half of each other's earnings. (Some, but not all of these obligations can be changed by agreement, but most people don't do this.) Second, and far more important, the social consequences of marriage are considerable. Society has so many conventions about marriage that by entering it, you inevitably make statements about your own values and, most importantly, about the nature of your relationship. Most people are unwilling to make those statements unless they are in a primary, committed relationship with the person they marry.

Because people generally don't get married to qualify for benefits, a health or pension plan that allows every employee to add one person of his or her choosing to the plan (an "open" plan) will always be more expensive that a plan that allows employees to add spouses. If a plan permits you to add anyone, you might well add a close friend who needed coverage, as long as your partner is covered elsewhere. You will be far less likely to do that if you have to marry your friend, especially if you have to divorce your spouse to do it. The open plan will have more people who were added because they needed coverage than the spouse plan. This means that more people will actually need care (some people will need coverage because they are self-employed, but some will need it because they are sick and, for example, can't work). This means the open plan will cost more.

If your domestic partnership policy is to work, and coverage for domestic partners is to cost the same as coverage for spouses, a domestic partner can't simply be anyone you name. If will have to be someone with whom you really have a committed, somewhat spouse-like relationship. Requirements and obligations help describe that, and, like the social and legal consequences of marriage, they discourage cheating.

37.4 The "Hearts and Flowers" Declaration

Many domestic partnership policies begin by describing the relationship as "intimate," "caring," "loving," "mutually supportive," "interdependent," etc. (See Appendix B, model A, sections 1,2[a].) These declarations are actually important for two reasons. First, the idea usually is to register people who are members of a committed couple, not just good friends or roommates. The declaration discourages people who don't fit it.

For example, a San Francisco pension administrator worried that fire fighters might declare domestic partnerships with sons of coworkers to give them an unjustified pension continuation. After being told that partners had to swear they had "chosen to share one another's lives in an intimate and committed relationship," had to live together, and could not be married to anyone else, the administrator agreed it might not be a problem after all.

37.4

The declaration also gives domestic partnership one of its great advantages to lesbian and gay couples: it provides convincing proof that two people aren't just roommates or good friends. (See section 34.4.)

37.5 The Marriage Requirements

Domestic partnership policies typically have the same minimum-age requirement that marriage does. This varies from state to state. They also typically say that you can have only one domestic partner and that you can't be married to anyone (this seems sensible regardless of whether you think of domestic partnership as a marriage substitute or as an alternative relationship).

Domestic partnership policies also tend to prohibit partnerships between people who are related so closely that they can't marry. To the extent this applies to parent/child, brother/sister, and aunt-uncle/niece-nephew relationships, this probably makes sense. If you want to include those relationships in a recognition or benefit plan, you don't need a new term to describe them. They are generally deliberately excluded from health and pension plans, and domestic partnership shouldn't be a way of bringing them in through the back door.

Many laws incorporate these requirements by referring to them instead of describing them (for example, the partners may not be related in any way that would bar marriage). But since most people have no idea of what the requirements are, it is much better to describe them. (See Appendix B, model C.)

37.6 Couples Requirements, Generally

Domestic partnership plans aimed at equalizing marriage related benefits or at providing a substitute for marriage often require domestic partners to have lots of the characteristics that the writers think are typical of couples. They tend to demand, for example, that to be domestic partners, people have integrated finances, as shown by joint bank accounts, and be jointly responsible for rent and mortgage payments.

37.4

Although many of these things are typical of married couples, few of them are actually required. Some people try to keep the requirements to those actually required for marriage, on the theory that others exclude important relationships and domestic partners should not have to meet requirements married people don't have to meet. The difficulty with minimizing couples requirements is that since you can't duplicate the social consequences of marriage, approximating some of its typical characteristics may be necessary both politically and to make benefit plans work. Some of those approximations are much more important to benefit plans and to the politics of selling a partnership policy than others are.

If you are designing a registration system that will (or might) be used in conjunction with a health plan, you may want to keep the registration system more flexible than the health plan would be. For example, you could put into the registration systems all the "couples requirements" that you think are necessary to make the policy politically acceptable, but leave out the additional requirements needed for a health plan. The health plan can then say that to qualify, you must register and then sign a declaration with the additional requirements. This lets the registration system be used with less benefit.

37.7 Requirements of Couples — Living Together

A shared place to live, although not required for married couples, is so typical of couples that it tends to be politically essential. It is also required by virtually every significant benefit plan. The definition of living together in the models in Appendix B have three important features. First, as long as the couple has a shared living space, they allow either partner to keep a place of his or her own as well. This keeps a lot of nonmarital relationships from being excluded, and it is common enough in marriage to be politically acceptable most of the time.

Second, the definition says the parties don't both have to own or be named on the rental agreement, and don't have to both pay for the home. This is very important. Many people in nonmarital relationships move into one partner's home or apartment and don't change the title,

37.7

for tax reasons, because the landlord might not consent, etc. Especially if one partner becomes ill, the other may pay all of the costs of housing. That shouldn't disqualify people from becoming domestic partners.

Finally, the definitions say the domestic partnership doesn't end if one partner leaves but intends to return. If your proposal has a "slob's dissolution" (see section 38.10.), you need this to make sure the partnership isn't automatically ended if one partner leaves for open-ended stay in, for example, a care facility or another city for a consulting job.

The definition doesn't say anything about principal residences. If a specific benefits plan requires that, you can piggyback it onto a definition used for a registration or for a bundle of benefit plans. (See section 38.3.)

37.8 Other Couples Requirements

Domestic partnership plans often say that couples must "share the common necessaries of life" or the "common necessities of life." The first phrase is taken from old law on marriages, and it means food, shelter, clothing, medical care, and other essentials. The second phrase is an open-ended phrase with no particular meaning. By themselves, both phrases are probably harmless. It is difficult to say what "sharing food and clothing," for example, means. But if coupled with a vague joint obligation, both phrases can be very dangerous. (See section 37.9.) Even without the vague obligation, either phrase could be interpreted to mean the couple has to share the costs of food, shelter, etc., which, again, can be a problem if one member isn't working, is self-employed, is ill, etc. It is just good practice to avoid vague descriptions of the relationship. If you want people to live together, say so.

Some policies are much more specific about what the couple must share, requiring shared finances, joint bank accounts, etc. Some give long lists of things and say the couple must have four or five. Since this kind of sharing isn't required of married couples, isn't done by a fair number, and isn't nearly as helpful in benefit plans as living togethers, none of it is necessary.

37.8

37.9 Financial Obligations

Most domestic partnership policies require the partners to make some promises of care and support to each other during the domestic partnership. These are usually very important to benefit plans. Some use very general language to describe the obligation, saying, for example, that the partners are "responsible for their common welfare" or "responsible for each other's basic welfare." This is a very bad idea, for two reasons. First, the partners don't know what they are obligating themselves to. They may find out only if a creditor of one sues and claims a right to get paid by the other.

Second, this kind of general language could be interpreted to cover all sorts of creditors' claims and serious costs like medical expenses. This is more likely if the definition also uses phrases like "sharing the basic necessaries."

Most health plans insist that if domestic partners are going to be included, the partners be responsible for each other's medical expenses that are not covered by the plan, just as married couples are. Fair as that may be when one partner gets coverage, people should know they are taking the obligation on. And it isn't fair to impose this obligation on people who are just registering but receive none of the economic privileges married couples do.

A better approach is to use relatively specific language for the obligations; for example, "the partners are jointly responsible for the cost of basic food and housing." (See Appendix B, models A and B. *Note*: The models define joint responsibility to mean one partner has to provide for the other if she or he can't provide for herself or himself. This avoids the problem of joint contributions if one person is sick, etc.)

You can resolve the dilemma of not putting too many obligations on people who just register while making the system work for benefits plans either by "piggybacking" additional requirements in the benefit plan (see section 38.3) or by putting a "floater" in the promise. A floater says that the obligations increase or decrease ("float") according to how the relationship is recognized. If a partner is added to a health plan, the partners are responsible for each other's medical expenses,

37.9

but not otherwise. (See Appendix B, model A.) Floaters can also be a potent political tool in arguments about the level of responsibility, since they say, in effect, "beyond a basic obligation, we'll take obligations on to the extent you recognize the relationship."

37.10 Time and Intent Requirements

Many policies and registration systems say that you can't enter a new partnership for a set time after you leave the old one, usually six months. These are very important to health plans in particular. They are the best guarantee against someone dropping a real partner to add someone who isn't truly a partner but who needs the coverage. Since it usually takes at least that long to get divorced, most people don't object to them.

Some benefit plans, especially health plans, require that the relationship exist for six months to a year before a partner becomes eligible. Others say domestic partners can only be added to a plan once a year at an annual open enrollment. There is no parallel restriction on married couples; employees can usually add spouses to a health plan immediately. But again, people rarely marry to qualify for health plans, and domestic partnership doesn't have the social disincentives that marriage does. This is a sensible way to be sure that, like spouses, only a small percentage of people become domestic partners to take advantage of the plan.

37.10

38. WRITING DOMESTIC PARTNERSHIP POLICIES – THE SYSTEM

38.1 Introduction: What this Chapter Covers

Appendix B has model domestic partnership policies. While these were pretty much state of the art when this was written, thinking may have changed by the time you go to work. Check with one of the national lesbian/gay rights organizations to see if there are newer models.

38.2 Two Mechanisms

There are two mechanisms for domestic partnership.

First, there are *registration* mechanisms. These set up a system for couples to create and end domestic partnerships. These are only set up by governments. (See section 38.3.) Second, there are *internal* mechanisms. These are systems set up by institutions, most often employers, to tell the institution that a couple has created a domestic partnership.

Both mechanisms can be used with either a recognition or a benefits policy. The employer, or other institution, can open its recognition system or benefit plan to couples who have registered, or it can make them available to any couple who uses an internal mechanism to establish that they are domestic partners.

Both mechanisms share three characteristics. First, each has a definition or description of what a domestic partnership is. (See chapter 37.) Second, each uses a document, usually called a declaration or affidavit of domestic partnership, to establish or prove the relationship. Finally, each has a system that uses the document, either simply to record the existence of the relationship (as with pure recognition systems) or to run a recognition or benefits system. (See section 32.2.)

38.2

38.3 Use a Registration Mechanism, If You Can

If you are designing a domestic partnership policy for anyone other than a government (like an employer, a hospital or a museum, or a gym or an auto club, etc.), find out if your local government has a domestic partnership registration system. If it doesn't, see if it might be possible to get it to adopt one. If your city has a registration system, you can have the employer, hospital, etc., in which you are working adopt its definition of domestic partnership and its system for having the couples create partnership. Many businesses have adopted domestic partnership policies using "internal" mechanisms instead of government registration mechanisms, so you can do that if you need to. But there are two drawbacks to "internal" systems.

First, internal systems focus on the business's needs. This means they are often ambiguous about aspects of the partnership that can be very important, such as when it starts, when it ends, and exactly what its terms are. Internal systems are usually designed, for example, to inform a human resources department that an employee is in a partnership. This means that they tend not to say when the partnership was created. Similarly, internal systems usually focus on telling the business when a benefit should end, but not necessarily when or if the partnership ended (for example, you might take your partner off your employer's health plan if it requires a contribution to the premium and she or he gets a job with a plan that does not).

Worse, some internal systems are ambiguous about the specifics of the relationship. Like registration systems, internal systems usually set out requirements to be domestic partners. But they often set up "minimum" requirements that they say the partnership must meet. Unlike registration systems, they usually don't say the partners don't have any obligation to each other apart from those requirements.

All this means that if there is a disagreement about some obligation —when it started, when it ended, whether it was included—an internal system may not answer it. But for many domestic partners the document from that system is the only document about the partnership they have. This ambiguity can be a serious problem if the internal system requires that the partners take on significant obligations to each other, or if the system suggests they may have obligations that are not spelled out.

Some employers shy away from government registration systems because they are typically based on a "basic" set of requirements, and the employers need more requirements for complex benefit plans like health plans and pension plans. (See section 37.3.)

This problem can be solved easily by having the employer "piggyback" the additional requirements onto the registration system's definition. The employer simply requires that the domestic partners be registered under the city's system, and that when the partners request the benefit, they sign a declaration stating that they meet the other requirements.

> **San Francisco city employees who want to add a domestic partner to the city's health plan must first register as domestic partners, something anyone who lives or works in the city can do. When they sign up for the benefit, they must declare that they have the same principal residence (the registration law requires only that they share some living quarters) and that both are responsible for each other's medical care (the registration law only requires that the employee who adds his or her partner to the plan be responsible for medical costs).**

While this may seem a little cumbersome, the use of the registration system eliminates most of the problems created by internal systems.

The other drawback to internal plans is that each tends to have its own description of domestic partnership. At some point, too many definitions may make working with domestic partnership unwieldy at best; for example, you shouldn't have to change the legal definition of your relationship because one of you changes job.

38.4 The Agreement Format

Under both internal and registration systems, the domestic partnership is actually created by the agreement of the partners; it is not created by the business of the government. (See Appendix B,

38.4

models A and B.) The idea is that the government or business in effect says to the couple: "If you meet these requirements [like an age or residency requirement] and have agreed to these things [like a support obligation], we will register your relationship [or put your partner on the health plan, etc.]."

The agreement format is very important. Most courts that have decided cases on the issue say two people can make agreements about their relationship the same way they can make other types of contracts. It is very doubtful, however, that a city or a business could "create" any sort of legal relationship.

38.5 The Declaration of Domestic Partnership

At the core of every domestic partnership system is a document, usually called a declaration or affidavit of domestic partnership. With registration mechanisms, the declaration is usually the agreement by which the partners create the relationship. With internal mechanisms, the declaration is usually a statement that the partners have made an agreement creating a domestic partnership at some point, a kind of "notice of an agreement."

Declarations for internal systems should say when the partnership was created. But they should be clear that the date marks when the relationship took on all the required characteristics and the partners made the agreement, not the date they became a couple. (See Appendix B, model A-2.)

Declarations typically have the partners say that they meet all of the requirements for domestic partnership. Registration declarations usually have the partners make whatever promises are required; internal systems typically have the partners say they have made the necessary promises. (See sections 2[d] in both models A and B in Appendix B.)

Declarations should be written straightforwardly, so that anyone can understand them. The declaration should also list the requirements and promises instead of just referring to them as a group (the "requirements to be domestic partners"). You want to make sure that people who sign up understand what they are saying.

38.6 Signing Requirements

To be an agreement, a declaration has to be signed by both parties. Even with an internal system where the declaration is a "notice of an agreement," it makes sense to have both partners say they have agreed, especially since the declaration is often the only written record for the agreement. Most declarations are either sworn or notarized or both. Requiring that the statement be sworn is some assurance that the people who sign it are serious.

Notarization is some assurance that neither signature was forged, since people have to appear in person before a notary and give proof of identification. Instead of requiring notarization, some registration systems require both partners to sign the declaration in front of the clerk who will file it. Notarization can also be a way to establish an informal registration system. (See section 38.8.)

38.7 Registration Systems

Most registration systems have the partners file the declaration with a local official, usually a city or county clerk. Some give the partners a stamped copy, showing that the original was filed. Others give the partners a certificate saying the declaration was filed.

Some registration systems restrict use to locals. If you plan to do this, make sure that registration is open to any couple that lives in the city, and any couple at least one of whom works in the city. Otherwise, local employers won't be able to use the registration system effectively.

In some states, filed declarations will be public records, available to anyone who want to see them. This is a matter of concern to some couples, especially lesbian and gay couples. Some worry because one or both are not "out" to family or at work; others worry that the system can be used to target lesbian and gay couples for harassment. Whether the declarations will be public records or not is usually a matter of state law, which you can't change by putting a confidentiality provision in your policy. Get your lawyer to find out. If the declarations will be public, make sure couples who go to sign up are warned, either on the declaration or in a flyer handout given to anyone who signs up. If you

38.7

can't make the declarations confidential, think about providing an informal registration system.

38.8 Informal Registration

A few registration systems allow couples to create domestic partnerships with an "informal" registration system. These usually require a sworn statement, a witness, and notarization. (See Appendix B, model A, section 3.) Informal systems usually require that the witness be given a copy of the declaration. That, along with the notarization, provides at least some independent record of the partnership.

38.9 Recognition, Registration, and Benefits: Hybrid Policies

If you plan to propose both a government registration system which will be generally available to couples and some type of benefit plan for government employees, you might want to keep the policies separate even if you decided to campaign for both at the same time. The government benefit plan is likely to have requirements you won't want to include in a registration system open to everyone. You also want to make sure people understand that only government employees are eligible for the benefits plan.

If you plan to advocate a government registration system and a government recognition system that will use the same definition as the registration system, you may want to keep them together. Typical examples of recognition systems include jail visitation policies and hospital visitation policies. Hospital leave policies are a bit tricky, since you want domestic partners to have access, but not over a patient's objections or if it might be truly harmful. (See Appendix B, model D-1.)

You can have your government agency adopt a general nondiscrimination policy; that is, a statement that it will treat domestic partners like spouses. This may make sense given the limited ways local government recognizes marriage. However, this kind of language can spark odious arguments about whether domestic partnerships are "equal" to marriage, and provide your opponents with fuel. (See section 34.3.)

38.8

You could adopt a government system that also requires private businesses, including employers, landlords, etc., not to discriminate. Provisions like these can have a limited effect. As explained in section 32.4, state and local government governments cannot require employers to include domestic partners in most benefit plans. They may be able to require domestic partnership to be included in recognition systems or benefit plans that are not financially significant.

They also may be able to require other businesses, like gyms, clubs, etc., which have couples rates, to recognize domestic partnerships. This is largely a matter of what kind of power your government has. (See section 32.2.) Mandatory nondiscrimination policies may be more trouble than they are worth. They almost automatically start equality debates (see section 34.3.), and they can make opponents out of businesses who would use the policy if it were voluntary. (See section 33.5.)

38.10 Ending the Partnership

Most registration systems set up a process for people to end domestic partnerships. Under all of the systems, either partner can end the relationship by sending a notice saying it is over to the other. If the declaration of domestic partnership was filed, the notice that it is over should usually be filed.

Some systems say the notice should be sent to the address shown on the declaration, and then allow people to amend the declaration to update addresses. A lot of people may not bother with that kind of bureaucracy, and for most partnerships, where the partner will be easy to locate, it seems unnecessary. It may be simpler and better just to say that you must give notice to your partner.

If the domestic partnership was used in any benefits or recognition systems, the domestic partner who told the system about the partnership usually has to tell it that the partnership is over. Usually, the partner must do that within a certain time, often sixty days of the day the partnership ends. Most laws provide that partnerships end automatically if a partner dies or gets married. In the first case, requiring a notice to end the partnership seems silly.

38.10

Ending the partnership automatically if either partner marries is designed to deal with a delicate problem. Marriage is created by state law. If the partners were to agree when they created the domestic partnership that neither would marry unless the partnership were first dissolved, the policy might be subject to legal attack as interfering with the state-created right to marry. Saying that the partnership ends automatically on marriage avoids the problem.

Some policies provide that the partnership ends if the partners stop living together. This is designed to take care of a very practical problem. Since domestic partnership doesn't have the social and legal consequences of marriage (see section 37.3), there is a greater risk that people will end their relationships simply by separating, and won't bother with the ending notice. The problem is that is the partnership carries obligations, the obligations would continue, and one partner could find him or herself responsible for a former partner's debts long after the partnership had dissolved.

Domestic partners are unlikely to foresee that possibility. Perhaps with a relationship to which society attaches the serious consequences and recognition that it give to marriage, it makes sense to let people who don't follow the formalities suffer the consequences. With a relationship as scantily recognized as domestic partnership that seems less fair.

If you include a "slob's dissolution" provision, make sure you say in your "living together" definition that the relationship won't dissolve if one partner leaves but intends to return. (See appendix B, model A, section 2-b.)

38.11 Spelling Out the Consequences

In addition to being clear about the obligations domestic partners have to each other, a good policy puts clear limits on those obligations. Couples who are domestic partners can have additional agreements between themselves, including legally enforceable agreements. They could agree, for example, to share earnings like married people do. However, the policy should make it clear that signing a declaration is evidence only of the obligations it describes, and that it neither creates nor implies any others. Neither a partner nor anyone else should be able to use it to suggest other obligations. (See Appendix B, model A.)

A registration policy should also make it clear that the promises the partners make to each other only cover obligations which are created while the partnership exists. (See Appendix B, model A.) Since internal policies don't generally address creating and ending the relationship, it is tough to include this limit in that kind of policy.

38.14

Appendix A

Each of these models needs some customizing. Places where you need to choose alternative wording, or where you need to supply local information, are shown in [brackets].

Most of the models also need a few words of explanation. The explanations are printed in regular type; the actual wording of the models is contained in *italic*.

Most of the models use the phrase "actual or perceived" after the words "sexual orientation." If you include a definition of sexual orientation in your proposal, the "actual or perceived" phrase should be in your definition, so you can drop it from the text of the law or policy.

MODEL A
The Drop In

The typical "drop in" repeats the whole text of whatever law or policy you are amending and simply adds the phrase "sexual orientation" at the end of each list of groups protected by the law. Many

A

drop ins also add a new section, defining sexual orientation. (See Model H for the wording of possible definitions.)

If you use this kind of a drop in, you'll probably need a short statement explaining the policy. Here is a suggestion:

> *This amendment to [name of city or business or other institution]'s nondiscrimination [law or policy] adds sexual orientation to the list of characteristics which cannot be used to discriminate. It adds the words "sexual orientation" to each list of people whom the [law or policy] protects.*

Here is an alternative model for a drop in; this model combines the drop in itself with the short statement, for a proposal that describes how the drop in works.

> *The phrase "sexual orientation" is added to each list of protected groups in [for a government, insert name and legal reference to civil rights law; for business or other institution, insert name of civil rights policy].*

MODEL B
The "Piggyback"

> *This [law or policy] makes discrimination based on sexual orientation (actual or perceived) illegal under [name of city or business or other institutions]'s [law or policy] which forbids discrimination based on race, religion, marital status, sex, national origin [adjust this list so it contains the groups covered by the existing law or policy] ([for a government, insert the name and legal reference to the existing law or policy here; for a business or other institution, insert the name of the policy]). [To explain the way the law works, you can add this:] To do this, this [law or policy] adds the phrase "sexual orientation" to each list of groups protected by [name of the civil rights law or policy you are amending].*

MODEL C
The Simple Statement

C-1. For a business, nonprofit, university, or similar institution, or for a government that is adopting a policy or a law that will apply to itself:

> *[Name of business, etc.] will not discriminate in any way on the basis of sexual orientation (actual or perceived).*

C-2. For a government that is adopting a policy or a law to require that those who do business with it agree not to discriminate:

> *Anyone who sells goods or services to the city under a written contract, or who rents property from the city, must agree not to discriminate on the basis of sexual orientation [if necessary (see below) add "in performing the contract or in using the property"]. Therefore, every written contract or rental agreement signed by the [name of city or other agency] will have the following term:*
>
> *[Name of business, etc.] agrees that it will not discriminate in any way on the basis of sexual orientation (actual or perceived) [if necessary (see below) add "in performing the contract or in using the property"]. This term of the contract is intended to benefit and may be enforced by anyone who is discriminated against.*

Some laws make anyone who has a contract with the city agree not to discriminate at all. The model does this if you **do not** include the words in quotes in the brackets. Some laws say that the person with the contract only has to agree not to discriminate in performing the contract. The quoted words in the brackets add that limitation.

Ordinarily, only one of the parties to a contract can enforce it. The last sentence makes it possible for a person who is discriminated against to enforce the agreement.

C-3. For a government that is adopting a law to eliminate discrimination in employment, housing, city services, and businesses throughout the area it governs:

A

279

> *Discrimination in employment, housing, city facilities or services or by businesses on the basis of sexual orientation (actual or perceived) is illegal in [name of city or county, etc.]. [Add one or more of the following, as appropriate: "This law can be enforced in a civil lawsuit for any appropriate remedy," "This law can be enforced with a complaint to the [insert name of local commission with the power to hear complaints]," "Violation of this law is a misdemeanor."*

MODEL D
The Stand Alone

The [insert the name of the board here] of [insert the name of the city or other agency here] ordains:

Section 1. Findings and Policy

(a) Policy. It is the policy of [name of city or agency] to make sure that no one in [the city or other description of jurisdiction] is subject to discrimination because of her or his sexual orientation.

(b) Findings. The [name of board] has held public hearings and has considered testimony and documentary evidence. The [name of board] finds that discrimination based on sexual orientation exists in [name of city or agency]. The [name of board] finds that discrimination is a serious threat to the health, safety, and general welfare of this community. Discrimination creates strife and unrest, and it deprives the city of its full capacity for development. By throwing able persons out of work and good tenants out of their homes, discrimination is expensive to [the city or other agency], both because of lost productivity and because it increases the demand for services from [the city or other agency]. The [name of board] finds that existing state and federal laws against arbitrary discrimination do not meet this community's needs, so

that it is necessary to pass local regulations adapted to the special circumstances which exist here.

(c) *Construction and Interpretation.* It is the intent of the [name of board] that this [law, ordinance, or policy] be interpreted broadly so that it will prevent as much discrimination as possible.

Section 2. Definitions

(a) *Business Establishment.* "Business establishment" means any person who provides goods, services, or accommodations to the public. A business which has membership requirements is still a "business establishment" if its membership requirements: (1) consist only of fees; or (2) consist of requirements under which five percent or more of the residents of this [city or other agency] could qualify; or (3) include requirements which are illegal under this [law, ordinance, or policy].

(b) *Discrimination.* To "discriminate" means to subject anyone to different or separate treatment because of her or his actual or perceived sexual orientation.

(c) *Person.* "Person" means any human being and any firm, corporation, partnership, or other organization, association or group of persons however organized.

Section 3. Illegal Practices

(a) *In General.* It is illegal for any person to discriminate against any person because of his or her sexual orientation in:

(1) *Employment:* any aspect of employment, opportunities for employment, or union membership;

(2) *Real Estate:* any real estate transaction, including the sale, repair, improvement, lease, rental, or occupancy of any interest in real property, and the extension of credit, financing, insurance, or services in connection with any of those transactions.

(3) *Business Establishments:* the availability or provision of goods or services from any business establishment;

(4) *City Services and Facilities:* the use or availability of any municipal service or facility; and

(5) *City-Supported Services and Facilities:* the use or availability of any service or facility that is supported by the city.

(b) *Association and Retaliation.* It is illegal to discriminate against any person in any of the areas mentioned in the section above because of the sexual orientation of any person with whom she or he associates. It is illegal to discriminate against any person because she or he supports this act, opposes any act which it makes illegal, exercises any right under it, or assists anyone in any way with exercising her or his rights under it.

(c) *Exceptions.*

(1) *Employment*:

(A) *Bona Fide Occupational Qualifications.*

(i) *Bona Fide Occupational Qualifications.* This [law, ordinance, or policy] does not prohibit hiring on the basis of a bona fide occupational qualification.

(ii) *Burden of Proof.* In any lawsuit under this [law, ordinance, or policy], if a party asserts that an otherwise illegal act of discrimination is justified as a bona fide occupational qualification, that party shall have the burden of proving: 1) that the discrimination is in fact a necessary result of a bona fide occupational qualification; and 2) that there exists no less discriminatory way to satisfy the qualification.

(B) *Seniority Systems.* It is not illegal for an employer to observe the conditions of a contractual seniority system as long as the system is not a subterfuge to evade the purposes of this [law, ordinance, or policy]. The terms of a seniority system will not provide an excuse for failure to hire any person.

(2) *City-Supported Services and Facilities.* Subsection 3(a)(5) of this [law, ordinance, or policy] does not apply to facilities or services which only receive assistance from the city which is provided to the public generally.

(d) *Notices.*

(1) *Requirements.* Every employer with fifteen or more employees, every labor organization with fifteen or more members, and every employment agency shall post in conspicuous places where notices to employees, applicants for employment, and members are usually posted, this notice:

> *"Discrimination on the basic of sexual orientation is prohibited by law. [Insert reference to this law]."*

(2) *Alternate Compliance.* This subsection may be complied with by adding the words "sexual orientation" to all notices required by federal or state law, and saying on the notice that discrimination on the basis of sexual orientation is prohibited by [insert reference to this law].

(e) *Advertising.* It is illegal for any person to advertise that he or she does or will do anything which this [law, ordinance, or policy] prohibits.

Section 4. Civil Remedy

Any person who violates any provision of section 3(a) will be liable for compensatory damages, costs and attorneys' fees, and a penalty of at least $1,000.00 and not more than $10,000.00.

Section 5. Criminal Liability

(a) Anyone who violates Section 3(a) or who aids or incites a violation, is guilty of a misdemeanor.

(b) Any person who willfully violates section 3(c) is guilty of an infraction. He or she may be punished by a fine of not more than Fifty Dollars ($50.00) for each offense.

Section 6. Civil Enforcement

(a) *Civil Lawsuit.* Any aggrieved person may enforce this [law, ordinance, or policy] in a civil lawsuit.

A

(b) *Injunctions*. Any person may bring a civil lawsuit to enjoin any person who commits or proposes to commit a violation of this [law, ordinance, or policy].

Section 7. Limitation of Lawsuits

Lawsuits must by filed within two years of the alleged discriminatory acts.

Section 8. Severability

If any part of this [law, ordinance, or policy] or any application of it to any person or circumstance is held invalid, the rest of the [law, ordinance, or policy], including its application to other persons or circumstances, shall not be affected and shall continue in full force and effect. To this end, provisions of this [law, ordinance, or policy] are severable and are intended to have independent validity.

Section 9. Waivers

Any agreement (written or oral) which says that anyone gives up any right under this [law, ordinance, or policy] is against public policy and void.

MODEL E
Exceptions

E-1. Exception for benefit plans

This [law or policy] does not prohibit the use of marital status limitations in health [and pension] plans if they are otherwise legal.

E-2. Quotas

This [law or policy] does not require [or permit] the use of quotas.

E-3. Quota and like devices

This law does not require [or permit] the use of quotas or other similar devices.

E-4. Free Exercise of Religion

This law does not limit the free exercise of religion guaranteed by the United States Constitution.

E-5. Free Exercise of Religion (descriptive)

This [law, policy, or ordinance] does not apply to employment of those who perform ministerial duties (teaching or spreading the faith, performing devotional services or church governance) for an organization whose primary purpose and function is religious. This law does not prevent that kind of organization from restricting membership, services, or use of its facilities to those who are members of the same religion.

E-6. Housing—Roommates

The section[s] of this [law or policy] on housing discrimination do not apply to renting space in a single housing unit.

E-7. Housing—Small Dwellings

The section[s] of this [law or policy] on housing discrimination do not apply to renting space in a building which is owner-occupied and which has fewer than four units.

MODEL F
Denials

F-1. Criminal Law Denial

This [law, policy, or ordinance] does not legalize any act which is illegal under [name of state] law.

F-2. Teaching Denial

This [law, policy, or ordinance] does not require the teaching of anything.

A

F-3. Approval Denial

This [law, policy, or ordinance] expresses neither approval nor disapproval of any person or group of persons.

MODEL G

Impact Sections

G-1. Impact Cases Are Covered

This [law, policy, or ordinance] applies to practices which have a disparate impact on the basis of sexual orientation.

G-2. Marital Status Impact Cases Are Covered

This [law, policy, or ordinance] applies to acts, practices, or policies based on marital status which have a disproportionate impact based on sexual orientation.

G-3. Business Necessity Defense to Impact Cases

Acts or practices which have a disproportionate impact on the basis of sexual orientation are not illegal if the person doing them can show they are job related and consistent with business necessity.

MODEL H

Definitions of Sexual Orientation

H-1. The Classic

Sexual Orientation. "Sexual orientation" means heterosexuality, homosexuality, or bisexuality, actual or perceived.

H-2. Lesbian or Gay

Discrimination Based on Sexual Orientation. "Discrimination based on sexual orientation" means any kind of separate or different treatment because a person is (or is perceived to be) a heterosexual, a lesbian, a gay man, or a bisexual.

(If you use the second definition in the "stand alone" (Model D), you should drop the definition of discrimination.)

A

Appendix B

DOMESTIC PARTNERSHIP

Places where these models need local information are shown in [brackets].

MODEL A

Basic Domestic Partnership Registration Law

Generally for use by governments (cities, counties, states, etc.).

Recognition of Domestic Partnerships

Sec. 1. Purpose

The purpose of this ordinance is to create a way to recognize intimate, committed relationships.

Sec. 2. Definitions

(a) *Domestic Partners.* Domestic partners are two adults who have chosen to share one another's lives in an intimate and committed relationship of mutual caring. The requirements to be domestic partners are:

1) the two must live together;
2) the two must agree to be jointly responsible for each other's basic living expenses during the domestic partnership;
3) neither person may be married or a member of another domestic partnership;
4) the two must not be related in a way which would prevent them from being married to each other;
5) both must be over 18;
6) the two must sign a Declaration of Domestic Partnership and establish the partnership under section 3.

(b) "*Live Together*." "Live together" means that two people share the same place to live. It is not necessary that the legal right to posses the place be in both of their names. Two people may live together even if one or both have additional places to live. Domestic partners do not cease to live together if one leaves the shared place but intends to return.

(c) "*Joint Responsibility for Basic Living Expenses*." "Basic living expenses" means basic food and shelter. It also includes any other costs (for example, medical care costs) for which a partner is receiving some reimbursement or benefit (for example, health-care benefits) because she or he is a member of a domestic partnership. "Joint responsibility" means that each partner agrees to provide for the other partner's basic living expenses if the partner is unable to provide for herself of himself. Anyone to whom these expenses are owed can enforce this responsibility.

(d) "*Declaration of Domestic Partnership*." A "Declaration of Domestic Partnership" is a form provided by [name official]. By signing it, two people swear under penalty of perjury that they meet the requirements of the definition of domestic partnership when they sign the statement. This form will require each partner to provide a mailing address.

Sec. 3. Establishing a Domestic Partnership

(a) *Methods*. Two persons may establish a domestic partnership by either:

1) presenting a signed Declaration of Domestic Partnership to

the [name official], who will file it and give the partners a certificate showing that the declaration was filed; or

2) having a Declaration of Domestic Partnership notarized and giving a copy to the person who witnesses the signing (who may or may not be the notary).

(b) *Time Limitation.* A person cannot become a member of a domestic partnership until at least six months after any other domestic partnership of which he or she was a member ended and a notice that the partnership ended was given. This does not apply if the earlier domestic partnership ended because one of the members died.

Sec. 4. Ending Domestic Partnerships

(a) *When the Partnership Ends.* A domestic partnership ends when:

1) one partner sends the other a written notice that he or she has ended the partnership; or

2) one of the partners dies; or

3) one of the partners marries or the partners no longer live together.

(b) *Notice the Partnership Has Ended.*

(1) *To Domestic Partners.* When a domestic partnership ends for a reason other than the death of one of the partners, at least one of the partners must sign a notice saying that the partnership has ended. The notice must be dated and signed under penalty of perjury. If the Declaration of Domestic Partnership was filed with the [name official], the notice must be filed with the [name official]; otherwise, the notice must be notarized. The partner who signs the notice must send a copy to the other partner.

(2) *To Third Parties.* When a domestic partnership ends, a domestic partner who has given a copy of a Declaration of Domestic Partnership to any third party in order to qualify for any financially valuable benefit (or, if that partner has died, the surviving member of the partnership) must give the third party a notice signed under penalty of perjury saying that the partnership has ended. The notice must be sent within sixty days of the end of the partnership. A third party who suffers loss as a result of fail-

ure to send this notice may sue the partner who was obliged to send it for actual loss.

(3) *Failure to Give Notice.* Failure to give either of the notices required by this subsection will neither prevent nor delay ending the domestic partnership.

Sec. 5. [Name of Official]'s Records

(a) *Amendments to Declarations.* A partner may amend a Declaration of Domestic Partnership filed with the [name of official] at any time to show a change in his or her mailing address.

(b) *New Declarations of Domestic Partnership.* No person who has filed a Declaration of Domestic Partnership with the [name of official] may file another Declaration of Domestic Partnership until six months after a notice the partnership has ended has been filed. However, if the domestic partnership ended because one of the partners died, a new declaration may be filed anytime after the notice the partnership ended is filed.

(c) *Maintenance of City Clerk's Records.* The [name of official] will keep a record of all Declarations of Domestic Partnership, Amendments to Declarations of Domestic Partnership, and all notices that a partnership has ended. The records will be maintained so that amendments and notices a partnership has ended are filed with the Declarations of Domestic Partnership to which they apply.

(d) *Filing Fees.* The City Council will set the filing fee for Declarations of Domestic Partnership and Amendments. No fee will be charged for notices that a partnership has ended. The fees charged must cover the cost of administering this [law/ordinance].

Sec. 6. Legal Effect of Declaration of Domestic Partnership

(a) *Obligations.* The obligations of domestic partners to each other are those described in the definition.

(b) *Duration of Rights and Duties.* If a domestic partnership ends, the partners incur no further obligations to each other.

MODEL B
Basic Domestic Partnership Policy

For use by businesses, universities, and other institutions when a benefits or recognition system needs a detailed definition of domestic partnership.

1. Domestic Partners.

The requirements for two people to be domestic partners are:
1) the partners must live together;
2) the partners must agree to be jointly responsible for each other's basic living expenses during the domestic partnership;
3) neither partner may be married or a member of another domestic partnership;
4) the partners must not be related in way which would prevent them from being married to each other;
5) both must be over 18;
6) neither partner must have had a different domestic partner in the previous six months (this requirement does not apply if the partner died);
7) the partners must sign a Declaration of Domestic Partnership.

2. Definitions.

"Live Together." "Live together" means that two people share the same place to live. It is not necessary that the legal right to possess the place be in both of their names. Two people may live together even if one or both have additional living places. Domestic partners do not cease to live together if one leaves the shared place but intends to return.

"Joint Responsibility for Basic Living Expenses." "Basic living expenses" means basic food and shelter. It also includes any other costs (for example, medical care costs) for which a partner is receiving some reimbursement or benefit (for example, health-care benefits) because she or he is a member of a domestic partnership. "Joint responsibility"

B

means that each partner agrees to provide for the other partner's basic living expenses if the partner is unable to provide for herself or himself. Anyone to whom these expenses are owed can enforce this responsibility.

"*Declaration of Domestic Partnership.*" A "Declaration of Domestic Partnership" is a statement signed under penalty of perjury. By signing it, the two people say they have agreed to take on all the obligations in the definition of domestic partnership and swear that they meet all the requirements of the definition. Each must provide a mailing address.

3. Ending Domestic Partnerships.

A domestic partnership ends when:

1) one partner sends the other a written notice that he or she has ended the partnership; or

2) one of the partners dies; or

3) one of the partners marries or the partners no longer live together.

4. Notice the Partnership Has Ended.

When a domestic partnership ends the partner/employee (or if that partner has died, the surviving partner) must sign a notice saying that the partnership has ended and give it to [name of department]. The notice must be dated and signed under penalty of perjury. The notice must be sent within sixty days of the end of the partnership. If [name of company] or any benefits provider suffers loss as a result of failure to send this notice, it may sue the partner who was obliged to send it for actual loss. The partner who signs the notice must send a copy to the other partner. Failure to give the notice will neither prevent nor delay ending the domestic partnership.

5. Effect of Domestic Partnership.

The obligations which domestic partners have to each other for this plan are those described in the definition. If a domestic partnership ends under this plan, the partners incur no further obligations to each other.

B

MODEL C
Domestic Partnership Declarations

C-1. Declaration for Registration Systems
Declaration of Domestic Partnership

We declare under penalty of perjury:

1. We have an intimate, committed relationship of mutual caring;
2. We live together (see definition on the other side of this page);
3. We agree to be responsible for each other's basic living expenses (see definition on the other side of this page) during our domestic partnership; we also agree that anyone who is owed these expenses can collect from either of us;
4. We are both 18 or older;
5. Neither of us is married and neither of us is related to the other as a parent, brother or sister, half brother or sister, niece, nephew, aunt, uncle, grandparent or grandchild;
6. Neither of us has a different domestic partner now and neither of us has had a different domestic partner in the last six months (this last condition does not apply if you had a partner who died; if you did, cross this out).

We declare under penalty of perjury under the laws of the State of [insert name of state; some states do not use declarations under penalty of perjury for sworn statements; use whatever form your state uses for sworn statements] that the statements above are true and correct.

Signed on _____ , 19 _____

in _____

Signature _____

Print Name _____

Signed on _____ , 19 _____

in _____

Signature _____

Print Name _____

YOU MUST ALSO FILL OUT THE OTHER SIDE OF THIS FORM

B

1. Definitions

"*Live together*" means that the two of you share a place to live. You don't both have to be on the rental agreement or deed. It is okay if one or both of you has a separate place somewhere else. Even if one of you leaves the place you share, you still live together as long as the one who left intends to return.

"*Basic living expenses*" means the cost of basic food and shelter. It also includes any other expense which is paid by a benefit you or your partner gets because of the partnership. For example, if you get health insurance from your job, and the insurance covers your partner, you will be responsible for medical bills which the insurance does not pay. You don't have to split basic living expenses to be domestic partners. You just have to agree to provide these things for your partner if he or she can't provide for him or herself.

2. Address: Each of you should fill in your mailing address here:

Name

_____

Address

_____

City, State & Zip Code

Name

_____

Address

_____

City, State & Zip Code

_____

3. The Last Step: To finish setting up a domestic partnership, you must EITHER:

     (1) File this form with the [name of city or county] Clerk; or

     (2) Sign this form in front of a Notary Public and have the Notary fill in the notarization at the bottom of this page.

[If your registration system will allow people the option of creating domestic partnerships by signing notarized statements instead of filing with the city or county, you should include whatever form notaries use in your state on the declaration form].

B

C-2. Declaration for Internal Systems

Declaration of Domestic Partnership

We declare under penalty of perjury:

1. We live together (see definition on the other side of this page);
2. We agree to be responsible for each other's basic living expenses (see definition on the other side of this page) during our domestic partnership; we also agree that anyone who is owed these expenses can collect from either of us;
3. We are both 18 or older;
4. Neither of us is married and neither of us is related to the other as a parent, brother or sister, half brother or sister, niece, nephew, aunt, uncle, grandparent or grandchild;
5. Neither of us has a different domestic partner now and neither of us has had a different domestic partner in the last six months (this last condition does not apply if you had a partner who died; if you did, cross this out).
6. We have been domestic partners since_____
   and we made the agreement described in paragraph 2 on
   _____   _____.

We declare under penalty of perjury under the laws of the State of [insert name of state; some states do not use declarations under penalty of perjury for sworn statements; use whatever form your state uses for sworn statements] that the statements above are true and correct.

B

Signed on _____ , 19 _____

in _____

Signature _____

Print Name _____

Signed on _____ , 19 _____

in _____

Signature _____

Print Name _____

YOU MUST ALSO FILL OUT THE OTHER SIDE OF THIS FORM

1. Definitions

"*Live together*" means that the two of you share a place to live. You don't both have to be on the rental agreement or deed. It is okay if one or both of you has a separate place somewhere else. Even if one of you leaves the place you share, you still live together as long as the one who left intends to return.

"*Basic living expenses*" means the cost of basic food and shelter. It also includes any other expense which is paid by a benefit you or your partner gets because of the partnership. For example, if you get health insurance from your job, and the insurance covers your partner, you will be responsible for medical bills which the insurance does not pay. You don't have to split basic living expenses to be domestic partners. You just have to agree to provide these things for your partner if he or she can't provide for him or herself.

2. Address: Each of you should fill in your mailing address here:

Name
_____

Address
_____

City, State & Zip Code
_____

Name
_____

Address
_____

City, State & Zip Code
_____

MODEL D
Special Sections

Model D-1. Hospital Visitation.

(a). When a health-care facility restricts a patient's visitors, the health-care facility shall allow every patient to name those individuals whom the patient wishes to allow to visit, unless:

(1) no visitors are allowed; or

(2) the facility decides that the presence of a particular visitor named by the patient would endanger the health or safety of a patient, or would endanger the primary operations of the facility.

(b). If a patient with whom visiting is restricted has not made the designation described in subsection (a), and if the patient has not stated that she or he wishes no visitors, the facility must allow the patient's domestic partner, the children of the patient's domestic partner, and the domestic partner of the patient's parent or child to visit, unless:

(1) no visitors are allowed; or

(2) the facility decides that the presence of a particular visitor named by the patient would endanger the health or safety of a patient, or would endanger the primary operations of the facility.

Model D-2. General Nondiscrimination.

The [city or name of other institution] will treat people who are related as domestic partners in the same way it treats people who are related as spouses.

Model D-3. Residents Only Limit.

[Add this section to your domestic partnership registration law if only those who live or work in the city can file official declarations.]

Section [fill in number]. The [name of official who will file declarations] will only file a Declaration of Domestic Partnership if:

1. the partners have a residence in [name of city or county]; or
2. at least one of the partners works in [name of city or county].

[Then add the following to the end of the declaration form:]

To be able to file this form with the [name of official], one of you must work in [name of city or county] OR both of you live together in [name of city or county] explanation below).

[ ] Check here to state that one of you works in San Francisco.
[ ] Check here to state that you live together in San Francisco.

You don't have to check either space if you finish setting up your domestic partnership by getting this declaration notarized.

Appendix C

ACLU FACT SHEET

AB 101 (FRIEDMAN)

AB 101 is legislation that gives lesbians, gay men, and heterosexuals the civil right to be free from discrimination on the job and in housing. AB 101 adds "sexual orientation" to the list of protected categories in the state Fair Employment and Housing Act.

Q: Doesn't the law already prohibit discrimination based on sexual orientation?

Employment. California law now says that state and local governments cannot discriminate on the basis of sexual orientation. It also says that private employers cannot discriminate against people who are openly gay. Private employment discrimination against lesbians and gay men who are not open, and against heterosexuals, is not now illegal. In addition, state and local employees and gay men and lesbians who are open cannot make complaints to the Department of Fair Employment and Housing, the special state agency that enforces our employment discrimination laws.

AB 101 would prohibit all job discrimination based on sexual orientation (except by small employers or religious employers, who are exempt) and it would give the Department of Fair Employment and Housing the power to enforce this law.

Housing. The courts have said that housing discrimination based on sexual orientation is now illegal under California's Unruh Act. Many people don't know that, however, since the Unruh Act does not actually mention sexual orientation. Adding "sexual orientation" to the Fair Employment and Housing Act will let everyone know what the law is.

Q: Are lesbians and gay men really discriminated against?

Reliable studies show that we need to include sexual orientation in the Fair Employment and Housing Act. For example:

* A 1970's National Institute of Mental Health study showed that 16% of all gay and lesbian workers experience employment difficulties and that 9% lose their jobs because they are lesbian or gay.
* A 1987 *Wall Street Journal* poll showed that 66% of the heads of Fortune 500 companies who answered a survey would hesitate to promote a gay or lesbian employee to a management position.

Q: Will AB 101 require affirmative action for lesbians and gay men?

No. AB 101 does not require any affirmative action; it does not establish quotas, goals, or timetables.

Q: Won't AB 101 give lesbians and gay men "special rights," and force employers to hire them?

No. AB 101 doesn't require employers to hire or promote lesbians or gay men. Employers can still fire and refuse to hire people who can't or won't do a job. Far from giving gay people special rights, AB 101 simply says that lesbians and gay men, like other groups that have been discriminated against, can't be refused work because of things that have nothing to do with their ability to do a job.

c

Q: Why should civil rights laws apply to people who decide to be gay? Doesn't the law prohibit discrimination based on things you are born with, like race and gender?

Civil rights laws generally prohibit discrimination based both on things a person is born with (like race and gender) and fundamental choices a person makes (like decisions about religious faith and marital status). No one really knows whether sexual orientation is something a person is born with or whether it develops when a person is very young. Few people who think about their own sexual orientation, however, believe it is something they could easily change. The point is, people shouldn't face the loss of a job for something that has nothing to do with ability.

Q: Will the churches have to comply?

No. Religious organizations are exempt from the Fair Employment and Housing Act.

Q: Will this law protect people with AIDS?

No. State law already prohibits discrimination against people with AIDS and people who have the virus that is believed to cause AIDS.

Q: Will this law protect people who commit sex crimes?

No. Neither AB 101 nor the Fair Employment and Housing Act protect illegal behavior.

Q: Doesn't this law force employers and landlords who are sued to prove that they don't discriminate? Won't innocent people be harassed with false claims?

No. The Fair Employment and Housing Act says that the person making the claim must prove that he or she was subjected to discrimination. Moreover, anyone who files frivolous charges can be held liable for the other person's legal fees.

Q: Will this law apply to people who rent out rooms in their homes?

No. The Fair Employment and Housing Act exempts any "owner-occupied single-family house" with "no more than one roomer."

Q: Will this law force employers to allow on-the-job sexual activity and cross-dressing?

No. AB 101 doesn't change an employer's right to set reasonable dress and conduct codes.

Q: Isn't this really part of an attempt to get state sanction for gay marriage?

AB 101 is the culmination of a fifteen-year fight to see to it that lesbians and gay men don't lost jobs and homes for reasons that have nothing to do with whether they are good employees or tenants. It is not tied to bills about same-sex marriage, or to any other bills.

Q: Don't most people favor discrimination against gay people?

State and national polls show that people think discrimination on the basis of sexual orientation is wrong. A national Roper poll taken several times since 1977 has shown that more than 50% of the people believe lesbians and gay men should be guaranteed equal treatment in jobs and housing. The most recent (1985 and 1987) versions show two-thirds of the people feel that way. Virtually every respectable poll shows similar results.

C

QUESTIONS AND ANSWERS ABOUT RIGHTS AND OBLIGATIONS UNDER SAN FRANCISCO'S DOMESTIC PARTNERSHIP LAW

1. Are domestic partners responsible for each other's debts?

Some of them. Domestic partners agree to be responsible for each other's basic living expenses. Sec. 2(a) of the law. The law says that means basic food and shelter. Sec. 2(c). Domestic partners don't have to split costs; they have to provide each other with food and shelter if that becomes necessary. Sec. 2.

2. Does a domestic partner have a right to part of his or her partner's income or property?

No. Domestic partners take responsibility to provide each other with basic food and shelter. There is no agreement to share income or assets. Sec. 2.

3. Could a domestic partner ever become responsible for his or her partner's medical expenses?

Yes, but only if his or her partner gets medical insurance through the domestic partnership. For example, if your employer allows you to add your domestic partner to its health plan, you'll be responsible for those medical expenses your partner has which the plan does not pay for. Sec. 2(c). Married people have the same responsibility. There is no responsibility for medical expenses if your partner does not get insurance through the domestic partnership. Sec. 2(c).

4. Are domestic partners responsible for each other after the partnership ends?

No. Domestic partnerships end when: 1) one partner dies; 2) one partner tells the other in writing that the partnership ended; or 3) the partners stop living together. Sec. 4. Once the partnership ends, the liability for new costs ends. Sec. 6.

5. Could a domestic partner be held responsible for some of his or her partner's bills.

Yes, bills for food and shelter. If a partner cannot provide his or her own food or shelter, the partner must provide it. If the partner does not, and somebody else provides it on credit, the creditor can insist that the partner pay. Sec. 2(c), (d).

6. What kind of food bills could a domestic partner be responsible for?

The obligation is for basic food. This would surely include groceries, and it would probably include average restaurant meals.

7. What does being responsible for your partner's shelter mean?

You've got to provide your partner with a place to live if she or he can't provide it for her or himself. This means you are responsible for your partner's share of the cost of the place you share. Sec. 2.

8. What kinds of bills could be included in the responsibility for shelter?

The cost of getting and keeping a place to live. This would include monthly rent (or a mortgage if you own). It would include water, garbage, heat, light, and similar utilities.

9. Could a landlord insist that I pay rent on the place we share if my partner can't pay?

Yes. But if the apartment is in both your names, you are both responsible for the whole rent anyway. In most cases, if the landlord knows that both of you are living in the apartment, both of you are responsible for the whole rent. And of course, if your partner's half of the rent is not paid, you'll both be evicted.

C

10. Could a bank insist that I pay my partner's half of the monthly mortgage payment if my partner can't pay?

Yes. But if you own the house together, you are almost surely both responsible for the whole payment under the note you signed for the loan.

11. If my partner and I split up, and my name isn't on the lease or the mortgage, could I be held responsible for rent or mortgage payments for my partner?

No. Once you stop living together, the domestic partnership is ended. You are not responsible for any bills which your partner runs up after the date you separate.

12. Could a domestic partner be responsible for the costs of a nursing home or board and care for his or her partner?

For some of the costs, perhaps. Usually, when a partner moves out, that ends the partnership. Sec. 4(a). The partnership does not end if a partner leaves but intends to return. Sec. 2(b). If one partner went into a nursing home but intended to return, and if he or she could get into the home on credit, his or her partner could be responsible for the part of the bill which covered room and food (but not care).